# Resilient Religion, Resilience and Heartbreaking Adversity

Edited by

Chris A.M. Hermans and Kobus Schoeman

LIT

This book is printed on acid-free paper.

**Bibliographic information published by the Deutsche Nationalbibliothek**
The Deutsche Nationalbibliothek lists this publication in the Deutsche
Nationalbibliografie; detailed bibliographic data are available on the Internet at
http://dnb.dnb.de.

ISBN 978-3-643-91500-9 (pb)
ISBN 978-3-643-96500-4 (PDF)


A catalogue record for this book is available from the British Library.

© LIT VERLAG Dr. W. Hopf Berlin 2023
Contact:
Fresnostr. 2   D-48159 Münster
Tel. +49 (0) 2 51-62 03 20   Fax +49 (0) 2 51-23 19 72
e-Mail: lit@lit-verlag.de   https://www.lit-verlag.de
**Distribution:**
In the UK: Global Book Marketing, e-mail: mo@centralbooks.com
In North America: Independent Publishers Group, e-mail: orders@ipgbook.com

# Contents

ACTING: PREACHING, NARRATING, AND
DISCERNING

FEELING, STORY, AND TRAUMA

# Introduction

*Chris Hermans & Kobus Schoeman*

## 1. The topic of resilience

Nowadays, resilience theory is the 'talk of the town' in the academic community across all disciplines, from ecology, sustainability science, disaster management, economics, sociology, psychology, social work, and developmental science to neuropsychology. The rise of resilience theory dates back some five decades ago and, according to many scientists, it holds the promise of formulating an integrative theoretical framework across disciplines.

Resilience theory has its roots in the study of adversity and an interest in how adverse life experiences have a detrimental impact on people (Van Breda 2018). In theology and biblical studies, resilience has a long tradition in Black theology and African theology, liberation theology, feminist theology, as well as pastoral theology and psychology. Despite this long tradition, theology has only recently begun to connect with resilience theory in other disciplines. In this introduction, we begin with an overview of theological theory regarding the concepts 'resilience' and 'resilient religion'. Next, we explain the questions that resilience theory needs to address. What are the main concepts and the relationship between these concepts in a theological theory on resilient religion? Finally, we give an overview of the contributions in this volume.

## 2. Theology and resilience: an overview

In theology and biblical studies, resilience has a long tradition in Black theology and African theology connected with the struggle from colonialism and White supremacy, building a hermeneutic of liberation for the marginalized, and inculturation of Christianity within the African culture.[1] The concept 'resilience' also figures in different forms of liberation theology, eco-theology, feminist theology, and queer theology.

The term 'resilience' has a long tradition in Black theology, from two perspectives. First, the term 'resilience' is anchored in social movements in the struggle against colonialism and White domination. Secondly, it has its own biblical hermeneutics that has developed in these communities, sometimes already with ancient roots, as the experiences of slaves in the USA show (Ross 2021).

---

[1] The concept of resilience figures also in different forms of liberation theology, eco-theology, feminist theology, and queer theology.

This also applies to so-called African theology, although representatives of this theology disagree as to whether, in the African context, the themes of liberation and inculturation go together (according to Tutu) or are considered to be distinctive (according to Mbiti) (Tshaka 2016). If we want to understand what resilience and a resilient religion mean, we must take as our starting point the experiences and stories from Africa of people who live (surviving) on the periphery of the city in poverty, socio-political exclusion, and culturally marginalized (Thsaka 2016:104). In African theology, biblical hermeneutics is developed as interpretative resilience, which helps marginalized people find their place within families and churches (West 2019).

Another field is pastoral theology and pastoral psychology. In a special issue of the journal *Pastoral Psychology*, 'reliance' is defined as the ability to bounce back from adversity and trauma. "Implied in this definition is the ability to recover strength, spirits, good humour, etc., and to do so quickly and with a sense of buoyancy." (Carlin *et al.* 2015:550). Theological resilience is conceptualized as the source of rich possibilities for life that are offered from religious language "from which human beings can draw in their efforts to discern, understand, gain clarity, and find truth" (Carlin *et al.* 2015:653). "From the perspective of theological resilience, optimism and pessimism are where faith and unbelief manifest." (Carlin *et al.* 2015:656). Typical for this field is a combination of both psychological and theological approaches to spiritual care. Resilience is considered to be "an outcome of caregiving relationships that help people spiritually integrate moral stress" (Doehring 2015:636). Other authors in this field emphasize that resilience necessarily comprises a "moral dimension" that is an adaptive process of (eventually) finding existential meaning in life. Finding meaning in life is considered a process of keeping oriented towards believable visions of the good life (Schuhmann & Van der Geugten 2017:525).

Then there is the work of Craig (notably his book *Resilience and the virtue of fortitude* [2006]). He brings theology in conversation with psychology on resilience through the theory of Thomas Aquinas on emotion and the role of reason. According to Thomas Aquinas, emotions arise from the attraction that emanates from a certain object. He assumes that reason influences the emotions, by assessing whether the object to which one is attracted is morally 'right' or 'wrong'. Reason exercises that control through the (cardinal) virtue of *fortitudo* (courage):

> fortitude is the special capacity to control fear and daring when
> resisting or overcoming [adversity].' Furthermore, fortitude can
> contribute to one's ability to resist or overcome adversity be-
> cause it includes capacities that regulate hope (magnanimity,
> magnificence, longanimity), and sorrow (patience, constancy)
> (Criag 2006:146-147).

Craig wants to control emotions through reason, which refers to man's life in the spirit (spiritual life). Whether he succeeds in it is another matter.[2]

A 'white raven' in theology is White and Cook's volume, entitled *Biblical and theological visions of resilience* (2020) The authors connect to the theory development of *resilience theory* in the academy. The model is derived from Windle (2021:157):

> the need for a significant adversity/risk, the presence of assets
> or resources to offset the effects of the adversity, and positive
> adaptation or the avoidance of a negative outcome.

The Bible and Christian theology constitute social and spiritual capital that makes it possible to reduce or transform the effects of adversity (White & Cook 2020:5). The focus of religion and spirituality in resilience is on ultimate purpose, meaning, and human flourishing (White & Cook 2020:6). How can people not only survive, but also thrive in situations of adversity?

What does this overview show about state of art of a theory of resilience in theology? The Bible, Christian faith, and Christian communities are highlighted as sources of resilience. They are a source of hope and meaning making, and Christian communities can be a social network of support in situations of adversity. It is not always clear as to what kind of processes theology is focusing on. The dominant orientation on process is psychological, where adaptation and bouncing back are the main focus. Some authors raise this question referring to issues of the moral good and the purpose of life (human flourishing, perfect happiness). A second issue is the question as to what kind of problem of adversity is religion dealing with? Is it psychological, social, or spiritual? If it is spiritual, what is this life in the spirit? And what kind of adversity is connected with this life in the spirit? A next observation is that the concept 'resilient religion' is almost completely missing in theological discourse. What is the outcome of resilience in terms of a resilient religion? Finally, we observe that some literature pays hardly any attention to the possibility that religion is not contributing to the resilience of people and systems (communities and organizations).

## 3.  Adversity and resilience

Resilience theory has its roots in the study of adversity and an interest in how adverse life experiences have a detrimental impact on people (Van Breda 2018). Initially, there is an emphasis in the theory building on seeking the causes that make people ill or cause a breakdown in social functioning or health. Next to this pathogenic focus, a salutogenic focus on resilience developed, with the focus on processes that mediate between adversity and negative outcomes (Van Breda 2018:3). In this instance, resilience centres on the mediating factors or processes

---

[2] See the critique of Cartagena (2021).

that enable positive outcomes in the wake of adversity. Finally, resilience as process can be distinguished from the outcome of the process, namely being resilient or a resilient system that is better equipped to deal with adversity, due to the process of resilience. Where adversity refers to the input, resilience as a process to the throughput, resilient refers to the outcome (see Figure 1). Based on these three elements, Van Breda (2018:4) defines resilience as "[t]he multilevel processes that systems engage in to obtain better-than-expected outcomes in the face or wake of adversity."

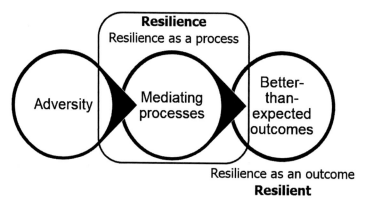

Figure 1: Resilience as process and as outcome (adopted from Van Breda 2018:4)

## 4. Building blocks of a theory on 'resilient religion'

What questions does a resilience theory on religion need to answer? A theory of religion consists of three building blocks, namely adversity, resilience as mediating processes, and resilient religion as outcome and the relationship between them. This means that a theory of resilience must provide an answer to four questions:

- What defines the kind of adversity in which religion is involved?
- What mediating processes characterize resilience in religion?
- What defines resilient religion?
- Which epistemology connects these three elements in a logically imitable way?

Before answering these questions, we ask some critical questions from the subject of our study, namely religion. Adaptation is the frame in which resilience theory is formulated: resilience processes are processes of adaptation, and a resilient system is better adapted to deal with adversities. Adaptation presupposes an existing order, and the best condition to deal with changes in this order. Adaptation is focused on the stability and continuity of an existing order. All those who are not strangers in Jerusalem, *i.e.* the field of religion, will know that it is not about existing order, but about the emergence of something new.

> Behold, I will do a new thing; now it shall spring forth; shall ye not know it? I will even make a way in the wilderness, *and* rivers in the desert (Isaiah 43:19; King James Bible).

The outcome of processes of resilience in religion will not be something considered to be better adapted to existing orders. A theory about resilient religion will have to indicate the problem of adversity in life which it addresses. The intrinsic value of resilient religion is to help people deal with this problem of adversity.

Secondly, what are the processes of resilience that help deal with adversity? The kind of processes are not related to adaptivity but to an openness to new beginnings. New beginnings of what is considered to be ultimate good, ultimate happiness, the admirable as such. These multi-level processes are related to persons within a dynamic relationship to systems (families, communities, organisations, public institutions).

Thirdly, we need to formulate resilient religion as the outcome of processes of resilience. In what way is resilient religion capable of avoiding a crisis due to the experience of adversity, or can it absorb the effects of adversity? What is specifically the role of God in this regard?

Fourthly, what binds the three elements together? Epistemology is about the logic of inference based on our beliefs and experiences about reality. All theory on resilience works with the concept of experience which is a vague and contested concept.

## 5. Outline of the book

The volume starts with a cluster of three chapters, in which Chris Hermans offers a map of a theory of resilient religion in theology. Experiences of adversity, processes of resilience, and resilient religion are the outcome of these processes.

## 5.1 Mapping THE FIELD

In Chapter 1, "*Heartbreaking adversity*", Hermans addresses the issue of the kind of adversity that religion addresses. Heartbreaking adversity is the experience of being separated from the good life with, and for others. Following Ricoeur, this kind of existential adversity finds its origin in the disproportionality of human beings. Viewed as a whole, human beings are thrown into time and space, in a body and a history, on the one hand, and have a spiritual life that transcends the given to the possible, to ideals and the *telos* of life, on the other. This aporia or paradox between the limitations of existence and the perfect infinity is part of the human constitution. It is part of the make-up of the human self, between the one self, as experience of the limitations of existence, and the other self, as experience of the greatness of the ethical vision. The demand for mediation or wholeness is a demand for mediation between one self and the other self. The chapter begins with an epistemological reflection on experience. How do we know what we know in experience? What is the truth of experiences? We cannot escape these epistemological reflections because the concept of experience is contested in theology. The author illustrates the problems we want to avoid in theological theories on human experiences of adversity and resilience, and offers an epistemological basis for the concept of experience based on the pragmatic theory of the American theologian Donald Gelpi.

Chapter 2, "*Processes of resilience*", deals with the question as to what processes of resilience help people deal with heartbreaking adversity associated with the absence of good with, and for others? According to Hermans, processes of resilience relate to experiences of the good in, and of our lives with, and for others, in a just and sustainable society. They promote awareness and experience of the possibility of a connection between good and concrete events in the reality in which we live. Resilience is the power of the human spirit that connects experiences of the self to the good in life events (here and now). The author distinguishes four processes of resilience: recognition of contingency; transcendental openness; experience of happiness, and handling tragedy.

In Chapter 3, "*Resilient religion*", Hermans defines religion as religious systems – in a dynamic relationship with other systems – that can prevent or process the loss of the good and/or the absence of God as a possibility *in and of* life events with, and for others, insofar as this becomes visible in the practical way of life that follows from the meaning of this experience. In resilient religion, God is the foundation of the synthesis of the self as openness to the unlimited, and the self as directed towards the limited. Against the experience of a person or community, in which there is no future and no possibility of moving forward, a resilient religion sets the belief and experience of God as Creator. Hermans then elaborates on the capability of discernment as a model for the art of living well with, and for others. Discernment is aimed at the awareness and experience of the ultimate good in reality that rests in God. Finally, the author elaborates on the concept of 'resilient religion' into three dimensions, namely thinking, acting, and feeling. To what extent are religion and spirituality helping people recognise the contingency of existence, and lifting them up to think, act, and feel in freedom? Hermans pays attention to the institutional dimension of religion and the agency of the actors. Institutions provide structures that support and enable the agency of individual actors, while simultaneously limiting and suppressing their freedom. A theory about resilient religion will have to accommodate both dimensions and be aware of the tension between religion as an institution and the freedom of individual agents.

## 5.2     The dynamics of THINKING

All religions can be viewed as a reservoir of imagination, centred on the mystery of perfect good, fulfilling happiness and human flourishing. Thinking is characterised by a disproportionality between taking a specific point of view and the meaning (truth) of the object of our thinking, *i.e.* the God symbol, and by the synthesis of perspective and meaning. How can we think God within the limits of a specific point of view? God as mystery is elusive, inexhaustible, incomprehensible. At the same time, human thinking about the infinite can only be done from a specific point of view, tradition, and context. How not to ignore the awareness of a specific point of view? And how to open up for the truth, as given in the God symbol that emanates from a specific perspective?

In Chapter 4, entitled *"Christian resilience, intellectuals and the God symbol. Interaction and changing shape"*, Rian Venter presents a broad *genealogical approach* to the interplay between large social and cultural upheavals, the creative role of intellectuals, and the re-figuring of the symbol of the Divine. Religions as living traditions encounter 'epistemological crises' that should be resolved, in order to address the criteria of truth, intelligibility, and rationality. These epistemological crises are embedded in social and cultural upheavals such as the exile of Israel or the two World Wars in the twentieth century. The author focuses on four trajectories of the God symbol: the crystallisation of monotheism (Assyrian Exile), the Empire, metaphysics, and substantial trinitarianism (fourth century A.D.), modernism and social trinitarianism (1970s; 1980s), and finally Auschwitz, alterity and anatheism (after 2000). Throughout history, one encounters intellectual *resilience* to make sense of the world, to keep the vitality of the faith alive, and to make a public contribution to understanding the human-embattled condition. Venter agrees that it is possible to design a shifting *sociology of the intellectuals* in every major historical period. But this misses the specific intellectual task of thinking as creative process of imagining the God symbol. God as central orientating symbol is imaginatively reinterpreted not only to reflect modes of thinking of the specific historical period, but also to convey the constantly surprising and disruptive impulses emanating from this reflection. The Divine meets the crisis through the intellectual activities as ever new and lifegiving. The task of intellectual thinking is to open oneself to the truth, as given in the God symbol that emanates from the specific perspective connected to the crisis of the world in which we live.

Dion Forster invites us to consider unique aspects of (South) African reality, identity, and sense-making in the dynamics between the human perspective and meaning (truth) of the God symbol, and the syntheses between perspective and meaning. In Chapter 5, entitled *"African realities and resilient religion? An invitation to Africanize the conversation"*, Forster starts with the argument that, for religion to be a responsible and appropriate source of fostering resilience for (South) Africans, it will also need to be "explicitly contextual". We need to question the colonial and imperial commitments that continue to lie behind the suffering that so many of our siblings face daily, before we turn to the pragmatic and utilitarian application of religion to foster resilience. We need to prioritise and process "un-thinking the West" before participating in the debate on resilience, adversity, and resilient religion in (South) Africa. In the debate on resilient religion, we shall need to remain vigilant so as not to merely perpetuate the pathologies of colonialism, either in the outright rejection of the West or in the uncritical adoption of what is described as African. According to Forster, we need at least three forms of decolonisation and Africanisation for a project such as ours on resilient religion. The first deals with the psychological and social wounds of colonial domination; the second addresses epistemologies, methods, and approaches to meaning making, while the third aims at re-centering African experiences and contributions in the conversation about resilient religion, African experience, and reality. Long before the missionaries arrived on Southern African shores, Africans had religious beliefs, a moral philosophy, culture, art, technologies, and law.

### 5.3    ACTING: Preaching, narrating, and discerning

Where is God in our life and the life of others? Our actions are characterised by a disproportion between the determinacy of our character as subject, and the excess of happiness related to the dignity (humanity) of every human being and God. Due to the limitations of our character, we fall short; the synthesis of our character and openness towards the happiness of the other and the self are not realized. Which practices in resilient religion aim to promote this synthesis of the limitations of our actions and excess of happiness?

According to Martin Laubscher, in Chapter 6, entitled *"Resilient preaching? A critical appraisal of Johan Cilliers' trilogy on 'grace'"*, preaching may represent the idea of resilience in more than one sense. On the one hand, there are the specific experiences and cases of dealing with heartbreaking adversity, but so too it might be important to take another step back and explore the idea of preaching as the embodiment of resilience itself. Besides the challenge to relate resilient religion and preaching to particular issues and scenarios, it might be even more helpful to re-imagine preaching as such, as a resilient endeavour. In other words, mere showing up, even before we say a single word, might "possess" within itself the gift of seeing things differently. Resilience is what preaching assumes and craves, but often fails to deliver. Instead of dealing with adversity, preaching can easily succumb into creating it. Laubscher uses the trilogy of the South African homiletician Johan Celliers (*"Space for grace"* [2016]; *"Time for grave"* [2019], and *"Grace for grace"* [2022]) to reflect on the relationship between resilience and preaching. First, space for grace seeks and voices an open, moving, dynamic, and relational space called "home", where we can discover "others" and "the

Other". It exposes spaces of fear emerging from the ideology of apartheid. Secondly, the hopeful tenor of all preaching is timing as pre-sencing the Presence of Christ in the present. The eternal truths become audible in the form of being simultaneously timely and temporal. Thirdly, grace upon grace refers to the self-awareness that we are fully being known. Although we move, we are neither drifting nor fading. This movement generates space and time, and there is destiny-and-certainty within the kairos of being under way. The art of healing in preaching guards against the temptations of quietism or pietism (being mere bench-sitters).

In Chapter 7, entitled "*Becoming a resilient Christian community: A narrative approach*", Eugene Baron argues that a narrative approach would contribute to resilient religion. This narrative approach within congregations would allow some vulnerable stories to enter the "sacred" spaces of churches. The author underscores the dependence of churches on propositional and foundational approaches. As example, he refers to the Reformed tradition, in which it has become important to focus on the Bible (*Sola Scriptura*), and its truth to be affirmed within congregational worship. The author aligns with Bosch who proposed an "expansion of rationality", where both reason and narrative would be equated, and both affirmed as avenues to "faith knowledge". The author discusses the evasiveness of a narrative approach and story forms in some Christian traditions, but also how narrative facilitates resilience within a Christian community. The church should facilitate a metanarrative (not oppressive), the story of the *missio Dei*, in which the community of faith is able to find ultimate meaning by providing space for the dialogical interaction between the 'personal' mundane story, and the sacred story (see Stephen Crites). Because of such dialogue, Christian communities and their members become more resilient in the face of adversity.

Kobus Schoeman, in Chapter 8, writes on "*The congregation as a community of discernment and practice – Enhancing resilient religion*". The author starts with the effect of the COVID-19 pandemic on congregational life. The ministry and activities of the congregation were put on hold; the use of online platforms became the norm, and the pandemic may even have affected their service in the community. Against this background of adversity, the main research focus of this chapter is formulated in the following question: *How does a congregation develop and enhance resilience in response to adversity in the community or society*? The author formulates a theoretical framework for the congregation's response to adversity. He analyses the congregation as a network of support in a situation of adversity. A resilient community develops the capacities of discernment and good practices that may enhance the experience of happiness and purpose in response to adversity. Congregational leadership plays a significant role in this process. Schoeman presents the results of an empirical research in the Dutch Reformed Church in South Africa during the COVID-19 pandemic. The response of the church and its leadership could be interpreted as a typically state church response: Do as the government says but add a little mercy and charity, and that would be your Christian responsibility. In the conclusion, he formulates some critical questions on the basis of the findings. What discernment capacities should congregations develop in recognizing the text and context and developing a resilient framework to develop a critical response in a crisis? What kind of listening, critical discerning, challenging adversity, and prophetic response should congregations develop, in order to be relevant and effective in crises such as the pandemic?

## 5.4    FEELING, story, and trauma

The heart longs for experiences of fulfilling happiness *in* life with, and for others. How to experience unlimited happiness in experiences of heartbreaking adversity? A synthesis of happiness and the concrete events of life are fragile. How can story help express feelings of experiences of crises, tragedy, and trauma? How can stories help heal the broken heart?

In Chapter 9, entitled *"Resilience and resistance in the Book of Job: An African socio-economic hermeneutical reading"*, Funlọla Olojede gives a hermeneutical reading of the Book of Job in the context of the major pandemics that have ravaged the globe and, specifically, the African continent. The methodology she uses to analyse the Book of Job is the African Biblical Hermeneutics (ABH) that is steeped in both resistance and resilience. ABH is the product of a radically resistant post-slavery, postcolonial and post-apartheid theology and hermeneutics that takes a swipe at traditional or conventional Eurocentric interpretations of the biblical text, Western indoctrination, as well as their imperialising realities and tendencies. The Book of Job, like most of the books of the Old Testament, was written or revised in the exilic/post-exilic period and calibrated in response to the trauma caused by the Assyrian-Babylonian captivity. Job verbally expresses his feeling with regard to his physical and emotional trauma. He talks about the unquantifiable weight of his grief, the bitterness and anguish of his soul, his feelings of shame and regret, not only about his life but also about his birth. The author stresses the impact of Job's economic loss – the loss of his business and ground staff in one day. He no longer had a source of livelihood. It appears that resistance fundamentally involves asserting one's capacity to act in the face of the domination of another agent. We see this in the radical resistance of Job to give in to pressure from Satan, his friends, or his wife. At the same time, Job also exercises resilience in the face of his heartbreaking adversity and existential crisis. Central to the process of resilience is hope. Job's resilience and his ultimate vindication and change are a testament of hope for those experiencing similar situations of tragedy and trauma.

Juanita Meyer, in Chapter 10, writes on *"Surviving my story of trauma": A pastoral theology of resilience"*. The *experience* of trauma might include the feeling that human life is threatened or that one's life is in danger, and this feeling might elicit urges such as fight, flight, or freeze. It also refers to feeling over-whelmed or annihilated, defeated and psychologically and physically over-whelmed. It is often through story that the experience of trauma lives. The author proposes that a theology of resilience is a collection of stories and narratives that tell us something about the character of the triune God as revealed through the stories of God in Scripture. Such a theology offers people an endless resource centre from which stories can be borrowed, incorporated, and embodied to remain resilient amidst inevitable experiences of suffering. Resilient religion finds its power through the theology of suffering that employs the therapeutic powers of lament, allowing a person to express pain, sorrow, and despair in the presence of God, who is the ultimate source for redemption and renewal. Resilient religion is about a person's ability to make the stories within the larger narrative of religion meaningful and to use that meaning to overcome adversity in the process. Finally, a resilient religion actively employs a theology of hope through a spirituality of reconciliation to renew relationships with the self, the other, and God. This sus-tains the reauthored metanarrative in the framework of the master narrative. Through hope and reconciliation, ownership can ultimately be taken of the story of trauma.

## Bibliography

Carlin, N., Capps, D. & Dykstra, R.C. (2015). Living stories of resilience, re-sistance, and resourcefulness. Pastoral Psychology 64:549-551. DOI 10.1007/s11089-015-0667-z

Cartagena, N.L. (2021). Resilience, emotion regulation, and Thomas Aquinas. The Heytrop Journal 62:485-497.

Craig, S.T. (2006). Resilience and the virtue of fortitude. Aquinas in dialogue with the psychosocial sciences. Washington, DC: The Catholic Univer-sity of America Press.

Doehring, D. (2015). Resilience as the relational ability to spiritually integrate moral stress. Pastoral Psychology 64:635-649. DOI 10.1007/s11089-015-0643-7

Ross, R.E. (2021). Black theology and the history of U.S. black religions: Post civil rights approaches to the study of African American religions. Religion Compass 6(4):249-261.

Schuhmann, C.M. & Van der Geugten, W. (2017). Believable visions of the good: An exploration of the role of pastoral counsellors in promoting resilience. Pastoral Psychology 66:523-536. DOI 10.1007/s11089-017-0759-z

Tshaka, R.S. (2016). How can a conquered people sing praises of their history and culture? Africanization as the integration of inculturation and libera-tion. Black Theology 14(2):91-106.

Van Breda, A.D. (2018). A critical review of resilience theory and its relevance for social work. Social Work/Maatskaplike Werk 54(1):1-18.

West, G.O. (2019). "Not peace but a sword" (Mt. 10:34): Recognising resilience but struggling for resistance. Stellenbosch Theological Journal 5(3):183-200.

White, N.H. & Cook, C.H. (2020). Introduction to biblical and theological visions of resilience. In: N.H. White & C.H. Cook (eds), Biblical and theological visions of resilience. Pastoral and clinical insights (Routledge [Ekindle]), pp. 1-16.

Windle, G. (2021). What is resilience? A review and concept analysis. Reviews in Clinical Gerontology 21(2):152-169.

# Chapter 1
# Human experiences of heartbreaking adversity

*C A M Hermans[1]*

## 1.1 Introduction

What defines the kind of adversity in which religion is involved? Any theory on resilient religion needs to answer this question. A common response would be situations of brokenness; all kinds of suffering (physical, social, mental); moral feelings of guilt and shame; the death of someone who is near to us or having an incurable illness. These experiences are also the subjects of other disciplines such as sociology, psychology, and medicine. What is the specific perspective from which these human experiences of suffering are studied in theology and religious studies compared to other disciplines? What is the 'stitch' in human experiences of suffering, masterfully represented by the dramatic words of Shakespeare, "To be, or not to be"? The kind of adversity that is the focus of religion is the experience of being separated from that which gives life lustre, perfect happiness, purpose; an ultimate reason to live. I will define the human experience of being separated from the good life with, and for others as heartbreaking adversity.

Human experiences of heartbreaking adversity are part of the anthropological make-up of human beings (see section 1.2). According to Ricoeur (1986), human beings are defined by a disproportionality between finite happiness – imperfect, transitory reality – on the one hand, and good, infinite, perfect happiness, on the other. The possibility of heartbreaking adversity will be situated in this disproportionality.

Such heartbreaking adversity is an existential possibility for both religious and non-religious persons. This raises the question: How can the relationship between religion and the experience of heartbreaking adversity be defined? According to Ricoeur, human self-understanding is associated with the greatness (grandeur) of the ethical vision of people and the world, of the good life with, and for each other. In line with this, I will interpret the relation between religion and the experience of heartbreaking adversity as the relationship between religion and morality (the good life). According to Van der Ven (1998), this relationship can be interpreted from different perspectives: morality as part of the integrated text of religion, as the context of the text of religion, or as a subtext of religion. I start

---

[1] His e-mail address is: chris.hermans@ru.nl

with a critical reflection on two theological positions that subsume the good under religion.

Adversity is an experience of human beings. We cannot speak on a life marked by adversity, without reference to human experience. In theology and philosophy, the concept of 'experience' is a contested one. How do we know what we know when we experience adversity? Experience is a vague concept with a dubious epistemological foundation. Can this be a good basis for building a theory of resilient religion? In the first section, I will formulate some core problems regarding the concept of experience in philosophy and theology. In what way is experience related to reality? What is the truth claim of our experiences? How do we come to conclusions based on our experiences? I reflect on these questions based on the American theologian Donald Gelpi's pragmatic epistemology. Gelpi's work is less known outside the USA, although he wrote all his life on epistemology in theology and was in conversation with many contemporary theologians. I argue that Gelpi offers a good theoretical basis for the concept of experience in a theory on resilient religion, which avoids the problems connected with the concept of 'experience'.

## 1.2 Experience: An epistemological foundation of a contested concept

The concepts of 'religious experience' and 'faith experience' play an important role in discovering the essence of religion (Bagger 2004:2). This is evident in the work of leading academics in Catholic theology such as Edward Schillebeeckx, Bernard Lonergan, Clodovis Boff, and Charles Heartshorne (Gelpi 1994). However, the concept of 'experience' employed by these authors is not unproblematic.

Epistemology focuses on the logic of inference, or on what reasoning our knowledge is based. How do we know what we know in experience? What is the truth of experiences? According to what categories do we evaluate experiences (Gelpi 1994:13)? In the following, I want to lay down an epistemological basis for the concept of 'experience', in order to avoid the above problems. I base my work on that of Donald L. Gelpi (Jesuit, 1934-2011) – specifically his book *Turn to experience in contemporary theology* (Gelpi 1994).[2] First, I briefly outline the epistemological problems to be avoided. I then touch on the main features of Gelpi's pragmatic epistemology required for a substantiation of the concept of 'experience' in building a theory on resilient religion. I begin with the question as to which four problems to avoid.

---

[2] Gelpi is considered an authority on the philosophy of Charles S. Peirce and so-called transcendentalism in American philosophy and theology (Corrington 2002; Oppenheim 2004). An introduction to the theology of Gelpi can be found in Markey & Zuschlag's article (2017). Of note is the enthusiastic reception for Gelpi's theology within the circles of Pentecostalism in America (Young 2014: section 3).

- Nominalism, in its strictest sense, recognises only one form of being, namely the being of a thing or fact. "Strict nominalists hold that a general rule is nothing but a mere word or couple of words" (Gelpi 1994:4). In addition, Peirce distinguishes a second form of nominalism, which he calls conceptualism. "The conceptualist recognises the reality of universals but allows them only the reality of thought" (Gelpi 1994:4). Common to both forms of nominalism is a denial that general laws of nature are reality. They exist only in the mind.

- For Peirce, individualism or subjectivism refers to the "spirit of Cartesianism [which] holds that philosophical thinking must begin with universal doubt, and it locates the test of certainty within consciousness" (Gelpi 2000:235). This view assumes that there are, first, principles that are self-evident to the human mind (intuitions). From these self-evident truths, we reason according to the truth of an experience (the logic of inference).

- Essentialism refers to a reification of ideas or immutable principles. For Plato, these are transcendent ideas; for Aristotle, immutable principles of being, inherent in things. These essences are immutable and separate from reality, from the observer's perspective and experience: "The term 'essence' designates a human evaluative response – a sensation, image, or conceptual perception – abstracted from the reality it perceives and from the one who does the perceiving" (Gelpi 1994:101).

- Dualism refers to the separation of body (*bios*) and mind, where body stands for the time-spatial reality and mind for a reality that transcends time and space (Gelpi 1994:103). Thus, the separation between body and mind simultaneously implies a separation between two realities. Starting from this separation, openness to transcendence is placed in the human mind. The consequence, however, is that transcendence and faith are considered, from this separation, in terms of two realities. In other words, the meaning of religious experiences can no longer be thought of in terms of temporal-spatial conditions, in and of this world.

According to Gelpi (1994:126-136; 2000:237-245), Peirce's pragmatic epistemology is realistic, triadic, and social. I will explain each criterion, and discuss what they mean for experiences of adversity, resilience, and religion.

### 1.2.1  Realism

The claim of realism implies that laws – or regularities – are tendencies of reality, and not simply ideas or thought constructs. Laws that the human mind understands are generalities that are present in reality. Statements convey the meaning of facts by grounding them in a law or general tendency (Gelpi 1994:15). If I claim that a certain experience is *a priori* part of being human, but this claim turns out to have no empirical basis in reality (*i.e.*, the sum of human experiences), then the claim has a weak foundation. Reality is a critical test for our claims because our claims cannot match reality.

Our views are fallible (weak rationality) and, therefore, reasoning must be subject to the principle of fallibility (fallibalism). "Fallibalism holds that the human mind has a better chance of reaching true belief if the mind in question admits that it can err than if it denies its capacity for error" (Gelpi 2000:241). Reasoning can lead to erroneous views. That is why they must be tested critically against reality, so that they have a better chance of being 'in accordance with' reality.

What does this epistemological criterion mean for the experience of adversity and resilience in religion? In beliefs such as the experience that 'the ground has been snatched away from under my feet', or the experience of 'happiness that completely filled me', people make a claim about the reality in which they live and not simply about a reality in their head. Reality is an 'opposite' – it can offer a rebuttal to our view, or a confirmation. Our views are fallible, especially when it comes to adversity, resilience, and religion. That is why our views must withstand the test of reality.

### 1.2.2   Triadic reasoning

The logical underpinning of our views (experiences, aspirations, and feelings) has a triadic character. Views such as 'the earth is round' are an expression of an argument made up of three elements:[3]

- a category (hypothesis, appreciative evaluation);
- a general rule (regularity, habitual orientation), and
- a concrete and definite fact (given, concrete experience) (Gelpi 2000:239).

Peirce distinguishes three kinds of reasoning, in which these three elements play different roles, namely abduction, deduction, and induction. What is crucial, however, is the assumption that, in any argument, all elements are assumed, but do not play the same role. Every argument is directed to a conclusion, but that conclusion is different in each type of reasoning: the conclusion of an abduction is a hypothesis (or possibility); the conclusion of a deduction is a certain fact, and the conclusion of an induction is a certain law.

I will illustrate this with an example (Gelpi 2000:236-237). Columbus observes that he first sees the flag on the mast of a ship entering the harbour, and that only gradually does the entire ship become visible. This fact is inexplicable if the earth is flat. He forms a hypothesis that could explain these facts, 'The earth

---

[3] Peirce refers to these three elements from his semiotic theory as firstness, secondness, and thirdness. Everything in reality is made up of these elements – so, not only opinions, but also experiences, aspirations, and feelings, etc. (Sonesson 2013).

is round'. This conclusion is the result of abductive reasoning. Note that Columbus does not formulate his hypothesis without observed facts; but these facts have not yet been tested. The facts are also not predicted by a general idea. Columbus has a suspicion of a general idea, which – together with the observed facts – leads to the hypothesis, 'The earth is round'. In a deductive argument, Columbus assumes the law that the earth is round. Based on this law, he can hypothetically predict that, when he sails west, he will reach Asia. When these facts actually occur, the law is correct. These facts are tested in an inductive argument. Facts in an inductive argument are theoretically interpreted (theory-loaded) (Samuels 2000:14). Hypotheses are then formulated about facts that occur on the basis of a certain law. The conclusion of an inductive argument is a generality (law) explaining these facts.

### 1.2.3   The pragmatic maxim

Peirce summarised the logic behind his substantiation of the truth of beliefs or experiences in the so-called pragmatic principle (or maxim). His last version (1905) of this principle reads as follows:

> In order to ascertain the meaning of an intellectual conception one should consider what practical consequences might conceivably result by necessity from the truth of that conception; and the sum of these consequences will constitute the entire meaning of the conception (Gelpi 2000:253).

There are three elements of the logic of inference in this formulation, namely hypothesis, certain facts, and a generally valid idea. The formulation begins with a hypothesis about determining the meaning of an intellectual conception. Two things are needed to determine the meaning, namely practical consequences and the truth of this view. The practical consequences refer to certain facts that may follow from this view. The word 'consider' has a deliberative, reflective, musing meaning that echoes the hypothetical character. The truth of this view refers to a generally valid rule such as human dignity or happiness. Facts correspond to the truth (the general validity) of a view.

The meaning of a belief (experience, action, feeling) is the totality of consequences whereby people live in practice. Typical of Peirce's pragmatism is that truth and meaning are linked. If we claim truth but do not live by it, beliefs are meaningless castles in the air.[4] The proof of the pudding is in the eating.

What does this triadic criterion mean for the experience of adversity and resilience, and the connection between the two? Triadic reasoning is not only

---

[4] "We never fix our beliefs in a purely theoretical way, because the fixation of every belief demands a practical commitment to stand by its consequences until we have a good reason to call that belief into question" (Gelpi 1994:37).

about facts and a generally valid idea, but also about the quality or point of view from which facts express an idea (hypothesis). The logic of inference always implies hypothesis building. There are no facts that belong to a particular idea; but, in a process of deliberation, different facts and different ideas are considered. A hypothesis is crucial to establish the connection between fact and idea, because a generally valid idea explains facts from a certain point of view. In experiences of heartbreaking adversity, the experience of the good (and God) in certain life events is lost. The ground on which we stand has fallen away from under our feet. I cannot connect the belief of a good life with, and for others with my life. Resilience rests on the hypothesis that the possibility of the good (and God) is experienced in the facts of my life – the good, not as an abstract idea, but as the truth in, or of my life.

### 1.2.4  Social

The human mind can fail to give a reasonable substantiation of the meaning and truth of a belief or experience. According to the pragmatic epistemology of Peirce, we need to test the truth in a community of inquiry and from a long-term perspective. As human beings, we belong to different epistemic communities in which we share assumptions about true knowledge: the democratic constitutional state, the church, education, the university, etc. In a community, people share knowledge; they question knowledge, by presenting it to others, and they create a social context for adjusting attitudes and experiences (Gelpi 2000:242).

There are several reasons for this. First, we must learn to substantiate our experiences and beliefs. The logic of inference is not innate, but it must be learned (Gelpi 2000:238). Secondly, our hope is that we will know the truth in a community of inquiry, conceived as a community without borders. History shows that both individuals and communities can be horribly wrong; this is why we need the most extensive possible testing of beliefs and experiences, based on dialogue and contradiction. Thirdly, we will eventually know the truth. This claim is not an asset (strong rationality), but it is based on a long period in which we test and adjust our beliefs. "Now I know imperfectly, but then shall I know fully, even as I myself am known" (1 Cor. 13:12).

What does this criterion 'social' mean for experiences of adversity, resilience, and the relationship between them? Beliefs are fallible, and there are no 'strong' claims to truth about the connection between the good (and God) and certain facts (events) in the lives of people. In line with the pragmatic, social criterion of truth, I advocate dialogue with, and contradiction by others in a community – without limits, and over the long term.

## 1.3 Heartbreaking adversity

Heartbreaking adversity is the kind of misfortune to which religion refers. Our heart can be broken by loss of love, loss of a career, or of good health. We can be agonised by doubt, guilt, or shame. We can be torn by not knowing what to do, or by whether we have done the right thing. All these examples show the possibility that persons can lose themselves, in the sense of becoming estranged from a part of themselves.

What have we lost in heartbreaking adversity? Can we be torn inwardly? Yes, because the human condition is characterised by disproportionality between the limitations (finiteness) of the concreteness and determinacy of human thinking, acting, and feeling, and the unlimitedness (infinity) of the human mind. The heart (feeling) is the place where this disproportionality connects with the experience, in the sense of self-being. This is my disproportionality. This is me!

The possibility of heartbreaking adversity is based on disproportionality that characterises man as spirit (a spiritual being). In human experience, the unity between finiteness and unlimitedness – between finiteness and infinity – can break. We can be broken, but without being a pile of misery that is not capable of anything good. If so, we would not know what we are separated from; no freedom could be attributed to us which makes us responsible for our thinking, (not) acting and (not) feeling. Disproportionality presupposes a connection between our self, directed towards concreteness or the finite, and the other self, directed towards unlimitedness or the infinite, and the possibility of a synthesis between the two.

I will elaborate on this thesis in two complementary ways. I start with William James – one of the founders of psychology, and the psychology of religion, in particular. He thematises this disproportionality through the concept of 'the divided self'. I will then approach this disproportionality from Ricoeur's philosophical anthropology, in particular from his book *Fallible man* (1986).[5]

### 1.3.1 Divided self

William James is known for his approach to religion from people's experiences. His famous book, *The varieties of religious experience*, has a section in which James (1903:166) makes a distinction between healthy-minded people and sick souls. Healthy-minded people report experiences of adversity in life without a complete loss of the good (happiness). Sick souls are people who find it difficult to experience the good *in or of* their life. The good they experience is simply too scarce and too transient to generate a positive attitude to a life of happiness. Moreover, the good is eventually destroyed by death (James 1903:166). This leads to an emotional life (heart) in which there is no balance, but which has great heights

---

[5] (Original) *L'Homme fallible* (1965).

and deep valleys. The biologically given feelings and impulses (animal feelings) are too strong and too conflicting for us to survive as spiritual beings (James 1903:137, 167). The interior of man (the heart) is a battlefield between an actual self and an ideal or spiritual self.

> There are persons whose existence is little more than a series of zigzags, as now one tendency and now another gets the upper hand. Their spirit wars with their flesh, they wish for incompatibles, wayward impulses interrupt their most deliberate plans, and their lives are one long drama of repentance and of effort to repair misdemeanours and mistakes (James 1903:166).

In his book *Sick souls, healthy minds* (2020), Kaag has deepened insight into these concepts from James' life history and Calvinist background. Kaag shows that James' life, in his twenties and thirties, was strongly determined by negative feelings of alienation and loneliness. He himself was a sick soul, whose negative feelings and impulses seemed inescapable. These heartbreaking feelings brought James to the brink of suicide. And yet he broke the circle of determinism, based on a belief in free will and the decision to act from this free will.

> … an individual's will could break the logical continuity of a mechanical series and be the initial cause of another series of phenomena. … The argument for free will might have a proof, but its validity and soundness were only reflected in the activity of life. Upon reading the second Essays, James resolved to do something: "My first act of free will", he asserted, "shall be to believe in free will." (Kaag 2020:49).

For James, this step is associated with an ineradicable optimism.

> James knows that 'looking on the bright side' is often not objectively warranted: life is harsh and cruel in all of the ways that the sick soul suspects. It is, however, practically warranted, deeply useful as what he called a 'life hypothesis' (Kaag 2020:62).

### 1.3.2   Disproportionality as spiritual being

In psychology, the human constitution is viewed from the perspective of dividedness, whereas, in philosophical anthropology, it is viewed from the perspective of man as entity (as a whole). Viewed as a whole, human beings are thrown into time and space, in a body and a present history, on the one hand, and they have a spiritual life that transcends the given to the possible, to ideals and the *telos* of life, on the other. My analysis is based on the book *Fallible man* (1986) by the philosopher Paul Ricoeur, which is part of his long search for free will. In this search, Ricoeur came to understand the polarity between freedom and freedom from a more comprehensive, fundamental polarity, which is between finality and infinity in human beings, and the need to mediate between them (Ricoeur 1986:XIIV). The vulnerability of man and his ability to experience himself as 'divided' lies in the failure of this process of mediation.

Ricoeur wrote *Fallible man* (1986) about this stage of his search. According to him, human self-understanding is associated with the greatness (grandeur) of the ethical vision of people and the world, of the good life with, and for each other, of ideals and ultimate values and perfect happiness. The affirmation of this greatness is primal to anything that a man does or experiences. Man has an ethical awareness of the good, and simultaneously realises that he is inadequate in living according to this standard. Human beings are marked by the greatness of their ethical orientation, and the limitations of their actual existence. Given this human constitution, man is a question about wholeness that is constitutive for the self (Ricoeur 1986:XLIX).

In *Fallible man,* this question of wholeness lies below the experience of brokenness of the heart (the "pathos of misery") – more precisely, in the aporia or paradox between the limitations of existence, failure and deficit and finiteness, on one side, and the greatness (grandeur) of the ethical vision, humanity, the perfect and infinity, on the other (Ricoeur 1986:1). This experience of brokenness is not something outside oneself; it is registered within oneself, as a disproportion between one self and the other self (*idem*). That is why the demand for mediation or wholeness is a demand for mediation between one self and the other self. It is incorrect to release the one 'self' from the other 'self', to separate the biological from the spiritual and then build the whole from the parts (Ricoeur 1986:4). The whole is more than the sum of its parts. The whole is an entity that exits before the dividedness.[6] Following Ricoeur, I will describe three forms of being torn apart (brokenness), namely in people's thinking, acting, and feeling.

### 1.3.3    In line with a pragmatic epistemology

As described in the preceding section, I interpret Ricoeur in terms of a pragmatic epistemology. This requires some explanation, as there are epistemological differences between Ricoeur and Peirce. Both authors derive the threefold structure of finiteness, infinity, and the mediation between the two from Kant (see Lowe 1986:xvii).[7] Ricoeur follows Kant in founding the necessity of this synthesis of

---

[6] The term 'synthesis' occurs 121 times in *Fallible man,* always as an indication of the mediation between two apparently mutually exclusive poles.

[7] Peirce is known to have read Kant's book on the critique of pure reason several hours a day for two years (Gelpi 1994:30). According to Peirce, Kant does not sufficiently distinguish between the three forms of logical reasoning. "As a result of that failure Kant's transcendental method formulates an unverified hypothesis about how the human mind works, and then presents it as an induction, a validated hypothesis, while calling it a transcendental deduction" (Gelpi 1994:31). Moreover, Peirce links this triadic reasoning with

finiteness and infinity in a transcendental synthesis (by reason alone). The synthesis of finiteness and infinity is more original than the rupture of reason (Lowe 1985:xviii). But Ricoeur does more: he precedes this transcendental synthesis with a pre-reflexive understanding of the relationship between finiteness and infinity in a case of heartbreaking misery. This phenomenological analysis forms a framework, within which the transcendental synthesis in thought takes place, in Ricoeur's construct (Lowe 1985:xx). He also extends this phenomenological approach in the analyses of acting and feeling, in order not to lock up the subject in itself, apart from reality as it shows itself.

This connection between thinking and reality is also characteristic of Peirce's pragmatic epistemology. However, Peirce thinks triadically; the relationship between finiteness, infinity, and synthesis is a triadic relationship between a certain fact, a general idea, and a hypothesis (possibility). This relationship has no other structure in thinking, acting, or feeling. The failure of the synthesis (hypothesis, possibility) is an abductive problem, i.e., no connection is made between the concrete and a generally valid idea (human dignity, love, happiness); between a concrete fact or event, and the ultimate good.[8]

### 1.3.3.1 Thinking

According to Ricoeur, thinking is characterised by a disproportionality between taking a specific point of view and the meaning (the ultimate good, the truth) of the object of our thinking, and by the synthesis of perspective and meaning. As embodied beings, we are open to the world from a particular place in time and space. Our openness is a finite openness. "Primal finitude consists in *perspective* or *point of view*. It affects our primary relation to the world, which is to 'receive' objects and not to create them" (Ricoeur 1986:24). This point of view is not the same as the 'receptivity' that exists in an openness to the world. Our finite openness is also not synonymous with physicality, which mediates our openness to the world. "It consists more in the role of the body's zero origin, in the original 'here' starting from which there are places in the world" (Ricoeur 1986:24).

The meaning of the world does not coincide with one's own perspective. Human beings also intentionally transcend a given situation towards the truth, which is objectively given in the world, i.e., in the object of our knowledge (Ricoeur 1986:26-27). However, this awareness of truth is only accessible through

---

reality, based on the assumption that the structure of the mind and that of reality correspond. Finally, Peirce distances himself from Kant's subjectivism and connects triadic logic with a social process of testing truth in the community.

[8] According to Peirce, religion, art, and aesthetics involve a specific form of abduction, namely 'musement'. Beliefs are the result of a creative process in which they 'befall' people (in Dutch, *gewaarwording*).

our concrete perspective on the world, which is a specific point of view. A synthesis can only be realised when we let ourselves be addressed by the world so that the truth, as given in the object itself, emerges in our concrete perspective on the world. This synthesis is fragile, because there is also freedom in the knowing subject, in addition to the intentional orientation towards truth. A subject has the possibility to deny what is given as truth in the object of our knowledge. A synthesis between a finite perspective and truth is not realised.

### 1.3.3.2 Acting

Acting refers to the will, to the motives (reasons) from which people act, to the desires and capacities to act ('I can'). Our actions are characterised by a disproportion between the determinacy of our character as subject, and the excess of happiness related to the dignity (humanity) of every human being. Every human being has the whole palette of motives from which subjects can act, namely good and evil motives, selfish and selfless. Nothing human is alien to us. On the other hand, our actions are open towards human dignity (humanity), which is universal and an unlimited possibility of our acting. There is a disproportionality between the infinite possibility of human dignity and the limitations of our character. We can fall short in our openness to human dignity. "My character and my humanity together make of my freedom an unlimited possibility and a constituted partiality" (Ricoeur 1986:61).

We can realise that we are trapped in our limitations and do not act from the point of view of the human dignity of the other. The synthesis of our character (limitation) and the human dignity of the other (as unlimitedness) may not come about. For example, our motives could be selfish and not focused on the other person and his/her fulfilling happiness. Human dignity is the ontological constitution of man. Respecting this dignity should underpin our actions. However, due to the limitations of our character, we fall short; the synthesis of our character and openness towards the happiness of the other does not come about.

### 1.3.3.3 Feeling

Feeling should not be equated with the inner world of a person, the inner self. There is a double movement in feeling, namely a practical binding to the world, and a binding of the self (Ricoeur 1986:89). Feeling connects us with the world that speaks to us; it binds us to ourselves through feelings of desire and love that are evoked by the world. Both movements are inextricably linked. However, the consequence of this double movement is that the fragility we encountered in thinking and acting comes together in feeling (heart). "All the disproportions that we have seen culminate in the disproportion of happiness and character would be interiorised in the heart" (Ricoeur 1986:82).

At the same time, a philosophy of feeling must not be a relapse into a pathos (*pathétique*) inaccessible to reason. According to Ricoeur, the key lies in the distinction between pleasure and happiness. The nature of the mediation or synthesis in sensual delight or pleasure is limited, while happiness is characterised by unlimitedness. An example of the first is the pleasure we can get from dancing or singing. Pleasure ends as soon as the dancing or singing is over. The joy of dancing and singing gives vitality to life. However, this solution will not help in a situation in which we feel existentially unhappy; if we no longer see any light at the end of the tunnel, and everything is heavy. These turns of phrase refer to the absence of a happiness that is limitless (Ricoeur 1986). This makes us aware that the ontological condition of man is a demand for unlimited happiness that gives fulfilment (being sufficient in itself). Ricoeur calls this fulfilling happiness a "spiritual joy" (Ricoeur 1986:92), the "Joy of YES!" (Ricoeur 1986:110), and "the only affective 'mood' worthy of being called ontological" (Ricoeur 1986:106).

The synthesis of our actual joy in a finite situation and this unlimited happiness is primordial to the individual parts. We cannot become aware of infinite happiness without realising the finiteness of joy, and vice versa. Just as we search in our mind for the truth of our synthesis, and in our action seek confirmation of human dignity (goodness), so the heart is focused on the experience of fulfilling happiness. However, this synthesis is fragile.

### 1.3.4   Three needs: to have, to be able, and to be valued

Ricoeur (1986:106-125) illustrates the human quest for fulfilling happiness through three needs that are characteristic of every human being: to have (*avoir*), to be able (*pouvoir*), and to be valued (*vouloir*). The joy of having is limited by the fear of losing, of not having something (any longer). When 'to have' replaces the 'innocence' (freedom) of being happy, then we are not free from fear. Then 'having' does not rest on possessing the other, or an object outside of ourselves, but on the experience of a fulfilling – and as such, also liberating – happiness (Ricoeur 1986:115).[9]

The joy of being able ('I can', 'I speak', 'I sing') appears concretely in an objective form linked to social roles and technological means, and in an institutional form in the public domain (education, care, police, etc. – for example, 'I

---

[9] Ricoeur calls this a utopia of the possible implicit in the experience of the good of 'having' (to possess). "I cannot imagine a suspension of having that would be so radical as to deprive the 'I' of any anchorage in the 'mine'. If man's goodness is to be possible, even as a past or future utopia, this goodness would require the innocence of a certain having. It should be possible to draw a dividing line that cuts not between being and having, but between unjust having and a just possession that would distinguish among men without mutually excluding them" (Ricoeur 1986:115).

teach', 'I take care of a patient', 'I speak justice', respectively). Without this connection with what lies outside us, we cannot experience the joy of being able. In this objective form, however, the ability (power) can take the form of coercion if the ability loses its innocence (freedom). It is not the infinite happiness of being able to, but of realising something (a work) that lies outside the self. We can experience this compulsion and loss of innocence as brokenness (heartbreaking misery). The experience of unlimited happiness is only possible if and only if we can imagine, desire, and realise the joy of being able as innocent power (freedom).[10]

Finally, there is the desire of people to be appreciated by the other. Appreciation or affirmation is fragile when it is outside of ourselves, in the words of the other, or the feeling that the other values us (Ricoeur 1986:121). In this case, the source of the appreciation lies outside ourselves and not in the realisation and experience of infinite happiness associated with our dignity as individuals. Appreciation always occurs in the limitation of the opinion of another, the one who expresses recognition (Ricoeur 1986:122). But we need to realise that, ultimately, a concrete joy does not lie in the judgment of the other, but in the infinite dignity of oneself as a person. Fragmentation arises when the synthesis of the concrete recognition and human dignity of the person does not come about. The result may be a longing for recognition without the possibility of finding meaning. This can result in a loss of self-esteem.

## 1.4 Religion and the experience of heartbreaking adversity

What is the relation between religion and the experience of heartbreaking adversity? The presumption is that the wholeness of the one "self – directed to infinity", and the other "self – directed to the finite", is prior to any differentiation. The mediation between the greatness of the ethical vision (the good life, perfect happiness, humanity) and the finite existence cannot be realised in certain situations in life such as enduring suffering, the terminal phase of a disease, being separated from a loved one. The awareness and feeling of the absence of the good in this situation defines the experience of heartbreaking adversity. Where is the good in my life? How is this existential experience related to the religious experience: where is God in my life? To structure my reflection on this question, I will follow a scheme which Hans van der Ven developed in his book *The moral self* (1998).

---

[10] "The fact remains that I could not understand power as evil if I could not imagine an innocent destination of power by comparison to which it is fallen. I can conceive of an authority which would propose to educate the individual to freedom, which would be a power without violence; in short, I can imagine the difference between power and violence; the utopia of a Kingdom of God, a City of God, an empire of minds or a kingdom of ends, implies such an imagination of non-violent power. This imagination liberates the essence; and this essence governs all efforts to transform power into an education to freedom" (Ricoeur 1986:120).

From the framework of religion as text, he examines the relationship between religion and the good from four perspectives: religion as an integrated text incorporating morality (*i.e.*, distinguishing between good and bad), morality as a context of religion, and morality as a subtext of religion. This distinction gives a structure for analysing this relationship between religion and the good from different angles.

### 1.4.1   The good subsumed under religion

Before I elaborate on this relationship according to the fourfold distinction described earlier, I want to reflect on the position that subsumes the good under religion. Or put differently, the claim that only religion can give access to the experience of the good. On what grounds does one claim subsuming the good under religion?

First, things are good because they express God's will, or commandment, or love. The authority for the good rests in God, not in the good(s) themselves (Nieman, 2011:16). A biblical story that expresses this argument *par excellence* is the story of Abraham at Mount Moriah. Real faith is to crucify the intellect, and to simply follow God's commandment even contrary to the reasons which people have of the good. "The demand to find reason after reason is at odds with a grateful acceptance of creation, and arrogant at that" (Nieman 2011:16). The argument against this position is found in the story of Abraham at Sodom. The core argument of Abraham in this story is that things are good in themselves. A claim based on the good is a universal claim. People who are innocent should be treated as innocent, whether they are known (friends, relatives) or unknown (strangers) (Nieman 2011:3).

Secondly, Abraham expresses a resoluteness in challenging every authority – even the highest – if it trespasses on this universal claim. "Abraham dares to remind the King of Kings that He's about to trespass on moral law. ... 'Let not the Lord be angry if I go on' is what precedes the line that bargains God down to thirty" (Nieman 2011:3).

Thirdly, moral judgment is not a matter of decisions made once and for all, but of keeping our eye on distinctions. We need to give arguments for the good. Numbers matter. Gradations matter (Nieman 2011:3). Moral clarity on the good is never absolute, but in need of argumentation and reasons. Claims about the good are never abstract, but concrete. The question of whether a concrete situation is a manifestation of the good can only be settled by argument.

A second argument for subsuming morality to religion is based on the theological argument that mankind is so alienated from the good by sin that he no longer has access to good (Hick 2010). If this argument is true, then any experience of a heartbreaking adversity is excluded, because people have no access to the good. Yet people experience an absence of the good, which is the 'stitch' of the experience of adversity. And this absence of the good is considered to be evil. Where does evil come from, if humanity is created by God in innocent perfection? One theological tradition understands the fall as being alienated from past good. Another tradition – of which Augustine was one of the founders – understands evil as *privatio boni* (the absence of good) (Hick 2010). According to this tradition, evil is the result of man's will, which does not do good. Man's sin, then, is turning away from God (*aversio Dei*), and turning to what is limited (*conversio ad creaturas*). In other words, the absence of good is the result of 'evil' will. "For when the will abandons what is above itself, and turns to what is lower, it becomes evil – not because that is evil to which it turns, but because the turning itself is wicked" (Hick 2010:60). This tradition does not run into the problem that man is completely alienated from the good, and therefore cannot explain the experience of absence of the good in the experience of heartbreaking adversity.

### 1.4.2   Religion as text

Before elaborating on the fourfold relationship between morality and religion, I will briefly introduce the concept of 'text', derived from Ricoeur (1991). The concept of text has four markers. First, "a text is any discourse fixed by writing" (Ricoeur 1991:106). A text is independent of speech. It inscribes directly, in written words, what the discourse means. Secondly, a text is characterised by a separation between the meaning of the text and the intention of the author. "The text is the very place where the author appears" (Ricoeur 1991:109), but the text also distances itself from the author. Thirdly, the meaning contained in a text is independent of an event, and at the same time reconnected to the world through signs (Ricoeur 1991:108). The direct reference of speech to the world is lost – yet the referential function of signs is preserved. "The text is not without reference: the task of the reader, qua interpretation, is precisely to fulfil the reference" (Ricoeur 1991:109). Fourthly, a text – in principle – is accessible to everyone. Any reader, in any context and time, can be part of the ongoing process of interpretation. This also implies getting into dialogue with other interpretations of the text by the community of interpretation, and into dialogue with other texts and the community of interpretation of those texts. A last remark: everything that meets all four characteristics is a text (Dupont 2010:77) – not only written pages, but also buildings (churches), rituals, a rule of action, clothes that people wear, actions, and material objects.

### 1.4.3   The relationship between religion and the good

In the first model, religion is approached as an integrated, structured text, in which the meaning of various elements can only be discovered through their interrelatedness (Van der Ven 1998:13). Morality is understood as a constitutive subtext of religion – perhaps even the most important subtext related to ortho-praxis. An example of this approach is to call hospitality a Christian value in education. This interpretation reflects the idea that morality is viewed as an inte-gral subtext of the Christian religion. "In the Bible, true hospitality is connected with unconditionality, openness and grace" (Broer *et al.* 2018). At the same time, the authors connect the biblical understanding to the analysis of hospitality by Derrida, who defines absolute hospitality as the virtue where one gives all to an-other without any compensation or reciprocity. They understand hospitality both as subtext of the Christian religion (part/whole relation) and as a non-religious moral good, grounded on morality shared by humanity.

In the second model, religion and morality are related as text and context. Religion as text must be understood from the context, and vice versa. Text and context are dialectically related to each other. Van der Ven (1998:15) gives an example of early Christianity in its historical context: "We see it being influenced by the Roman Empire, by Greco-Roman culture, and by urban life in this culture, while in turn influencing this culture and society". In the Graeco-Roman culture, the religious text of Christianity existed next to other texts such as those of Juda-ism, Stoicism, and Epicureanism. "Within this intertextuality, it is not easy to determine which is the genotext and which is the phenotext" (Van der Ven 1998:15). Within this model of text and context, morality (the good) is not viewed as completely independent and grounded on religious authority (Christian or other traditions). Intertextuality is a process of mutual interaction.

A third model regards morality as a subtext of religion. The main ques-tion is: What happens to non-religious morality when it is incorporated and inte-grated in religion? According to Van der Ven (1998:16), we need to distinguish two different levels of influence on morality so that it becomes a subtext of reli-gion: the immanent and transcendent levels.

At the immanent level, religion performs three functions of integrating, orienting, and criticising morality, while at the same time accepting morality as an autonomous field based on critical moral reasoning.[11]

- "First it integrates external ideas, beliefs, values and norms by relating them to the main Christian themes, that is creation, alienation, literation, and eschatological completion. In this way it establishes connection" (Van der Ven 1998:16).
- Second, in the course of this integration process, it "orients them toward the future, which is a future of surprise, gift – not a futurum that is the product of extrapolations from the past and the present, but an ad-ventus, a new coming era" (Van der Ven 1998:16).
- "Third, within this orientation process, religion carries out a moral cri-tique of historical developments, assessing how well or how badly they

---

[11]Auer (1971) is one of the founding fathers of the theory of autonomous morality in Catholic theology.

fit into the intrinsic value of nature and humanity as aimed at in God's creation" (Van der Ven 1998:16).

At the transcendent level, religion places morality in a qualitatively different perspective, thereby changing its very character. This change of character does not mean that on an ethical and moral plane, Christian faith adds something to the predicates 'good' or 'obligatory' as applied to action (Van der Ven 1998:17). Following Ricoeur (1992), Van der Ven points to two changes of character. First, morality is characterised by a question-and-answer structure. The question refers to what is good or bad, and the answer to specific epistemic criteria.

> In the realm of religion, 'question' takes on the meaning of a call, while 'answer' refers to the response to this call. Here, the question is 'Where are you?', and the answer is 'It's me here – here I stand for you, I cannot do otherwise' (Ricoeur 1992:22, 24, 352) (Van der Ven 1998:17).

The second change or character of morality through religion refers to a recapitulation of morality by the names we use to indicate God.

> Biblical *agape* belongs to an economy of the gift, possessing a metaethical character, which makes me say that there is no such thing as Christian morality, expect perhaps on the level of the history of *mentalités*, but a common morality ... that biblical faith places in a new perspective, in which love is tied to the naming of God (Ricoeur 1992:25) (Van der Ven 1998:17).

## BIBLIOGRAPHY

Auer, A. (1971). Autonome Moral und christlicher Glaube. Düsseldorf: Patmos-Verlag.

Bagger, M. (2004). Religious experience, justification and history, Cambridge: Cambridge University Press.

Broer, N.A., De Muynck, A., Potgieter, F.J., Van der Walt, JJ.L. & Wolhuter, C.W. (2018). Religieuze tolerantie vraagt onderwijs in gastvrijheid. HTS Teologiese Studies/Theological Studies 74(4), 4859. https://doi.org/10.4102/hts.v74i4.4859 .

Corrington, R.S. (2002). Reviewed work(s): Varieties of transcendental experience: A study in constructive postmodernism by Donald L. Gelpi. Transactions of the Charles S. Peirce Society 38(3):457-463.

Dupont, J. (2010). Identiteit is kwaliteit: De identiteitstheorie van Paul Ricoeur als voorstudie voor een verheldering van de identiteit van katholieke basisscholen in Nederland. Budel: Damon.

Gelpi, D.L. (1994). The turn to experience in contemporary theology. Mahwah, NJ: Paulist Press.

(2000). Varieties of transcendental experience: A study in constructive postmodernism. Collegeville, PA: Michael Glazier Books.

Hick, J. (1903). Varieties of religious experience William James, The varieties of religious experience. Boston: Longmans, Green, and Company.

(2010). Evil and the love of God. London: Palgrave MacMillan.

James, W. (1903). Varieties of religious experience William James, The varieties of religious experience. Boston: Longmans, Green, and Co.

Kaag, J. (2020). Sick souls, healthy minds. Princeton, NJ: Princeton University Press. Kindle Edition.

Lowe, W.J. (1986). Introduction, In: P. Ricoeur, Fallible man (revised translation by Charles A. Kelby) (New York: Fordham University Press), pp. vii-xxxii.

Markey, J.J. & Zuschlag, G. (2017). The foundational theology of Donald Gelpi, SJ. American Journal of Theology & Philosophy 38(2-3):167-178.

Nieman, S. (2011). Moral clarity: A guide for grown-up idealists. London: Vintage books.

Oppenheim, F.M. (2004). Gelpi's History of American religious philosophy. Transactions of the Charles S. Peirce Society 40(3):477-486.

Ricoeur, P. (1986). Fallible man (revised translation by Charles A. Kelby). New York: Fordham University Press.

(1991). From text to action. Essays in Hermeneutics II. Evanston, ILL: Northern University Press.

(1992). Oneself as another. Chicago/London: The University of Chicago Press.

Samuels, W.J. (2000). Signs, pragmatism, and abduction: The tragedy, irony, and promise of Charles Sanders Peirce. Journal of Economic Issues 34(1):207-217.

Sonesson, G. (2013). The natural history of branching: Approaches to the phenomenology of firstness, secondness, and thirdness. Signs and Society 1(2):297-326.

Van der Ven, J.A. (1998). Formation of the moral self. Grand Rapids, MI: Wm B. Eerdmans.

Young, A. (2014). The dialogical spirit. Christian reason and theological method in the third millennium. Cambridge, UK: The Lutterworth Press, James Clarke & Co.

# Chapter 2
# Processes of Resilience

*C A M Hermans*[1]

## 2.1 Introduction

What processes of resilience help people deal with heartbreaking diversity associated with the absence of the ultimate good with, and for others? I define resilience as follows:

> Multi-level processes of systems that are in a dynamic relationship with other systems, that make us aware and experience the reality of the good as a possibility in and of events in our lives with and for others, and a just and sustainable society, insofar as this is visible in the practical life that follows from the meaning of this experience.[2]

Processes of resilience relate to experiences of the good in, and of events in our lives with, and for others, in a just and sustainable society. They promote awareness and experience of the possibility of a connection between the good and concrete events in the reality in which we live. Resilience is a power of the human spirit. Resilience allows people to experience the good in life events (here and now). And this experience gives meaning to life, offers unlimited happiness, and helps handle situations of tragedy. In line with this, I distinguish four processes of resilience, on which I will elaborate in this chapter.

- Recognition of contingency;
- Transcendental openness;
- Experience of happiness, and
- Handling tragedy.

The definition speaks of multi-level processes in dynamic systems. Resilience processes take place in multiple domains or levels of the social ecology in which people live (Van Breda 2018:4). The term 'systems' can refer to units of various sizes such as individuals, families, communities, and organisations (institutions). These systems interact dynamically. For example, how we deal with tragedy is

---

[1] His e-mail address is: chris.hermans@ru.nl

[2] This definition of resilience has the structure of Peirce's pragmatic maxim (see Chapter 1, section 2, in this volume). The truth of an opinion and experience is connected with the consequences that become visible in the practical life of systems (persons, groups, organisations).

related to processes in systems such as family, friends, a religious community, and the dominant culture of a society that influence us. These systems can support each other in processes of resilience, but also work against or conflict with each other. Systems are marked by agency (capacities) and structure of institutions, as well as the interaction between the two (Van Breda 2018:10). Agency refers to "the freedom that individuals have in their lives and social environment and the influence they exert on it, while structure reflects the macrosystems that facilitate but also limit the choices and opportunities of individuals" (Van Breda 2018:10).

## 2.2 Contingency

"And behold it happened ..."; "It came my way ..."; "I did not see it coming ...". These statements express experiences of contingency. First, I will define contingency as the ontological mode of existence of man. Next, I will discuss different ways of dealing with contingency and finally, I will elaborate on the recognition of transcendence in connection to experiences of contingency.

### 2.2.1   Ontology of contingency

Contingency refers to the feeling of unpredictability and uncertainty in human existence (subject becoming). It refers to the moment when an opportunity actually arises, and that it happens unexpectedly is new by definition and different from what we expected. The following description of contingency is taken from Agamben:

> [w]hat is not, from the possibility to be, and what is, from the
> possibility not to be (Van der Heiden 2014:260).

This description is in line with the analysis of the pathos of misery, which we interpreted as a discord between two 'selves': one thrown into time and space, concrete and determined, and one with a sense of infinity, the greatness ('grandeur') of the ethical orientation and perfect happiness. Human beings are simultaneously both and the whole of both parts, but this synthesis is a possibility that does not always come about. Contingency is the experience that what is (the good) can possibly not be and that what is not (the good) contains the possibility of being. We are not the masters of the synthesis of finiteness and infinity. That's what the experience of contingency explains.[3]

---

[3] "Man is not master of the possibility of synthesis because he is not master of infinity, human dignity, and perfect happiness. That which I *am to be* is denied in the feeling that it was not necessary that I be such as I am, nor even that I exist, that it was possible for me to have been another and even not to have been. This feeling cannot be stated without absurdity since the imagination of my being-other stands out against the background of the unquestionable presence of this body and of this life that excludes *ipso facto* all other

Contingency is a characteristic of our human condition (ontology) and not 'in the facts', but a characteristic of the experience and interpretation of our 'subjectification' (becoming subject). An experience of contingency is subjective. The same event can be interpreted as a contingent by one person and not by another. The essence of being is what happens.

> The event concerns the singular occurrence by which our world changes, since it interrupts something in our world or interjects something new in it (Van der Heiden 2014:17).

Characteristic of an 'event' is the possibility of an actuality that was not foreseen, nor can be traced back to given facts. The essence of an ontology of contingency is the 'new beginning'. This beginning is a possibility of something completely different, something that cannot be foreseen, controlled, or calculated.

### 2.2.2   Definition of philosophy of religion

What is the experience of contingency? The German philosopher of religion, Kurt Wuchterl (2019:147), defines the experience of contingency as follows:

> A personal conviction is religious-philosophically contingent if and only if the facts addressed in the conviction are judged to be ontologically contingent; moreover, [if] that state of affairs resists all attempts by human action to eliminate the present non-necessity; [if] this fact is also accompanied by existential interest, and finally, [if] the circumstances of the person involved trigger the need to deal with the phenomenon.

The first feature in the definition refers to the ontology of contingency, as developed above.[4] The event is possible, not necessary, yet actual (Hermans 2019). Secondly, a human actor cannot remove the non-necessity of the event by human action (by himself or others). For example, a person of a specific racial and ethnic group shares characteristics such as culture and physical markers that cannot be undone. The non-necessity of these markers cannot be undone. Thirdly, there is an existential interest in the non-necessity of this situation or this event. A person experiences a rift between self and self. The term 'existential' refers to an awareness of what is missing: a better world, human dignity, perfect happiness (the telos or purpose of human life). This awareness manifests itself primarily as a feeling: a desire or passion, or the opposite, resistance or protest. It is not simply

---

possibilities; but the brute fact of existing in such a way, here and now, when it is measured against the demand for totality, emerges as existence that I do not produce, that I do not posit. Existence is discovered to be *only* existence, *default of being-through-self*. The imagination that forms the possibility there was of not being is, as it were, the revealer of that default of being-through-self" (Ricoeur 1986:139).

[4] The first marker is the epistemic element in the definition (Wuchterl 2011:36).

this event, but it is about the meaning of the whole of our existence (the synthesis).[5] A contingency experience leads to uncertainty or disrupture about the possibility that this life (or the life of others) ultimately has meaning. Fourthly, the event provides food for thought, so that it does not let go of a person (any longer). A person must give this experience a place in his/her own life story and organise his/her thoughts about it (Wuchterl 2011: 37). This leads to the need to reorganise a life narrative.

### 2.2.3   Three ways to deal with contingency

People deal with unforeseen events differently. Wuchterl (2011:40-44; 2019:175-176) distinguishes three forms (modes) of dealing with contingency. The first mode is controlling contingency (German 'Kontingenzbewältigung'). The term is confusing because, in the subjective experience of the person, there is no control at all. What Wuchterl calls "control" refers to reasonable explanations that people give. For example, getting cancer can be explained by smoking, radiation, or a wrong diet. For some people, this is a sufficient explanation for the cancer that this person has (and not someone else). In this mode, the person accepts only reasonable explanations, based on natural laws (biological, chemical, etc.). Based on this presumption, there cannot be a subjective experience of contingency.

The second mode is recognition of contingency. Experiences of experience recognition are marked by the four characteristics mentioned earlier, namely ontological contingency, they cannot be undone by any action, having an existential importance, and the experience gives rise to thinking.

Wuchterl calls the third type a contingency encounter (German 'Kontingenzbegegnung'). Encounter refers to an experience of the unexpectedly possible because a person opens him-/herself to what is considered to be outside the limits of reason. This experience of new possibilities is the argument why contingency encounter must be distinguished from the experience of contingency. Contingency encounter can be defined as contingency recognition plus transcendental openness. In the next section, I will elaborate on transcendental openness as an experience beyond contingency.

### 2.3 Transcendental openness and musement

Transcendental openness is the second process of resilience to the experience of a heartbreaking adversity provoked by the absence of the good. Transcendental openness focuses on the event in which the good appears in a reality, while this

---

[5] See Chapter 1:section 2.2. This ties in with the disproportionality that manifests itself in the experience of torn apart. This reference is absent in my previous publications on the experience of contingency (Hermans 2020), just as it is absent in Wuchterl. Ricoeur's analysis in *Fallible man* led me to this connection.

event is experienced as contingent. Transcendental openness is aimed at the appearance of the good life (God) in religion, ethics, and art. Raposa (1989; 2012) calls this process of experiencing a transcendent reality "musement", based on the pragmatic epistemology of Peirce.

### 2.3.1  Transcendental openness

Transcendental openness refers to an event in which infinity, human dignity, or fulfilling happiness unexpectedly manifests itself in reality. Joas (2008:7) defines self-transcendence as follows:

> This means experiences in which a person transcends herself, but not, at least not immediately, in the sense of moral achievements but rather of being pulled beyond the boundaries of one's self, being captivated by something outside of myself, a relaxation of or liberation from one's fixation on oneself.

Transcendental openness refers to experiences in which the self is pulled beyond its own boundaries. Wuchterl describes this as a contingency encounter (see above), where encounter refers to an unexpected event, in which a new possibility (a new beginning) becomes reality. This event is contingent, in the sense that the person realises that paradoxically this actuality can also not be there. But, in transcendental openness, this possibility of 'not be' is set aside. In the experience of the actuality, the possibility of 'not to be' is annihilated.

> In the actualization of potentiality, the potential not to … is set aside. To actualize is a 'nullification' of the potential not to be that is, when nothing in it has the potential not to be and when it can, therefore, not not be (Van der Heiden 2014:240).

How can this potential not-to-be disappear? Joas gives a clue by characterising self-transcendence as (German) '*Ergriffensein*', that is, being apprehended or overwhelmed. It does not depend on one's freedom whether new possibilities appear. In the experience of being overwhelmed by the ultimate good, the freedom is liberated from the burden of having to choose and desire something. A person who feels overwhelmed can only surrender to the realised possibility. Wholeheartedly!

### 2.3.2  Musement

How does an openness come about for the perfect good (God)? Can this be understood as abductive reasoning, aimed at generating hypotheses and tentatively accepting them (Tschaepe 2014:117)? Yes and no. When it comes to religion, ethics, and aesthetics, specific demands must be placed on the process of abduction because of the indeterminacy of the infinite (Raposa 1989:150) and there can be no testing of hypotheses. In line with Peirce, Raposa calls this particular form of abduction "musement", derived from the word 'muse'. According to the *Oxford Dictionary*, 'muse' refers to "a person or spirit that gives a writer, painter, etc. ideas and the desire to create things"[6] (Tschaepe 2014:117) Musement has a connotation of receptive perception, amazement, noticing, contemplating, letting oneself be touched. Raposa (1989; 2012), Cooke (2018), and others describe musement as a process with different phases. These phases should be viewed as a whole, in which there is an interplay between the elements.

### 2.3.3   First phase

The first phase involves the pure play of ideas that arise in a person's mind (Cooke 2018:1).[7] A play in itself has no purpose or interest other than the joy of playing (Raposa 1989:128-129). The intrinsic joy is an expression of a desire (inspiration) and not the result of agreements made or following rules. The human mind is in a state of freedom, receptivity, and wonder. If there is any law in pure play, it is the law of pure freedom (Raposa 1989:128-129; Cooke 2018:6).[8] There is receptivity with as little control as possible by the self. Finally, this phase is characterised by an attitude of wonder, in which the beauty of ideas, nature, music, or a symbol can have an attraction. In sensation, a person is gripped by an intrinsic sense of delight or joy.

### 2.3.4   Second phase

The second phase focuses on the observation of remarkable facts or events (*noticing*) (Cooke 2018:10-11). In daily life, we usually look at something without noticing it, because we see what we expect to see.[9] In the case of musement, we see something as new, remarkable, and surprising. This may involve an extraordinary or abnormal experience. But we can also see something with new eyes, as if we were seeing it for the first time. This observation of a remarkable fact is thought provoking. It may be a question that a person has asked him-/herself before, but with a remarkable fact a person is touched by an event (Cooke 2018:13). Being touched brings about involvement with, and care for this remarkable event. The question evoked by an event does not let go and creates a desire to understand the meaning of this event.

---

[6] https://www.oxfordlearnersdictionaries.com/definition/american_english/muse_1

[7] Peirce is indebted to Friedrich Schiller's concept of 'Spieltrieb' (English: play instinct) (Raposa 1989:128).

[8] In this instance, Peirce refers to John 3:8: "It bloweth where it listeth" (Cooke 2018:7).

[9] Normal experiences simply do not catch our attention because life goes on without notice. This is the result of predictive processing, which aims at error management. When something unexpected happens (for instance, my brother calls to tell me, his wife died in a car accident), this moment becomes different from normal experiences (Hermans 2015:38).

### 2.3.5   Third phase

The third phase is a generative process, in which a person seeks a hypothesis that could explain this remarkable event. Although the process of sensation occurs freely and without purpose, it does not happen without a judgmental or evaluative element. In the process of perception, there is also a reasonable substantiation, but then not from a goal, but from an ideal (Cooke 2018:11). In the case of ethical orientation, this is the idea of the '*bonum commune*' and, in religion, the idea of God as the ultimate good (Raposa 1989:137-138). The generative moment in amusement can be viewed as a play with ideas through which consequences become visible. Cooke (2018:12) warns us that "there is no possibility for error in musement, in contrast to inquiry, in general. In musement the free-playing mind cannot go wrong because it does not aim at anything in particular".

### 2.3.6   Spiritual prayer

'Spiritual prayer' is the last phase referring to the awareness and feeling of the soul of being connected to the perfect good (God, the beauty of nature, etc.). It is not a conscious prayer or form prayer, but an instinctive inclination (attitude, disposition), embodying the felt reality of this idea or ideal (Raposa 1989:139). A feeling that can happen to a hiker in nature at sunrise. The person feels part of the whole, and this feeling gives focus and direction to his way of life (ethos).

### 2.4 Happiness

Happiness is the experience of the perfect, unlimited good in an event in life with, and for others. This experience of happiness has several characteristics. Following Stephan Strasser, I will distinguish several markers of the experience of happiness.[10] Next, I will discuss the fact that the realisation of the perfectly good in an event takes on different forms, depending on the practice in which this realisation takes place.

### 2.4.1   The experience of happiness

What is happiness in relation to the experience of the presence of good in a concrete situation or event? Strasser (1977:37) defines happiness as follows:

> Happiness consists in a transcending anticipation. It is a deficient anticipation of the experience of fulfilment, a precision

---

[10] I quote from the English translation *Theory of feeling* (1977); original *Das Gemüt* (1956).

limited to single aspects, an imperfect presentment of the final completion of our own existence.

The experience of happiness anticipates the perfect good, which is greater than is manifested in this event. The realisation of the good keeps something in reserve with regard to the ultimate fulfilment. It is the perfect good that takes shape, but only insofar as this event can be transparent to the perfect good. It is adequate in the sense that it is a realisation of the perfectly good, but this realisation comprises only some aspects and not the totality of the perfectly good. That is why Strasser calls it an imperfect realisation of the ultimate completion of our own existence.

Being able to perceive possibilities that are experienced as absolute shows that man is a being gifted with spirit ("logos").[11] The highest form of human becoming is defined as the soul, "the bearer of the idea of man as a being which is also spiritual" (Strasser 1977:170). On the level of the spirit, human beings are able to project completely abstract values such as peace, health, beauty, and truth.

Strasser identifies five characteristics of this experience of happiness.[12] His claim is that all characteristics play a role in the experience of happiness as the anticipation of the perfectly good (Strasser 1977:370-372). However, that does not mean that each characteristic is equally strong in every experience.

- First, happiness implies the realisation of a transcendent moment in, and of reality. It is a partial anticipation of fulfilment, but nevertheless the awareness of fulfilment is there.
- Secondly, this experience of happiness is characterised by a state of mind, which Strasser describes as euphoric, delirious, and blissful. A person cannot experience the infinite that emerges in the concrete and definite without stepping outside of himself. "The 'object' of this blissful experience is such that a subject is overwhelmed by its richness, inexhaustibility and boundlessness" (Strasser 1977:370).
- Thirdly, happiness is an experience of harmony with the world as a whole, and of one's place in it. Harmony requires a certain balance and the right proportions. The passionate impulses must be in proper proportion to each other; not delirious and not hypothermic. An example of this is the harmonious experience of happiness from an intimate connectedness with nature.

---

[11] Strasser uses Logos in the sense in which it is used in ancient Greek philosophy and early Christian theology, referring to the divine reason implicit in the cosmos, ordering it, and giving it form and meaning (https://www.britannica.com/topic/logos). For an introduction to the relationship between "pneuma" ("spirit") in the Gospel of John and "logos" ("word" or "mind") in the prologue of John, see Engberg-Pedersen (2012).

[12] Part of this text is also published in the article by Hermans & Kornet (2020), *Spirituality as passions of the heart.*

- The fourth characteristic of happiness is contentment or the experience of peace with oneself. "The experience of happiness will always be his concrete experience, and thus will be limited by his capacity to assimilate the inexhaustibility of the good-in-itself" (Strasser 1977:372).13 It is marked by the feeling of being at peace with oneself and living within the confines of the circumstances in which the ultimate good is concretely experienced.
- Finally, happiness is both a possibility that can become a reality in life, and a risk, because this happiness cannot be enforced. A person can have fun, but not enforce lasting and fulfilling happiness. Some religious practices promote an attitude to life that is centred on the experience of the perfectly good (see Chapter 2 in this volume), but even these do not necessarily lead to experiences of anticipation of the perfectly good.

### 2.4.2 Appearances of happiness

People do not have the same idea of happiness. According to the sociologist Ferguson (1992:104, ekindle), different appearances of happiness refer to different ideas of the good life. Forms of happiness are linked to different sociocultural environments and practices, in which different experiences of happiness can arise and thrive. Different environments and practices generate different experiences of the self, as realisation of the perfectly good. In a theory of resilience and a resilient religion, it is important to distinguish different appearances of happiness, as they may offer a different kind of resilience in dealing with heartbreaking misery.[14]

Ferguson distinguishes five modalities of happiness in the history of Christianity, namely surrender of faith, creed, morality, passion, and sensuality. These manifestations can be placed on a continuum from a strong inner experience of happiness to a strong outer experience, from a transformation of the subject to a transformation based on self-expression. I will now briefly elaborate on these five appearances of happiness. Ferguson describes them as forms of Christianity in Western society, which have developed one after the other.[15] He claims

---

[13] This distinction between '*his* concrete experience' and the 'inexhaustibility of the good' connect to the idea of disproportionality of human beings between self and self by Ricoeur (see Chapter 1).

[14] Ferguson also suggests this in the title of his book: *Religious transformation in Western society: The end of happiness* (1992).

[15] This description is not exhaustive. In what modalities has Christianity found its way into non-Western cultures? Which modalities can be distinguished in other religions in different cultures? For an introduction to the theology of Africa, see Tshaka (2016); in philosophy, see Ugwuanyi (2014).

that each form was dominant in a certain period, without the other forms disappearing. I present the appearances without claiming that it is exhaustive.

### 2.4.3   Surrender of faith

The self in a surrender of faith (faith) is determined by an inner acquiescence and merging with the ultimate good, or God: "In relation to God, which is an inward relation, Faith, there is no 'distance' and no 'estrangement' between the longing subject and the object of longing" (Ferguson, 1992:1456, eKindle). In the surrender of faith, there is a direct influence of God (as the ultimate good) in the redemption of man. In the inner relationship with God, all distance and division is absent. This experience of happiness, according to Ferguson, is so successful because the reality of God as love could be experienced directly in human feeling (soul). That is why Christianity was able to spread so well in the first centuries among small craftsmen, slaves, women, and lower classes in the cities of the Roman Empire, because it did not use the dominant culture of the civilian population in these cities for its spread.

### 2.4.4   Faith as belief

According to Ferguson (1992, Chapter 2), this form of the experience of happiness emerges from the moment Christianity becomes a state religion.

> The immediate link between God and man was broken and dissipated in a complex variety of customs and cultures. The universality and objectivity of Belief, therefore, replaced the inner certainty of having been exclusively chosen (Ferguson 1992; 2101, eKindle).

Faith as an inner belief is mediated by institutional structures, orthodoxy, a universal creed, liturgy, and other institutional practices. The universality and objectivity of faith replaced the inner certainty of the person as being chosen by God (Ferguson 1992:707, eKindle).

### 2.4.5   Personal morality

With the rise of capitalism and the loss of social connections and structures, Ferguson (1992, Chapter 3) sees a new form of happiness emerging in a personal morality (the so-called 'Protestantische Ethik'). Happiness is the personal experience of success in life. Man experiences this success inwardly as a sign of the perfectly good, without ascribing this success to himself.

### 2.4.6   Authentic self

The promise of happiness as a search for one's own passions or motives as an authentic self throws the subject in back into himself (Ferguson 1992, Chapter 3). God as perfect good is hidden in the depths of the soul. Transcendental openness is an openness to the depths of the soul: the perfect good as the inner compass, hidden in the soul of man.

### 2.4.7   Sensuality

The fifth form of happiness is sensuality, which includes both body and mind and sensuality, as source of the spiritual in the experience of happiness (Ferguson 1992, Chapter 5). Happiness is a sensuous, embodied experience that is fulfilling, yet sought over and over again and sometimes found. This has to do with the volatility of embodied experiences.[16]

### 2.5 Handling tragedy

Tragedy is characterised by the absence of happiness. For example, someone can passionately long for love, justice, or freedom, but this longing is not experienced as reality in life: not by him-/herself nor by the other. Is there also happiness for me, or this other person? Are we or is the other morally guilty of this absence of happiness? Is it simply a misjudgement that anyone could make, or is it a major, culpable mistake? I will now first give a definition of tragic experiences. Then I will distinguish four kinds of tragedy. Finally, I will connect dealing with tragedy with the absence of the ultimate good, or God.

### 2.5.1   A definition

What defines a tragic experience?
- First, this experience presupposes a recognition of contingency: a person experiences the situation as completely unexpected and does not have a schema that offers a sufficient explanation for what happened (Van Dalen, Scherer-Rath, Van Laarhoven, Wiegers & Hermans 2019:234-235).
- Secondly, the tragic person feels powerless because s/he has not been able to prevent the loss of ultimate good (Van Dalen et al. 2019:237).
- Thirdly, the person cannot give up the meaning of the ultimate good in his life with, and for others, even if this good is not experienced in the reality of this event (Van Dalen et al. 2019:237). The experience of the absence of good (God) makes itself felt in the experience of tragedy.

---

[16] A reviewer of Ferguson's book calls this 'therapeutic religion' (Johnson, 1995:125). Heelas & Woodhead (2005) describe this form of ultimate happiness.

- Fourthly, the person uses a moral scheme to measure the absence of ultimate meaning in his/her life. Am I (or is the other) guilty of what happened? Is it fair what happened? (Van Dalen et al. 2019:237)?

## 2.5.2 Four types of tragic experiences

Cancer is not only a clinical problem, but also a violation of the moral order of human life. Experiences of a tragic loss of happiness can be distinguished along two dimensions: pitiable and threat (Golden 1976:32).

> The term 'pitiable' is applied to situations in which a fall from happiness to misery involving the undeserved misfortune of others is depicted while the term 'fearful' refers to these same situations when viewed as occurring to ourselves.

Along these two dimensions, tragic experiences can be classified into four types: pitiable and threatening, pitiable and non-threatening, non-pitiable and threatening, and non-pitiable and non-threatening. I will only illustrate the first type of tragedy: pitiable and threatening.[17]

> When an event is experienced from both pity and fear, there are often forces at work that drive a person to actions he would not normally perform, or psychological, social, and health-related conditions that make a good life with, and for others impossible (such as a chronic illness, or the bankruptcy of a business that a person has built up throughout his life). When this is a personal experience, someone feels sorry for him-/herself. Why is this happening to me? I do not deserve this. Pity is the result of a confrontation between this event and a moral scheme (justice, (in)nocence) that the person uses: if I am not guilty of this event, then I do not deserve this to happen to me. Yet it happened to that person, and therefore s/he experiences this as unjust. "The good is not for me", people say. This interpretation can only be understood from a moral scheme in which the good should also be available for the just and the innocent. The absence of the good in life is 'what should not be'.

## 2.5.3 Handling tragic experiences

How can a person handle a tragic experience? Following Ricoeur (2007), I distinguish four tasks that are all related to the experience of a pathetic state of misery, *i.e.*, the experience of loss of the good in an event such as a chronic illness, the death of the mother or father of a 10-year-old child. In this situation, there is a connection between the loss of this mother or this father and the happiness that

---

[17] "In the purest and most intense form of tragedy ("high tragedy") both pity and fear must be present but in its widest and most common manifestation ("pathetic tragedy") pity alone occurs in any significant degree and fear is greatly attenuated or wholly absent" (Golden 1976:32).

disappeared in the child's life. The concrete other (mother or father) is the appearance of the good in life. The process of handling a tragic experience focuses on this connection between the reasons related to the loss of the concrete other and the reasons for the loss of the good life. Is the loss of the other an appearance of the ultimate good *eo ipso* also the loss of the good?

- The first task is the confirmation of the pathos of not knowing, not being able to act, and not feeling happy: "I don't know why, I can't change it, I feel unhappy" (Ricoeur 2007:69). If this suffering is innocent, then we must first affirm this innocence. If we are guilty of this suffering, we must first confess guilt.
- The second task is a lament: "How long, Lord?". On the one hand, the lament is an expression of the sorrow and emptiness that are unbearable and without end. On the other hand, it expresses the impatience of the hope of happiness that (does not) "come", the life that fulfils (Ricoeur 2007:70).
- The third task aims to separate the reasons for believing in God from the reasons for the tragedy. Despite the suffering, people believe in God as "Future that begins", also for them and over and over again. Ricoeur connects this disconnection with the aporia to which speculative thinking about evil leads (Ricoeur 2007:70). There is no reason for the necessity of evil. God (good) has the last word. Evil is the absence of good (Latin: privatio boni).
- The fourth task is to let go of the wound caused by the loss and emptiness. This implies letting go of the arguments why we should not have been affected by this existential torn. These arguments may be related to the desire to be rewarded for an exemplary life, to be spared suffering, or that the other had not died (Ricoeur 2007:70). Letting go of these arguments is a final step out of the circle of restoring what has been lost. This paves the way for recognising God as Creator, as Job did. In this way the believer confesses that fulfilled happiness and the good life are more original than the suffering that can befall a person (see also Chapter 3, The role of the Creator)).

**BIBLIOGRAPHY**

Cooke, E.F. (2018). Peirce on musement. The limits of purpose and the importance of noticing. European Journal of Pragmatism and American Philosophy X-2:1-18.

Engberg-Pedersen, T. (2012). Logos and pneuma in the Fourth Gospel. In: M.M. Mitchel & D.P. Moessner (eds), Greco-Roman culture and the New Testament (Supplements to Novum Testamentum 143) (Leiden: Brill), pp. 27-48. DOI: https://doi. org/10.1163/9789004226548_004

Ferguson, H. (1992). Religious transformation in Western society (Routledge Revivals). Taylor and Francis. Kindle edition.

Golden, L. (1976). Toward a definition of tragedy. The Classical Journal 72(1):21-33. https://www.jstor.org/stable/3296879?refreqid=excelsior%3Abe37bcaf6fec67177f64c4e33df99cef.

Heelas, P. & Woodhead, L. (2005). The spiritual revolution: Why religion is giving way to spirituality. Hoboken, NY: Wiley-Blackwell.

Hermans, C.A.M. (2015). Towards a theory of spiritual and religious experiences. A building block approach of the unexpected possible. Archive of the Psychology of Religion 37(2):141-167.

(2019). God as pure possibility and the wonder of possibilisation. Acta Theologica 39(2):9-30.

(2020). Unexpected possible. A building block approach to spiritual and religious experiences revisited. Acta Theologica Supplementum 30:5-33.

Hermans, C.A.M. & Kornet, L. (2020). Spirituality as passions of the heart. An empirical study into the character, core values and effects of the passions of the heart of general practitioners. Acta Theologica Supplementum 30: 182-209. doi.org/10.18820/23099089/actat.Sup30.8

Joas, H. (2008). Do we need religion? (The Yale Cultural Sociology Series). Taylor and Francis. Kindle edition.

Johnson, D.C. (1995). Review: Religious transformation in Western society: The end of happiness by Harvie Ferguson. Journal for the Scientific Study of Religion 34(1):124-126.

Raposa, M.L. (1989). Peirce's philosophy of religion, Bloomington, IN: Indiana University Press.

(2012). Musement as listening: Daoist perspectives on Peirce. Journal of Chinese Philosophy 39(2):207-221.

Ricoeur, P. (1986). Fallible man. Revised translation by Charles A. Kelby. New York: Fordham University Press.

(2007). Evil. A challenge to philosophy and theology. Translated by John Bowden. London: Continuum.

Strasser, S. (1977). Phenomenology of feeling. An essay on the phenomena of the heart. Pittsburgh, PA: Duquesne University Press.

Tschaepe, M. (2014). Guessing and abduction. A collaborative critical conversation on Philip Kitcher's Preludes to pragmatism. Transactions of the Charles S. Peirce Society 50(1):115-138.

Tshaka, R.S. (2016). How can a conquered people sing praises of their history and culture? Africanization as the integration of inculturation and liberation. Black Theology 14(2):91-106.

Ugwuanyi, L.U. (2014). The question of happiness in African philosophy. South African Journal of Philosophy 33(4):513-522.

Van Breda, A.D. (2018). A critical review of resilience theory and its relevance for social work. Social Work/Maatskaplike Werk 54(1):1-18.

Van Dalen, E. (2019). Interpretatiecrisis bij ongeneeslijke kankerpatiënten. Een religiewetenschappelijk onderzoek naar verklaringen, het onverwachte, tragiek en de gewaarwording van het andere. Munster: LIT Verlag.

Van Dalen, E., Scherer-Rath, M., Van Laarhoven, H., Wiegers, G. & Hermans, C.A.M. (2019). Tragedy as contingency acknowledgement: Towards a practical religious-scientific theory. Journal of Empirical Theology 32(2):232-250.

Van der Heiden, G.J. (2014). Ontology after ontotheology. Plurality, event and contingency in contemporary philosophy. Pittsburgh, PA: Duquesne University Press.

Wuchterl, K. (2011). Kontingenz, oder das Andere der Vernunft [Contingency, or the other-of-reason]. Wiesbaden: Frans Steiner Verlag.

(2019). Religious-philosophical contingency and empirical theology. Journal of Empirical Theology 32(1):169-187.

# Chapter 3

# Resilient religion

*C A M Hermans*[1]

## 3.1 Introduction

A resilient religious system can prevent an experience of heartbreaking adversity, or it can process this experience in such a way that the system does not collapse. 'Preventing' refers to the preventive capacity of a system, while 'processing disruptive experiences' refers to the curative capacity of a system that is able to absorb changes or disruptions. 'Resilient religion' refers to religious systems that have a dynamic relationship with other systems as a result of processes of resilience. Systems can be individuals, families, communities, and institutions. My assumption is that religion is always both institutional and individual. By choosing a system approach, I want to encompass both the institutional and the individual perspectives on religion. I start with a definition of resilient religion on which I will elaborate in this chapter.

> A resilient religion consists of religious systems – in a dynamic relationship with other systems – that can prevent or process the loss of the good and/or the absence of God as a possibility in and of life-events with and for others, insofar as this becomes visible in the practical way of life that follows from the meaning of this experience.

I want to develop a theory on resilient religion that is not simply the variety of traditions within the Christian religion, but all religions. The concepts within this theoretical frame religion find their origin in the study of the Christian religion (theology, spirituality, religious studies, sociology, philosophy). My claim is that they are open to understand resilience in all religions and the role of religion in dealing with heartbreaking adversity. If this is also true, it needs to be settled within the academic community of inquiry.

In the first section, I will first reflect on the idea of God as Creator. In resilient religion, God is the foundation of the synthesis of the self as openness to the unlimited, and the self as directed towards the limited. Against the experience of a person or community, in which there is no future and no possibility of moving forward, a resilient religion sets the belief and experience of God as Creator. In

---

[1] His e-mail address is: chris.hermans@ru.nl.

God as Creator, the ultimate good that man desires is more primordial than brokenness and heartbreaking adversity. I develop my ideas on God in resilient religion from Hannah Arendt's lecture on Augustine, especially thinking about love in Augustine's theology.[2] Why Arendt? First, Arendt gives a philosophical analysis of the theologian Augustine on the idea of God as creator. Her analysis is not restricted to the varieties of the Christian religion, but to the role of religion in human life with, and for others. Her analysis may not fit all religions, but that needs to be established in an academic debate. Secondly, I want to offer a concept of God that aligns with two features of the frame of reference of our late modern time, namely the acceptance of free will and an ontology of contingency. Why do we need to do so? We need to move away from concepts of God that are grounded in an ontology of the general and common that has been decisive for Western thinking since Ancient Greece (Van der Heiden 2014:15). The core issue in this ontology is that of the 'first beginning', in the sense of causation and sufficient ground. When God is 'hidden' as the first beginning in ontology, we speak of ontotheology (Van der Heiden 2014:16). In ontotheology, free will disappears, because the causes completely determine the possibilities to act. In an ontology of contingency, the core idea is the event in which a new beginning is made. The focus is on new beginnings and new possibilities to emerge. Arendt is a philosopher whose ideas are deeply embedded in the ontology of contingency and the acceptance of the free will (Canovan 1999; Helleloid 2014: Ballacci 2018). Her analysis of Augustine presents a strong analysis of the idea of God as creator which does justice to contingency and human free will.

Next, I will elaborate on the capability of discernment as a model for practical living, or the art of living well with, and for others. Discernment is aimed at the awareness and experience of the ultimate good in reality, which rests in God.

Finally, I will explain the concept of resilient religion into three dimensions, namely thinking, acting, and feeling. To what extent are religion and spirituality helping people recognise the contingency of existence, and lifting them up to think, act, and feel in freedom? Religious systems can be individuals, families, communities, and institutions. In each section, I will pay attention to religious institutions and the agency of human actors. Institutions provide structures that support and enable the agency of individual actors, but simultaneously limit

---

[2] Arendt developed the concept of natality (new beginnings) in her interpretation of the concept of love in the works of Saint Augustine. Literature has largely ignored this relationship between love and Augustine. Vecchiarelli Scott & Chelius Stark (1998) provided insight into this connection in their edition of Hannah Arendt's dissertation (*Love and Saint Augustine*). Arendt began reworking her original Augustine dissertation at various points in her life, but never finished the project. A final note: The context of the concept of natality in Arendt's reworking of her dissertation on Augustine is more existential (meaning of life, happiness) and less related to social and public life, compared to Arendt's later works.

and suppress their freedom. Religious institutions operate in a social field of competition and monopolisation, not only with other religious institutions, but also with the state (Bax 1987). Inwardly, to a greater or lesser extent, they exercise control over their members (orthodoxy check). A theory about a resilient religion will have to accommodate both dimensions and be aware of the tension between religion as an institution and the freedom of individual actors.

## 3.2 God as Creator

According to Augustine, human longing for happiness and love has its origin in the awareness of being created. Being born makes man aware that he is not his own origin. Perfect happiness does not depend on man; it is given in God prior to human birth. In God, the unity between the good (unlimited) and reality (limited) is more primordial than the brokenness and heartbreaking adversity that people experience. Next, I will show that man participates in God's creative action, because a person can make a beginning (in word and deed) to the good life with, and for each other.[3]

### 3.2.1  Human life as quest for happiness

The essence of man as a spiritual being is a longing for happiness, defined as when the perfect good is experienced as reality in life such as meeting a life partner, or the birth of a child. Happiness is neither an innate idea nor a future state that, it is hoped, will arise, but is based on memory and gratitude.

- Happiness is not an innate idea, because we do not know what ideal or ultimate happiness is.
- Nor is happiness the result of our hope, for this hope may be in vain.

The experience of heartbreaking adversity is evidence that happiness is not a certainty. In life, happiness does not last forever. At the same time, we experience in ourselves a longing for ultimate happiness which does not perish. If this desire is based on our brokenness, our desire for happiness is uncertain, unless the unity between the good and reality precedes and is more original than the brokenness. This whole is the synthesis between the self that is limited and the self that anticipates the perfect.

### 3.2.2  Happiness as memory of being created

Happiness is based on our memory of God as Creator, who is outside us and precedes us. Why remembrance? For Augustine, everything we know exists in

---

[3] Part of this section is based on my article entitled 'Unexpected possible: A building block approach to spiritual and religious experiences revisited' (Hermans 2020a:section 2.4).

memory, which to him equals consciousness. If we have forgotten something, we do not know that we have forgotten it. If it is something in the future, but not part of the consciousness from which we act, then it is meaningless to our life:

> the decisive fact determining man as a conscious, remembering being is birth or 'natality'; that is, the fact that we have entered the world through birth (Arendt 1998:Part II, 1. The Origin = eKindle 1187).

Man knows the idea of God as Creator only through memory, because creation came before our existence.

> The Creator is in man only by virtue of man's memory, which inspires him to desire happiness and with it an existence that would last forever: 'Hence I would not be, my God, I would not exist at all, if you were not in me', namely, in my memory (Arendt 1998:Part II, 1. The Origin; eKindle 1145).

In memory, human beings become aware of a boundary, beyond which lies what was 'before' or which 'preceded' human existence. Human beings do not exist by themselves.

> Seen from the perspective of human life, this Being has as its outstanding characteristic that it was before life began, will be when life has passed away, and therefore lies ahead of it in the future. Being relates to human life as that from which it comes and to which it goes, and is 'before' (ante) man in the twofold sense of past and future. Through remembrance man discovers this twofold 'before' of human existence (Arendt 1998:Part II, 1. The Origin eKindle 1168).

This awareness that God is the origin of our existence is aptly expressed in the name of God expressed as 'Future that Begins' or simply 'Beginning'. A 'Beginning' precedes birth and will be when life ends.

### 3.2.3 Contingency and free will

Does this relationship with God as Creator do justice to contingency and human free will? To answer this question, we must distinguish between *initium* (new beginning) and *in principio* (in the beginning) in Augustine's idea of creation.

> *In principio* refers to the creation of the universe – 'In the beginning, God created the heavens and the earth' (Gen. 1:1). However, *initium* refers to the beginning of 'souls', that is, not just of living creatures but of men. Augustine writes that 'this beginning did in no way ever exist before. In order that there be such a beginning, man was created before whom nobody was (Arendt 1998: Part II, 1. The Origin eKindle 1255).

The first beginning of a living creature is the product of the Creator, as Lord of heaven and earth. *Initium* is not about the first beginning, but about the possibility of a new beginning. With the creation of man, the Creator initiated the possibility of novelty (*novitas*), of contingency and free will. Without the possibility of a new beginning, people's lives with, and for each other would be determined by the conditions of the past. If we were determined by our biological condition, death would be the end.

> Hence, it was for the sake of *novitas,* in a sense, that man was created. Since man can know, be conscious of, and remember his 'beginning' or his origin, he is able to act as a beginner and enact the story of mankind (Arendt 1998:eKindle 261).

With man existing as a spiritual being, a being has appeared that has the capacity to 'begin'; that is, to be the originator of a 'new' action, speech, belief, desire, or experience. To 'begin', or to appear as a 'spirit being', is a capacity of individuals being born. Arendt repeatedly quotes this statement from Augustine: "In order that a new beginning might be made, man was created."

> Beginning, before it becomes a historical event, is the supreme capacity of man; politically, it is identical with man's freedom. *"Initium ut esset homo creatus est"*, 'that a beginning be made, man was created', said Augustine. This beginning is guaranteed by each new birth; it is indeed in every man (Arendt 1998:eKindle 2641).

This 'beginning', based on the creation of man, cannot yet be understood as factual or historical reality. It is the ability to 'begin', which all people receive at birth.

### 3.2.4  Love

What is the focus of the desire for happiness in people? Desire is a feeling, and the direction of this feeling determines the nature of the desire. Augustine distinguishes between love for the limited/finite (*cupiditatas*) and love for the unlimited/infinite, or love for God (*caritas*). The desire for the limited keeps man imprisoned in what is limited. This desire makes human beings 'un-free' because they become dependent on what lies outside themselves. "In *caritas,* whose object is eternity, man transforms himself into an eternal, non-perishable being." (Arendt 1998:eKindle 541).

A longing for God's love opens man to this love of God. This love sets us free because it is fulfilling, healing, perfect happiness. This love liberates us from fear, because God as the object of our love is 'before' actual existence (primordial). The person who acts as a 'beginner' from this love, acts from goodwill, on love for others (both aimed at the good life with, and for each other, or love for the other (both known and anonymous) (Arendt 1998:eKindle edition 630).

In the event that people act out of love for God, God becomes reality in the good life with, and for each other.

### 3.3 Discernment directed towards a practical way of life

Resilience is noticeable and demonstrable in the practical life of people if they live in the presence of God. Life events can lead to a loss of this experience. Where is God? Why did this happen to me (the other, our community, this group)? A resilient religion can (possibly) prevent this experience or help systems (people) cope with this loss and experience a new beginning of happiness in their lives. In order to be able to do this in life, systems need to acquire discernment. Discernment can be viewed as a compass with which to keep a course towards God in the storms of life (Waaijman 2013b).

I will now briefly discuss different tradition(s) on discernment in the Christian tradition, which help us understand that models of discernment are always contextual and open to transformation. Then I will distinguish five dimensions in which models of discrimination differ. Finally, I will outline a model of discernment.[4]

### 3.3.1   Contextual and open for transformation

In Christian spirituality, discernment is ambivalent, decidedly plural, and perhaps more inconsistent than is sometimes recognised (Hense 2016:10). Discernment follows two different lines in the Christian tradition (Waaijman 2013a:2-3). The first is about discernment of the spirits (*discretio spirituum*) and the second about the virtue of discretion (*discretio* in Latin, *diakrises* in Greek). The same authors sometimes connect the lines, in different ways, but there are also authors who are clearly in a certain tradition. In the New Testament, Paul of Tarsus uses the phrase 'discernment of the spirits' as one of the eight charismata, or gifts, to develop the community (1 Cor. 12:8-10). But the term is vague, and open to many interpretations. According to Hense (2016: 8), there is a coherent theme of discernment in the Christian tradition as far back as the writings of Origen (born AD 185/186) and Athanasius (born AD 295). All models of discernment are contextual and serve the specific needs of individuals or a community in a particular context.

### 3.3.2   Different dimensions

The differences between the models of discernment can be mapped along five dimensions. I describe each dimension as a continuum with two poles. Concepts

---

[4] The first part of this section is based on my article entitled 'Discernment as predictor for transformational leadership: A study of school leaders in Catholic schools in India' (Hermans 2021:section 2.4).

of discernment lie somewhere between the two poles within each dimension (Hermans 2021:394-395).

The first dimension is 'individual' versus 'collective'. "On the one hand, there is discrimination for an individual by an individual, accompanied by an individual. However, there is also a group distinction, performed by the group for a person or for a group" (Waaijman 2013b:5). These poles are not isolated from each other as if the subject were outside the social domain, but discernment is sometimes viewed as a quality of the individual, and sometimes as a quality of the community.

The second dimension concerns the origin of the good, either as a first beginning or as a new beginning. In the tradition of the discernment of spirits, the origin of the source (spirit) of the good determines the quality of discernment: the fallen human nature, demons, Satan, or God and his helpers (Nissen 2012:18). In the tradition of *discretio*, discernment is focused on new beginnings that God makes in events in this world (the Kingdom of God, the Holy Spirit, forgiveness, etc.).

The third dimension concerns the focus of discernment on exceptional situations versus situations in general. A situation is exceptional when people's normal judgmental capacity is unable to decide what is right or wrong in that situation (Vecoli 2014:87). In this situation, an exceptional authority (for example, religious authorities, the king) is needed to be able to judge. On the other hand, discernment as judgment in general refers to a capacity that enables spiritual growth or incarnation (Waaijman 2013b). This idea is voiced by Waaijman when he refers to discernment as the compass used on the high seas of life. "If we define these high seas as a life characterised by contingency, then we may consider this just part of becoming a subject, and not as exceptional." (Hermans 2021:396).

The fourth dimension concerns the focus of discernment on a penultimate goal versus a last goal. The ultimate goal of discernment is union with God (a blissful vision of God, glory, heavenly paradise). The penultimate purpose of discernment is a purity of heart, conceived as a stable, restrained, and rightly directed disposition.

> A volitional dimension insofar as it involves scrutinising and freeing one from improper desires and redirecting them towards 'spiritual things' … An epistemic dimension in that it plays a crucial role in developing a positive orientation towards cognitive states such as illumination, contemplation, and the vision of God, as well as fostering a steady pursuit of them (Aquino 2017:163).

The fifth dimension in which models of discernment differ concerns the source of trust or authority to grow in discernment such as ethics, dogmas (including the Bible), or a spiritual director (Hense 2016:190). In models of discernment, we select a particular source or a combination of sources. A 'spiritual director' is a person who has achieved a certain growth and quality in (a certain tradition of) discernment. 'Dogma' refers to the authority of religious institutions (church) and/or of the Bible (institutional authority of scriptural interpretation). 'Ethics', or 'ethical' orientation refers to the finality of human life (the good, or *telos*) and the development of virtues (*habitus*). This ethical orientation is characteristic of every human being as a spiritual being. This model of discernment is inextricably linked, in the Christian tradition, with the theologian Thomas Aquinas, who equates the power of discernment with practical prudence (*prudentia*) (Kolsky 1995; Sultana 2012).

> Prudence is characterised on the one hand by the finality of all human life, which plays the role of universal principle, the starting point of reasoning; and on the other hand by the singular act of reasoning. It is therefore conceivable to see, with Thomas Aquinas, prudence as an application of the universal in the singular; or, going further, an implication of the universal in the singular (Guery 2013:12).

### 3.3.3 Process of discernment

Different models of discernment have been developed in the Christian tradition. In this section, I describe a model that is connected to the assumption developed in this volume: new beginning(s), oriented to both the individual and the communal, and decision-making in general, oriented towards purity of heart (the penultimate goal), where the ethical orientation and the experience of happiness are the source.[5]

### 3.3.3.1 First step: Generative seeing and listening

Discernment begins with perceiving and hearing differences and remarkable facts. Perceiving and listening are generative in a focus on the new, the unpredictable, the unexpected possible in which the good can appear. First, this refers to a form of seeing and listening in which we become sensitive to different beliefs, experiences, and perspectives (Waaijman 2013b:20).[6] Secondly, this form of perceiving and listening characterises the good as a new beginning that becomes visible *in or of* reality.

### 3.3.3.2 Second step: Reflection and self-examination

Discerning the good requires reflection and self-examination into the feelings and motives that play a role in our judgment. To discern the good, we need a pure

---

[5] For a more extensive discussion, see Hermans (2021).

[6] This form of seeing and listening creates an openness for the way in which God 'looks' at the world (Waaijman 2013b:13).

heart. What motives drive our actions? These motives can lead us away from the right path (negative) or onto the path to the good (positive). Do my motives come from the good that wants to emerge in a situation, or from the motives of the ego? The self-examination can take place intra-personally and/or interpersonally, in conversation with oneself or with another.

### 3.3.3.3 Third step: Collect and weigh

Collecting refers to the ability to gather all the wisdom that can help give direction in a particular situation or event. This process requires an open attitude, in which the good can emerge;[7] it can be done individually or collectively. What is the good that wants to emerge in reality? It is not about what one person sees and/or what another sees, but what wants to be seen from an open, receptive attitude in which all beliefs, all experiences, and all awareness of the good are collected. All the wisdom that is collected also needs to be weighed in a critical process. Waaijman (2013b:2) calls this combination of collecting and weighing '*collatio*'. In this process of collecting and weighing, the good in reality 'resonates' in the heart of the person, and there is a heartfelt connection between participants in the weighing process (Hermans 2021).

### 3.3.3.4 Fourth step: Prudent deciding and virtuous acting

Prudent decision-making is the ability to decide what action, in a concrete situation, can be considered wise and sensible. What is wise in terms of the good with, and for others will have emerged in the previous step. What is sensible depends on the possibilities and impossibilities of giving shape to the good in a given situation. In many instances, this is not so clear. Take, for example, the situation of young people on the Cape Flats of Cape Town, living in poverty, and with poor expectations of finding work, housing, and a sustainable future. The complexity of their situation, according to the theory on scarcity (Mullainathan & Shafir 2013), can be viewed as a poverty trap. The practices in which they are involved, their mindset, and the structure of the society in which they live all keep them in a circle of poverty. "If we want to be successful, we need to start from the specific configuration of the problem situation of the people we want to help; and together with them, co-construct a plan of action" (Hermans 2017:48).

The person who judges must also be virtuous in his/her actions, whether that be in his/her own life or in carrying out a decision in an organisation. Two cardinal virtues are important at this stage: the courage to resist when carrying out a decision in practice, and the test of justice and fairness, which any decision should endure in a concrete situation (Dupont 2010:230-233).

---

[7] This refers to the process of 'transcendental openness and awareness', which is explained in Chapter 2: Processes of resilience, in this volume.

## 3.4 Thinking

All religions have a religious or spiritual capital, in the form of texts, rituals, symbols, and images to offer resilience in a heartbreaking situation. Religious institutions may have a weak (pluralistic) or strong (exclusive) claim to the truth of their religious capital. From the perspective of human agency, religion can be viewed as a reservoir of imagination, centred on the mystery of perfect good, fulfilling happiness, and human flourishing. God as mystery is elusive, inexhaustible, not owned, and cannot be monopolised. At the same time, human thinking about the infinite can only be done from a specific point of view. This implies that we must be aware of the limitations of thinking about God.

### 3.4.1   Religious capital

For discernment, wisdom and insight are needed about the ultimate good and about which way of life will relate to this ultimate good. A system (in a dynamic relationship with other systems) that has never considered existential adversity and resilience is less able to discern. A system (an individual or a community) that possesses a richer religious-cultural capital is better equipped to discern.

Institutionalised religions, as well as non-institutionalised forms of spirituality are sources of religious-cultural capital for a good life with, and for others, and for good sustainability (Verter 2003; Hermans & Anthony 2020). Both between and within religions, there is a diversity of views on the good life with, and for others, as well as conflicting truth claims. Monistic truth claims consider only one religion to be true; pluralistic truth claims assert that truth is found in different religions and spiritual ways of life (Knitter 1995: 2002). These truth claims affect discernment in different ways. From a pluralistic truth claim, people are open to capital from different religions and spiritual traditions. In order to be able to discern better, the focus must be on a richer and more differentiated insight into heartbreaking adversity and beliefs about the ultimate good. A monistic approach is characterised by a strong commitment to faith (effort and time investment) and an absolute idea of what is good and what is evil. Discernment can be strengthened from both positions; in situations in which one religion is a minority religion, the two approaches (monistic and pluralistic) can simultaneously strengthen the capacity for discernment (Hermans & Anthony 2020).

### 3.4.2   Forms of imagination and cultural thinking

According to Ward (2018:171), imagination has its origin in mythical thinking or mythical sensitivity. He refers to an intuitive layer of consciousness that "makes us think" and evokes a response of awe and inspiration (Ward 2018:60). Mythical sensitivity is a felt presence of this intuitive layer, which shows itself in reality.

No language can capture this intuitiveness, not even our language of self-transcendence or a category such as the 'numinous' that refers to an essential and universal experience of ultimate reality (Ward 2018:60).

Cultural imagination is the result of mythical resonance (Ward 2018:167). Mythical resonance in the imagination is brought about by the mythical sensitivity in which the unspeakable is experienced as present. In the imagination, the unspeakable becomes communicable through symbols, stories, objects, rituals, and paintings. Throughout history, this mythical resonance has constantly changed, as certain forms in which mythical sensitivity is displayed have been reused, rejected, and transformed (Ward 2018:174).

Different forms of individual and collective imagination of the mythical can be identified (Ward 2018:184-185):

- the cultural imagination, as the totality of possibilities of mythical resonance;
- cultural values, or the ethos that arises in dealing with this cultural imagination, and
- the forms in which we institutionalise and organise this imagination in our social imagination.

There is a layering between these forms, but it is not hierarchical in nature. In time and space, there is an interaction and a dynamic relationship between these layers, resulting in change and renewal. At the same time, Ward points out that the cultural imagination and cultural values are embodied in social relations and social organisations. The social imagination arises from the activities of the cultural imagination and cultural values and, in turn, generates cultural imagination and values (Ward 2018:185).

What certainty do we have that, in our thinking, we do get a view of God as ultimate reality or the ultimate good? Can thinking not lead to a misunderstanding of God? Yes, it can, because thinking is done from a certain point of view, with language and concepts from a certain time and context. The imagination (first naivety) must be purified by thought. A good example of this is Ricoeur's analysis of the question 'Where does evil come from?' The starting point for Ricoeur (2007) is biblical symbols and stories: about the fall from paradise, the stain, and the punishment. The imagination can lead to erroneous interpretations and must, therefore, be purified by critical thinking that is aware not to think too much ('thinking speculatively') and to think differently ('thinking differently'). This requires analytical thinking that exposes the structure of thinking from multiple perspectives, and from the consequences that become visible from each of these perspectives (Van Heusden 2010). This calls for a dialogical process in a community without borders, open to anyone who asks critical questions (see Section 2).[8]

## 3.5 Acting

From an institutional point of view, one can view religious practices in two ways (Hermans 2003:188-189). From a structure-oriented approach, practices are maintained and promoted by social systems through rules, sanctions, and power. From a culture-oriented approach, practices are regarded as meaningful acts that support and symbolise, reproduce, and sustain processes of resilience. In this section, I focus on a culture-oriented approach, because I am interested in the construction of meaning in religious practices. How can religious practices prevent or process the loss of the good and/or absence of God as a possibility *in and of* life events with, and for others? Next, I will elaborate on acting from the point of view of human competence (agency). In religion(s), the emphasis is on character formation. In a resilient religion, the good is anchored in the character (good qualities) or virtues of human beings.

### 3.5.1   Religious practices

Religious practice is not a natural fact but an institutional fact, created by constitutive rules. In the following, I base my point of view on John Searle's theory of social facts (Hermans 2003:188-214).

1.   By constitutive rules, water becomes baptismal water, a book becomes a holy book, and the laying on of hands becomes a blessing. Without these rules, there is still water, or a book; but no religious status is attributed to them. An act is only a religious practice if the participants attribute a religious status to it. This status function refers to God as Creator of heaven and earth, in whom the possibility of 'new beginnings' rests (see above).

2.   The participants in a religious practice collectively share the same constitutive rule(s) (Hermans 2003:181-187). For the members of the community, water in a baptismal ritual creates a new beginning as a child of God. The participants form a community in the sense (and only to the extent) that they act in this practice from a shared 'we' intention.[9]

3.   The authority of the tradition plays a major role in the assignment of a status function. By participating in practices, we recognise the authority of the tradition that assigns a certain status function (holy book, baptismal water, etc.) to an act or agent. In baptising a child, for example, the minister has the authority.

---

[8] In addition to analytical thinking, acting, and feeling can also purify our interpretation, according to Ricoeur (2007). (See Chapter 2, Section 4: Handling tragedy.)

[9] Searle (1995:104) sums up collective intentionality with regard to power status functions in the following formula: We accept S has the power (S does A).

4.   In a religious practice, besides the collective intentionality, there are also
     rules that are mediated by the cultural tools of that religious practice. Every
     practice has an action structure, context, actors, and material things that
     mediate the meaning of this practice. Religious rituals such as eucharist/the
     Lord's supper, baptism and '*lectio divina*' have a strongly rule-led charac-
     ter through which the meaning of practices is mediated. To put it differ-
     ently, the status function is transferred to the cultural tools that are used in
     a religious practice (Hermans 2003:192).

5.   The status function of religious practices refers to God as the ultimate
     good, the perfect happiness. A certain practice (praying, singing, meditat-
     ing, fasting, reading the Bible, etc.) brings people into a relationship with
     God. The status function of religious practices is characterised by a binary
     code, in which transcendence (limitlessness) is linked with immanence
     (limitation). The establishment of the connection between transcendence
     and immanence is a quality attributed to religious practices by traditions.
     Religious practices are culturally set apart because they can bring people
     into a relationship with God.

6.   Religious practices are influenced by systems, both by the religious insti-
     tutions that promote these practices and by public and private institutions
     in society as a whole. Within religious institutions, there are power con-
     stellations and ideologies that determine which practices are promoted and
     when there is a deviation from the status function of religious practices.
     Within religions such as Christianity, there are religious groups and
     churches with different views on religious practices such as baptism and
     the Lord's Supper. Finally, religious practices are influenced by public in-
     stitutions. For example, by the laws and regulations of the state, law sys-
     tem, and municipalities.

### 3.5.2   Character/Virtues

Virtues are morally good character traits that aim at living a good life with, and
for each other. They are dispositions that keep human beings directed to the good
that is pursued in action. We must distinguish between virtues of the will such as
faith, hope, and love and ordinary virtues such as the cardinal virtues of courage,
measure, prudence, and justice (Dupont 2010). Ordinary virtues can be acquired
by doing and, by putting them into practice, we can become better at them. Virtues of the will are also called theological (divine) virtues: faith, hope, and love.
They are virtues in which God (good) works in us without a decision of the will,
and they are, therefore, not merely the result of human self-development (Van
Tongeren 2020:155-158). They are infused in human beings by God, in the sense
that the possibility of 'new beginnings' rests in God as Creator. What does this
mean in a situation of brokenness, in which the will to love is missing? The one
"self" trapped by limitations (*i.e.*, unwillingness) is unconnected to the self that
is directed to unlimitedness (*i.e.*, the human dignity of the other). A will that is

liberated from its limitation is a will that is focused on boundless love (Van Tongeren 2020:166). Processes of resilience[10] can edit the transformation of the will. Love as a theological virtue is possible, but not necessary (contingency). It can happen, but it need not happen. The event in which we are 'moved by love' presupposes an anticipation of infinity (self-transcendence) and is experienced as fulfilling happiness.[11] This happiness convinces us of the perfection of good, without being able to comprehend the boundlessness of this love (Hermans 2017). Is this the end of what we call 'free will'? When we are moved by love, we are freed from the 'unwillingness' to love. Freed from the burden of willing, human beings give themselves wholeheartedly to the object of their love. In other words, we cannot 'not love'. And, in this love, we experience full happiness as the purpose of existence.

Good character traits (virtues) help us act 'in one piece'. Keeping course on the path of good is not easy, because our actions are often reactive (to what someone says or fails to do) or impulsive (from unconscious feelings). What does this mean for the virtues of hope, love, and faith? Cloninger (2004; 2007) connects hope with self-direction, love with focus on the 'dignity' of the other and cooperation, and faith with self-transcendence.

- Self-direction (hope) is characterised by responsibility (versus blaming others), purposefulness (versus aimlessness), solution orientation (versus incompetence), and self-acceptance (versus inferiority).
- Cooperativeness (love) is characterised by tolerance and kindness (versus prejudice and unkindness), empathy and support (versus insensitivity and hostility), and compassion (versus retaliation).
- Self-transcendence (belief) is characterised by good judgment and openness (versus no appreciation and closedness), and by inventiveness and spiritual experiences (versus convention and one-dimensionality).

Finally, we like to stress that virtuous acting plays a role in discernment connected with prudent decision-making (see above). Prudent decision-making is the ability to decide what action in a concrete situation can be considered wise and sensible. What is sensible depends on the possibilities and impossibilities of giving shape to the good in a given situation. Discernment starts with seeing and listening to the people in situations of poverty, violence, and suffering. According to the theory of scarcity (Mullainathan & Shafir 2013), the complexity of situations of heartbreaking adversity demand that we co-construct plans that fit the specific situation of the persons we want to help.

The person who acts must also be virtuous in his/her actions, whether that be in his/her own life, or in carrying out a decision in an organisation. Two cardinal virtues are important at this stage: the courage to resist when carrying out a

---

[10] See Chapter 2 in this volume,

[11] See Chapter 2 in this volume.

decision in practice, and the test of justice and fairness, which any decision should endure in a concrete situation (Dupont 2010:230-233).

## 3.6 Feeling

The heart longs for experiences of fulfilling happiness *in* life with, and for others. How to experience unlimited happiness? A synthesis of happiness and the concrete events of life is fragile. First, I will elaborate on how religious institutions can offer pedagogies of the heart, which support experiences of happiness. The pedagogy of the heart is linked to religious practices, whose religious status function is given. Next, I will describe the experience of happiness related to the agency of people. In this instance, I will focus on the formation of the character of the person related to the passions of the heart.

### 3.6.1   Institutional pedagogies of the heart

From an institutional point of view, the formation of the heart happens from an existing order of spirituality that is embedded in rules, practices, spiritual guidance, etc. The schools of spirituality related to religious orders in Christianity such as the Benedictines, the Carmelites, and the Jesuits have their own distinct spirituality (Waaijman 2002). Some focus on a life in silence and prayer, others in works of charity or in taking care of sick people. In the growing attention paid to spirituality in the Protestant churches in recent decades, a confessional criterion for spiritual practices is the doctrine of justification by grace and faith alone (Marchinkowski & De Villiers 2020:430).

A second characteristic of an institutional approach is that the heart is viewed as a battlefield between different powers that want to form the heart from their conception of the good life (Hermans 2020b). For example, Paul (2017) describes secularisation as a force to be combated that wants to form the heart of people. For Smith (2016:21), the main battle is with consumerism in our society: "So, in the practices of the shopping mall we acquire the consumer habit of a dispositional inclination to seek the gratification of buying products." Smith (2016:137) defines practices as liturgy in the sense that they materialise conceptions of the good life (human flourishing) in reality in a way that resonates deeply with the cultural imagination. It is not simply about a struggle between beliefs, but about the formative role of practices, with a focus on a particular conception of the good life.

A last characteristic of institutional pedagogies of the heart is the formation of the longing of a person. It is not merely a channel for the dissemination of information; these practices shape our orientation of the heart, our desires, and our love (Smith 2013:12). In this instance, Smith refers to a central idea of Augustine: a man is determined by what he desires. The desire Augustine describes is not so much curiosity as hunger; so, not so much an intellectual puzzle to be solved, but rather a desire for food for life (see Ps. 42:1-2) (Smith 2016:8).

### 3.6.2    Passions of the heart

From the point of view of the human agent (agency), the formation of passions of the heart is a central concept in spiritual formation. In line with the foregoing, we assume that the human mind is characterised by a transcendental openness to the infinite, which can be experienced in human feelings. Defining passions of the heart, according to Strasser (1977:294), is a meta-intentional sense of what is good and perfect, fulfilled happiness, human flourishing. The human soul is the embodiment of a finite mind, but with a desire for the absolute (Tallon 1992:356). At the level of the mind, man is able to project completely abstract values such as peace, health, beauty, and truth. From these values (*telos*), a completely new situation of freedom and possibility arises, because man makes the good the primary object of his will and can transform reality from there.[12]

The longing for God is not a different kind of passion of the heart to other passions. As I explained earlier, the synthesis of the good and concrete events in life is in God as Creator more primordial than any heartbreaking adversity that people can experience. God is the ultimate good, and at the same time the basis of 'new beginnings' in which people experience the good. New beginnings can manifest in different areas of life, not only those related to religious practices as identified in schools of spirituality. From the point of view of agency, each of these passions of the heart can be an expression of a desire for God.

Following Strasser (1977:294-295), I distinguish four markers of passions of the heart (Hermans 2020b; Hermans & Kornet 2020):

1.    Passions are characterised by a transcendent orientation: they make absolute a field of value (the good) that gives fulfilment to life. The ultimate good surpasses everything we have experienced previously, in fullness, perfection, and value. The acceptance of this value is final, in the sense that it is confirmed once and for all.
2.    Passions are characterised by receptivity, which refers to an experience of being apprehended or overpowered by something stronger (God). When we are drawn to the ultimate good, we can 'react' in no other way than with unconditional receptivity. This strong receptivity reflects the experience of being apprehended by the perfect good (God).
3.    Passions have the power to give direction and focus in life. The behaviour of the passionate person is characterised by consistency, perseverance, calmness, and awareness of goals. Someone who is passionate can devote him-/herself unconditionally to one thing, which is in itself meaningful and fulfilling.
4.    Passions of the heart have an ethical orientation towards some area of value such as peace, care, sustainability of nature, or love. This abstract value

---

[12] Resilience in religion is not about adaptation to the existing order, but about freedom to transform reality! Theology and religious studies thus add an essential and different point of view to the theories of resilience from the social and natural sciences.

becomes visible in reality: in concrete persons and events, in organisations and systems. Characteristic of passions of the heart is a drive to transform reality in the direction of good. This passion manifests itself as "an increase in power ... the intensity of the will, in preparedness for sacrifice, the gift of sensitivity for the discovery of means, and, in general, in the productivity of the heart" (Strasser 1977:295).

## 3.7 Conclusion

What is a resilient religion good for? Religion keeps a sense of the 'human measure' alive in society, namely:

- in thinking: the awareness of the unlimited purpose (*telos*);
- in acting: the focus on human dignity and the common good, and
- in the heart: the demand for fulfilling happiness, peace, and love.

We should not diminish human beings, but we should understand human beings as spiritual beings related to purpose, human dignity and fulfilling happiness, peace, and love. This creates an entirely new situation of freedom and possibility in people's thinking, acting, and feeling. From the perspective of purpose, human dignity, and fulfilling happiness, people are willing and able to transform existing reality, and each realisation of the good has something in reserve for its ultimate fulfilment.

But a human measure also implies an awareness that human beings can fail, and do not focus on the good in thinking, acting, and heart. A society without religion is in danger of hardening and becoming ruthless. The awareness of the possibility of failure is not a weakness, but a sign of resilience. And that is what religion is good for.

## BIBLIOGRAPHY

Aquino, F.D. (2017). Spiritual formation, authority, and discernment. In: W.J. Abraham & F.D. Aquino (eds), The Oxford Handbook of the epistemology of theology (Oxford: Oxford University Press), pp. 157-172.

Arendt, H. (1998). Love in Saint Augustine. Edited and with an interpretive essay by J. Vecchiarelli Scott & J. Chelius Stark. Chicago: University of Chicago Press. (Kindle edition).

Ballacci, G. (2018). Politics as transcendence and contingency: Hannah Arendt. In: J. Ballacci, Political theory between philosophy and rhetoric. Rhetoric, politics and society (London: Palgrave Macmillan), pp. 149-181. https://doi.org/10.1057/978-1-349-95293-9_6.

Bax, M. 1987. Religious regimes and state formation: Towards a research perspective. Anthropological Quarterly 60(1):1-11.

Canovan, M. (1999). Terrible truths: Hannah Arendt on politics, contingency and evil. Revue Internationale de Philosophie 53(208):173-189.

Cloninger, C.R. (2004). Feeling good. The science of well-being. Oxford: Oxford University Press. https://doi.org/10.1097/SMJ.0b013e318070d177.
(2007). Spirituality and the science of feeling good. Southern Medical Journal 100(7):740-743. https://doi.org/10.1037/a0012933.

Dupont, J. (2010). Identiteit is kwaliteit: De identiteitstheorie van Paul Ricoeur als voorstudie voor een verheldering van de identiteit van katholieke basisscholen in Nederland. Budel: Damon.

Guery, B. 2013. La prudence selon Thomas d'Aquin: Un éclairage pour le mana-ger contemporain. *Conference Paper Philosophie du management, ESM-IAE Metz,* 15 Mai 2013. https://www.gracerecherchefr/wp-con-tent/uploads/2016/02/
GUERY_Prudence_GRACE.pdf

Helleloid, E. (2014). Hannah Arendt's phenomenology of the will: Contingency, temporality, and the nature of moral judgment. Unpublished PhD thesis, University of Georgia. https://esploro.libs.uga.edu/esploro/outputs/doctoral/Hannah-Arendts-phenomenology-of-the-will/9949334557902959

Hense, E. (2016). Early Christian discernment of spirits. Munster: LIT Verlag.

Hermans, C.A.M. (2003). Participatory learning. Religious education in a glob-alizing society. Leiden: Brill.
(2017). Love in a time of scarcity. An event-hermeneutical interpretation. Acta Theologica 30(2):30-50.
(2020a). Unexpected possible. A building block approach to spiritual and religious experiences revisited. Acta Theologica Supplementum 3:5-33.
(2022b). Battle for/in the heart: How (not) to transform the heart. In: C.A.M. Hermans & J-A. van den Berg (eds), *Battle for the heart. How (not) to transform church and society* (Munster: LIT Verlag), pp. 9-29.
(2021). Discernment as predictor for transformational leadership: A study of school leaders in Catholic schools in India. Journal of Beliefs and Values 42(3):393-408.

Hermans, C.A.M. & Anthony, F. (2020). On the high sea of spirituality. Ante-cedents and determinants of discernment among school leaders in India. Acta Theologica Supplement 30: 34-59.

Hermans, C.A.M. & Kornet, L. (2020). Spirituality as passions of the heart. An empirical study into the character, core values and effects of the passions of the heart of general practitioners. Acta Theologica Supplementum 30:182-209.

Knitter, F. (1995). One earth, many religions: Multifaith dialogue and global re-sponsibility. Maryknoll, NY: Orbis. (2002). Introducing theologies of re-ligions. Maryknoll, NY: Orbis.

Kolski, H. (1995). *Ueber die Prudentia in der Ethik des hl. Thomas von Aquin.* Würzburg: Engelke.

Marchinkowski, G. & De Villiers, P.G.R. (2020). The rediscovery of spiritual practices within Protestantism. Stellenbosch Theological Journal 6(1):429-456.

Mullainathan, S. & Shafir, E. (2013). *Scarcity. The new science of having less and how it defines our lives.* New York: Picador.

Nissen, P. (2012). Het goede kiezen en delen: Over onderscheiding der geesten. [Choosing and sharing the good: On discernment of spirits]. *Speling: Tijdschrift voor Bezinning* 67(1):14-23.

Paul, H. (2017). De slag om het hart. Over secularisatie en verlangen. [The battle for the heart. On secularisation and longing]. Utrecht: Boekencentrum.

Ricoeur, P. (2007). Evil. A challenge to philosophy and theology. Translated by John Bowden. London: Continuum.

Searle, J.R. (1995). The construction of social reality. New York: The Free Press.

Smith, J.K.A. (2013). Imagining the kingdom. How liturgy works. Grand Rapids, MI: Baker Academic.
(2016). You are what you love. The spiritual power of habit. Grand Rapids, MI: Brazos Press.

Strasser, S. (1977). Phenomenology of feeling. An essay on the phenomena of the heart. Pittsburgh, PA: Duquesne University Press.

Sultana, M. (2012). On conscience and prudence. The Heytrop Journal 56(4):619-628.

Tallon, A. (1992). The Concept of the Heart in Strasser's Phenomenology of feeling. American Catholic Philosophical Quarterly 66(3): 341-360.

Van der Heiden, G.J. (2014). *Ontology after ontotheology. Plurality, event and contingency in contemporary philosophy.* Pittsburgh, PA: Duquesne University Press.

Van Heusden, B. (2010). De structuur van cultuur, of: wat weet de schildpad? Inaugural lecture, Universiteit van Groningen.

Van Tongeren, D.R. (2020). Face to face with death: The role of religion in coping with suffering. In: K. Vail & C. Routledge (eds), The science of religion, spirituality, and existentialism (San Diego, CA: Elsevier Academic Press), pp. 37-50.

Vecchiarelli Scott, J. & Chelius Stark, J. (1998). Rediscovering Hannah Arendt. In: J. Vecchiarelli Scott & J. Chelius Stark (eds), H. Arendt, Love in Saint Augustine (Chicago, ILL: University of Chicago Press), pp. 115-212.

Vecoli, F. (2014). Le discernement spirituel dans le christianisme ancien. Le problème de la décision. *Théologiques* 22(2):69-97.

Verter, B. (2003). Spiritual capital. Theorizing religion with Bourdieu against Bourdieu. Sociological Theory 21(2):150-174.

Waaijman, K. (2002). Spirituality: Forms, foundations, methods. Leuven: Peeters Publishers.
(2013a). Discernment and biblical spirituality. An overview and evaluation of recent research. Acta Theologica Supplementum 17:1-12.

(2013b). Discernment – the compass on the high sea of spirituality. Acta Theologica Supplement 17:13-24.

Ward, G. (2018). *Unimaginable: What we imagine and what we can't.* London: I.B. Tauris.

# Chapter 4

# Christian resilience, role of intellectuals, and the centrality of the god symbol: interaction and changing shape

*R Venter[1]*

## 4.1 Introduction

In conditions of adversity, an instinctive reflex of Christians is to revert to the benevolence of God: God's presence, love, and wise will. This helps them make sense of suffering and pain. It is a valid pastoral manoeuvre. However, to gauge the dimension of resilience in religion, one arguably needs fundamental notions of 'big history', of religious symbols, and of religious cognitive mutation. The historical resilience of religions can be understood only within this context. This chapter intends to explore a *basic insight* - in extreme historical conditions, the re-interpretation, by the intellectuals of that time, of central symbols, specifically the one of the Divine/God, facilitated the continued vitality of the religious tradition. This 'insight' can obviously be rephrased as the central *research question* of this chapter: Do we encounter in the history of the Hebraic-Christian tradition sufficient evidence that there exists close connection between deep crisis situations, the re-conceptualization of God by the thinkers of the specific era and renewed re-vitalization of the religion? The contention of the chapter is that this could indeed be argued, and furthermore, that such a perspective would result in a *nuanced understanding of religious resilience*. The argument would also point to a second *conclusion*, namely, that a contemporary task for theologians crystallizes in the process: the God-symbol should be re-imagined to make sense for a contemporary condition.

The chapter focuses on the Hebraic-Christian tradition, and describes *four major* historical conditions, the role of intellectuals, and the new trajectories of speaking God. It discusses the Babylonian exile, the Patristic period amidst Empire, Modernity, and the post-Auschwitz horizons. The chapter explores the intellectuals' creative re-imagining of the notion of God in terms of crystallization of monotheism, substantial trinitarianism, social trinitarianism, and anatheism. This inevitably prompts questions about the naming of the present, the task of the intellectual, and the notion of God that would serve a resilient self.

---

[1] His e-mail address is: rventer@ufs.ac.za

## 4.2 Religion as intellectual tradition

A number of *assumptions* underlie the basic thesis proposed in this chapter. First, the relatively new academic discipline of 'Big History' that attempts to suggest direction and structure to the complex history and development of mankind functions in the background. Excellent sources on this are also available.[2] Secondly, a multidimensional understanding of the phenomenon 'religion' is imperative. The work by the scholar of religion Smart (1996) is enlightening in this regard. He distinguishes various dimensions that are structurally present in all religions: the doctrinal, the ritual, the narrative, the emotional, the ethical, the social, and the material. I am interested in the doctrinal and philosophical dimensions.[3] Religions, in various forms and manifestations, do have an interpretative aspect, making sense of life. Thirdly, the notion of religion as a 'tradition' consisting of internal diverse traditions is also required for the development of the proposal. The contributions by the philosopher MacIntyre may be fruitfully employed in this argument. MacIntyre (1985:222) understands a living tradition as "an historical extended, socially embodied argument...about the goods which constitute the tradition". He couples this with the emphasis on 'epistemological crises' which traditions encounter, and which should be resolved, in order to address the criteria of truth, intelligibility, and rationality (MacIntyre 1989:141).

My proposal is based on a broad *genealogical approach*, describing four social and intellectual crises, and four major trajectories which the God symbol assumed in the Hebraic-Christian sense as the result of intellectual argument. The notion of 'genealogy' alludes to the work by the French philosopher Foucault,[4] and at the same time to books published on the development of conceptions of God.[5] In far-reaching crisis situations intellectuals have re-visited traditional understandings of God. These complex situations had obviously also additional dynamics. People have started to see themselves differently and the very ways of thinking had been affected. One may even refer to a re-constructed 'self' and, to complicate matters, to re-conceptualized categories. To address resilience in religion in broad and fundamental terms, one should configure all five elements - *crises, intellectuals, God symbol, self, and conceptual categories*. In genealogical terms, one should delineate their histories.

---

[2] See, for example, Harari (2011), Christian (2018), and Fernández-Armesto (2019).

[3] See Smart's full discussion (1996:27-69).

[4] 'Genealogy' fits into Foucault's historiography, and his interest in a so-called 'history of the presence', his emphasis on the link between knowledge and power, and on hidden determinants of contemporary institutions. Garland (2014:372) captures this well: "Genealogical analysis traces how contemporary practices and institutions emerged out of specific struggles, conflicts, alliances, and exercises of power, many of which are nowadays forgotten". A genealogical approach could be productive to investigate the interplay between crises, God-re-conceptualizations and epistemic work.

[5] The titles of books by Armstrong (1993) and Wright (2009) come to mind respectively – *A history of God*, and *The evolution of God*.

## 4.3 The God symbol: crises and trajectories

The *four trajectories* of God thinking form important elements of a *genealogy of the divine* in a Hebraic-Christian sense, but they do not exhaust the entire narrative. Two prior developments should be mentioned. The *origin of religion* and the belief in divine beings, and the mutation of tribal religion into *Yahwism* are most crucial phases in this story. A large and excellent corpus of scholarship is available on these topics; one can merely refer to two relevant texts – Torrey, *Evolving brains, emerging Gods: Early humans and the origins of religion* (2017) and Van Oorschot & Witte, *The origins of Yahwism* (2019). The seminal text by Bellah, *Religion in human evolution: From the paleolithic to the axial age* (2011), should also be acknowledged in this regard. In the following brief and fairly dense treatment the focus will mainly be on the identification of the historical crises and the shifts or mutations in the understanding of God. Brief references will be made to the role of thinkers, and the changed human self-understanding and the new ways of thinking.

### 4.3.1   Exile and monotheism

The crystallisation of monotheism – the existence of one single divine reality – is widely considered a revolutionary occurrence in the history of religion. There is ample scholarship on this theme in Israelite religion and there are also different theories to explain the phenomenon. Generally, this is distinguished from *monolatry* – the worship of one God amidst a recognition of the existence of others, The critical insight in scholarship is the conviction that the emergence of monotheism should be linked to the Babylonian exile of 597/587 BCE.[6] The impact of the events, described in 2 Kings 24-25, on the conception and transformation of Yahwism, is found in Deuteronomy 4 as post-exilic literature and in Deutero-Isaiah (Is 40-55). Increasingly, one finds studies that describe the political, social, and psychological devastation of these events for Judah – deportations; violence against women, children and the elderly, and plundering of the temple and the city. A most fruitful shift in scholarship has been the explicit exploration of the exile in terms of *trauma* studies. Carr deserves special mention.[7] In a recent article, Markl (2020) consolidates research and extensively links exile, monotheism, and trauma; he refers to the 'birth trauma of monotheism' (2020:2). The crisis led to intense theological reflection. What one encounters in Deutero-Isaiah is a counter-narrative, and the claim is repeatedly made "there is no other" (Is 45:5, 6, 14, 18, 21, 22), and the uniqueness of YHWH is emphasised (e.g., Is 42:8, 43:10-11, 44:6, 8). Smith (2001:193, 179-194) refers to a "new stage of rhetoric"

---

[6] Excellent treatments and discussions are found in Albertz (1994:414-426) and Römer (2015:210-241).
[7] See Carr (2014:67-90).

found in Israelite religion. Markl's (2020:19) comment is most applicable to the thrust of the chapter: "The monotheistic claims in Deutero-Isaiah are a powerful instrument of resilience against the background of Exile as cultural trauma." The connection between monotheism and exile is fairly obvious. Views about the *intellectual dynamics* behind Deutero-Isaiah and the eventual impact of Judean *self-construction* remain speculative. Text production in the ancient world was a complex phenomenon. Blenkinsopp's (1995) older study on the sages, the priests and the prophets as intellectual leaders remains relevant for background orientation. Albertz's (1994:414-426) view is exceedingly important for Deutero-Isaiah. It was produced by a group of theologians gathered around a master who came from circles of temple singers and cult prophets with nationalist sentiments (1994:415). The message of the text was innovative and offensive. It was based on a fundamental conviction about the power of YHWH in history (1994:416, 417, 418). Their re-interpretation of God tended towards universalism, but also towards a critique of domination, and the fusion of the divine and political power was dissolved (1994:420, 424). In this instance, Albertz views "a clear transformation of traditional notions" (1994:421), which was also an "ongoing process of reflection" (1994:423). The impact on monotheism is a complicated field of enquiry. The work by the Egyptologist Assmann should be acknowledged in this context. Monotheism amounted to a transformation of the world; it shaped the Western image of man, but came with a 'price' – exclusion; a certain kind of truth emerged: absolute, metaphysical, and fideistic (Assmann 2010:15). One could only speculate about the *monotheistic self*: the human who is more secure, more integrated, but also dangerously prone to certainty.

### 4.3.2 Empire, metaphysics and substantial Trinitarianism

The next trajectory requires a 'jump' to the *fourth century AD*: the establishment of the 'trinitarian canon'.[8] The importance of this century for the establishment of the specific Christian understanding of God can hardly be overemphasised. Anatolios (2007:432) claims that "[t]he Trinitarian controversies of the fourth century constitute the most crucially formative period in the development of the Christian doctrine of God" and the interested student is served by excellent scholarship (see for example, Ayres 2004). At stake, in this instance, is the *confession* that God is one in substance/nature/essence, and simultaneously differentiated as three persons – Father, Son and Spirit. It took the church a long time to reach a satisfactory understanding of the unity and diversity of the Divine, and the role of most creative intellectual work by outstanding thinkers cannot be stressed enough. Two specific councils – Nicaea 325 and Constantinople 381 – are crucial for the final terminology such as *homoousios* and the acceptance of the so-called 'Cappadocian settlement'. The *crisis*, in this instance, was specific – the Arian controversy about the precise ontic relationship of Jesus Christ to the Father. At

---

[8] For the term 'trinitarian canon', see Barnes (1998:47).

the same time, a wider horizon of exigency was operative: the challenge of Greek metaphysics, the domination of the Roman Empire, and the destabilisation by internal polemics. Early Christianity was in the grip of multifaceted threats; their very identity and their central religious symbol were at stake. The trinitarian controversies of the fourth century cannot be appreciated without a long *prior history*. This intricate narrative can be truncated and distilled to three brief references. Jewish believers, who were strict monotheists, were deeply unsettled by the person of the historical Jesus, the trauma of his death, the ambiguity of his post-resurrection appearances, and the experiences of salvation. This inevitably prompted the formulation of multiple *Christologies*.[9] The emergence of an early *binitarianism* – that is, belief in God and worshipping of Jesus – was most unique in terms of the history of religion (Schnelle 2020:470f). Finally, the availability of the *logos* concept in Greek metaphysics enabled early Christian thinkers to make sense of Jesus' unique divine status; the Ultimate reality was mediated to creation in the form of the Word. This played out in various proposals. For the church, *Sabellianism* – the appearances of God in various forms – was unacceptable. In a world deeply configured in terms of hierarchy (by Greek philosophy and empire politics), *subordinationism* – Jesus as unique, but not of the same nature as the immutable God – was a most attractive option, as particularly articulated by Arius. The precise nature of the *intellectual endeavours*, of the debates and of the discourses requires detailed study. Excellent sources are available, for example, on individual thinkers such as Origen, Athanasius, Hilary of Poitiers, and the Cappadocians; on the rise of the so-called early Christian intellectual (Ayres & Ward 2020), and on the nature of Patristic rationality (Williams 2009). The role of catechetical schools and the establishment of a Christian *paideia* (Young 2006) affirm a significant intellectual quality to the life of Early Christianity. The title of MacMullen's (2006) work on the councils, '*Voting on God*', is significant. However, something more fundamental may be at stake: *the very identity of God was born in intellectual labour*, an activity that was in essence about hermeneutics and ontology. *Two intellectual achievements* should be specifically identified. First, the use of the term *homoousios* at Nicaea to name the very co-substantiality of Jesus Christ with the Father.[10] This fundamentally redefined Divinity. Secondly, the Cappadocian insight that being is never 'bare', but intrinsically personal and relational (Zizioulas 1995:52ff). The implications of this for understanding human identity, for example, are exceedingly important. The *effect* of the work of Early Christian intellectuals was far-reaching. The *resilient efforts* to navigate myriad options stabilised the identity of a young religion and granted it

---

[9] For an excellent overview, see Capes (2019). Schnelle's (2020:92) comment is worth taking note of: "At the beginning of the new movement stood a thoroughly creative process."

[10] See the recent volume of essays Kim (2021).

a particular attractiveness to the wider environment.[11] The imaginative and resilient re-construction of the central symbol invested the Christian faith with *immense vitality*.[12] Neither internal divisions, nor metaphysical lure or imperial power could deprive the church of its own unique identity and life.

### 4.3.3    Modernity and social Trinitarianism

The next trajectory brings one to the twentieth century, at the height of developments in the 1970s and 1980s, with the articulation of major texts on the so-called social trinity, which forms part of the wider movement, the 'Trinitarian Renaissance'. These texts are conventionally associated with the two Karls – Barth and Rahner. Seminal texts were published by, for example, Moltmann (1981:171ff) and Boff (1988:134ff) who argue that God has a life of God's own, that God's very nature is relational, and that God is a divine community.[13] The assumptions were emphatic: the starting-point for trinitarian reflection is the *oikonomia*, the work of God in history; the three persons should be taken seriously, and God is affected by history. Insights into the economic Trinity should inform thinking about God's eternal life, that is the immanent Trinity. This relationship between immanent and economic Trinity and the reality of history are central in the discourse (see Kärkkäinen 2009:12). Why the new focus on the three divine persons, and why the shape the new interest has taken? These are complex questions, and one cannot give a simplistic answer. It is crucial to consider 'history' as a category for thinking. Several interpreters find the impetus for the new interest already with Hegel (e.g., Sanders 2012:23) and his turn to history. This had several implications: it was part of the quest for a new category for dynamic thinking, specifically relational ones (Shults 2003:11-36), and the occupation with concrete history. From a philosophical perspective, the background is modernity, and from a political perspective, the great twentieth century upheavals such as the two world wars. This third trajectory engages a multi-faceted *crisis*, and cannot be easily distilled, but a view that argues for a reaction to *modernity* and its political violent manifestations could not easily be rebutted. Barth's reaction to the First World War and nineteenth-century liberal theology fits into this explanation, as well as Moltmann's entire theology as one happening in the shadow of his own experiences of the Second World War. Theology was confronted not only with a new metaphysics that prioritises relationship and process, but also with the violent political manifestation of a modernist rationality and its dehumanising ramifications. Boff (1988:111-122) refers correctly to "the doctrine of the Trinity in

---

[11] Both Hurtado (2016:62ff) and Schnelle (2020:470ff), New Testament and Patristic scholars, emphasise the attractiveness of the Christian concept of God, especially its emphasis on love.

[12] In a fascinating discussion about the role of the Roman empire, Rieger (2007:91-100) argues that the trinitarian concept has a resistance factor to any imperial condition. The empire could never use the Christian divine notion to control people.

[13] For a detailed description, see Thompson (1997).

changed cultural situation". To re-envision the Divine in terms of relationship enables the Christian faith to accomplish several aspects: to integrate new categories of thinking, and to counter violent social attitudes with a vibrant social ethic that embraces otherness. The resistance to this re-imagining has been and continues to be intense. Holmes (2012:2), for example, explicitly claims that the ideas found in the new discourse "cannot be found in patristic, medieval, or Reformation accounts of the doctrine of the Trinity". Whether the work of a large number of major theologians really amounts to such a rupture can be debated; the point of the debate, however, underlines the insights of the chapter: new situations prompted theology to revisit and re-construct the conventional vision of the Divine. The *effects* of the Trinitarian Renaissance are fascinating: it revitalised a doctrine that many considered arcane and without any practical relevance. A large number of studies employed a trinitarian optic to rethink a wide scope of challenges, from identity questions, faith-science dialogue to interest in aesthetics. Re-imagination stimulates life: the social God creates a *relational self*,[14] a self that embraces the other, that is gifting, hospital and generous.

### 4.3.4   Auschwitz, alterity and anatheism

The fourth trajectory must be placed primarily within the discipline of Continental Philosophy of Religion, which has also influenced theology. The text *Phenomenology and the 'theological turn'*, edited by Janicaud (2000, originally 1991), signalled the new sensibility under way. A constellation of ideas converged in this instance: Heidegger's rejection of onto-theology and the ethical turn to 'the face of the other' in the philosophy of Levinas.[15] The broader material horizon of the atrocities of World War Two should be borne in mind. One encounters a farewell to the metaphysical God of classical theism, the so-called 'omni-monster', but also a dismissal of traditional theodicy efforts (see the discussion by Eggemeier 2012). The presence and agency of God in a conventional sense has become immensely problematic. The Jewish philosopher Jonas (1987:3) voiced a widespread consensus: "Auschwitz calls...the whole traditional concept of God into question". The title of the major volume by Korpel and De Moor (2012), *The silent God*, captures the sentiment. The historical conditions of the twentieth century and the philosophical critiques of Western metaphysics converged in postmodern philosophers of religion such as Marion (1991), Caputo (2006), and Kearney (2001). The titles of their major books convey the sentiments: *God without being, The weakness of God,* and *The God who may be,* respectively. This is clearly a 'new' approach to name the divine. The power and action of the divine has become greatly problematic; 'God' should happen in the ethical encounter with the Other. Substantial or relational categories of thinking have been replaced by a dynamic one of 'event'. Kearney's (2009:175) notion of

---

[14] See the apt title of Grenz's book (2001).
[15] For an excellent treatment, see Gschwandtner (2013).

*anatheism* is an apt denotation: it offers faith *after* atheism. There is an element of the eschatological: there is the possibility of a surprise, but it takes the form of a 'wager' "to be made and remade again and again" (Kearney 2009:183).[16] The work of the Christian systematic theologian Tracy should be appreciated in this regard. He agrees with most of the emphases of these philosophers of religion, but has a greater appreciation for some continuity with the Christian tradition, and with Trinitarianism. To name God, in a postmodern sense, as 'The Impossible', he suggests that God be understood as the incomprehensible, the hidden, and the excessive loving One (Tracy 2011:124-127). The very loose network of thinkers *conveys* not only the resilience of the symbol of the Divine, but also the imperative of re-interpreting it in the face of new ways of thinking and experiences. We find in this trajectory clearly new categories of speaking, of a re-location of the presence of the Divine, but also an explicit framing in terms of the ethical. The *self* that emerges is complex: it is no longer burdened by an illusion about Divine intervention; however, it remains open to some form of horizontal transcendence, mediated by the relationship with the other. Interestingly, one also comes across references to the mystical.

### 4.4 Preliminary conclusion – an expanded version of resilience and a response to hermans

The proposal advanced in this chapter acknowledges that *different approaches* to theologising resilience are possible, and even desirable. It focuses on the interplay among large social and cultural upheavals, the creative role of intellectuals, and the re-figuring of the symbol of the Divine. It is intentionally multidisciplinary and places emphasis on large systemic dynamics.

It has become clear in the discussion of the previous section that the Hebraic-Christian religious tradition experienced far-reaching *changes* as well as political and philosophical developments from which immunisation was impossible. It is a *narrative* of empires, of metaphysics and of the modern and postmodern saga of human rationality. Throughout this history, one encounters intellectual *resilience* to make sense of the world, to keep the vitality of the faith alive, and to make a public contribution to understanding the human-embattled condition. It is possible to design a shifting *sociology of the intellectuals* in every major historical period. But crucially important, the intuitive reflex of these intellectuals was to take recourse to what matters most: God as central orientating symbol. And this very symbol was imaginatively reinterpreted not only to reflect modes of thinking of the specific historical period, but also to convey the constantly surprising and disruptive impulses emanating from this reflection – the Divine meets the crisis through the intellectual activities as ever new and life-giving. In light of the historical overview in the previous section one may come to a *warranted*

---

[16] The work and notion of Hermans (2019) – "God as pure possibility" – should be mentioned.

*conclusion*: there are sufficient grounds to claim that *resilience, crises, the God-symbol* and the role of *intellectuals* be thought together and in their interaction.

The *resilience* of the Hebraic-Christian traditions has allowed believers to maintain the 'courage to be', to continue facing life. But, and this is most cardinal, resilience has been more than mere existential comfort; the very struggles were *productive*, the new vitality affected life beyond the confines of the community of faith; it has had *public* ramifications. Resilience has been fecund.

The work of *Hermans* on resilience calls for critical engagement. He deserves credit for initiating the research reflected in this volume of articles, and he availed participants of his reflection in progress (Hermans 2022a, 2022b, 2022c). His constructive work is comprehensive, multi-levelled and, to some extent, even fairly complex. In the development of the argumentation, a large spectrum of multidisciplinary scholars prompt the issue of the coherence and integration of his entire project. I will not address this formal question, in this instance. A great number of prominent motifs such as experience, epistemological criteria, pragmatic notion of truth, disproportionality, religion as morality, contingency, happiness, and heart-breaking adversity function as building-blocks for his theoretical edifice. When taken as a form of Gestalt and scrutinised, one cannot but wonder whether there are two basic and potential weaknesses in his overall project: a *privatised* (and, to some extent, even a bourgeoisie) notion of resilience, and a fundamental *a-historical* account of forms of adversity. Nowadays, the trend in scholarship is to display much greater sensitivity to communal and concrete realities. Life happens in conflictual situations and the vitality of religion should transpire precisely here. The proposal of my own contribution concentrates on large macro-historical events, on adversity as entanglement of metaphysical, political, and existential realities, and the intentional creative rethinking of the grammar of the central religious symbol – God. It attempts to place the question of a resilient religion in a broader and more fundamental framework than the one of Hermans. 'Adversity' is complex; it can refer to immense suffering due to exile; disorientation as a result of empire and philosophical impact; trauma as a consequence of war, and utter disillusionment. The *process* of establishing resilience is thoroughly marked by intellectual and hermeneutical endeavour. In no way does it question the validity of resilience in terms of privatised therapeutics, but the adequacy of such an approach. To address the question of resilience, for example, in an African context, requires an approach in the direction of the one I suggested. The statistical growth of Christianity in the South, and the issue of its vitality within a new context with its own cultural heritage and distinctive forms of adversity require *a non-bourgeoisie conception* of resilience. The various forms of African theology in its inculturation, liberation, and decolonial trajectories hint at a religion that is resilient in its ability of translatability. Occurrences of a resurgence of Traditional African Religion may be evidence of situational collapses of resilience, failures to re-interpret the Christian faith and its central symbols to make sense in a cultural and liberative manner. With its complex reality and myriad challenges, Africa may historically become a test-case whether the Christian faith is a resilient religion, or whether it remains a Western and colonial artefact. The proposals advanced by Herman and by myself may eventually contribute to the construction of a version of resilience that may be adequate to the African reality.

## 4.5 Resilience as theological task - discerning the present and naming God

In a strict Foucauldian sense 'genealogy' has to serve a 'history of the present' (see Garland 2014). One should at least intimate some direction about our own time considering the proposal advanced in this chapter: how to name the present, how to profile the intellectual, how to re-imagine God, and how to re-construct the self.

Quite recently a major work was published by Scandinavian theologian Henriksen and sociologist Repstad with the provocative title *God after the church lost control* (2022). This study underlines the fundamental tenet of this chapter, namely, that the continued existence of a religion is intimately linked to a understanding of God that remains relevant to a changing society. This multi-disciplinary exploration is precisely about the interaction between God and social shifts. Having discussed problematic emphases in traditional approaches to God, the two scholars eventually propose (2022:140-150) a notion of God as 'vulnerable love'.

It is difficult to name our polyonymous *time*, as it has too many names. Each one of the labels heuristically employed carries some crucial aspect of *our horizon.* One cannot ignore 'globalisation', 'anthropocene', 'fourth industrial revolution', or 'post-colony'. The COVID-condition has awakened us to the 'Black Swan' character; our time is one of deep insecurity and surprises. 'Vulnerability' has become an apt cypher to convey the character of the present. In Africa, the situation is even more complicated, especially with regard to religious life; the pervasive hybrid combination of traditional systems of thought and of Christianity persists and causes continued uncertainty. There is not a single denominator that captures and represents the multiple challenging forces threatening the flourishing of life. At best, in doing theology, one should at least consider the catalogue of challenges and indicate which one to address among the many challenges. Maybe this Lilliput approach may strangle the giant of our condition.

Interest in the *figure of the intellectual* continues unabatedly. Interesting work has been done by Bauman (1987), who distinguishes between modernist and postmodernist intellectuals and the identification of them as 'legislators' and 'interpreters', and more recently on the so-called 'post-colonial intellectual' (Ponzanesi 2021). Seldom does one find material on the theologian as intellectual; but the wide scholarship on theological methodology may convey something on how the role is implicitly being understood. It is clear that one thinks along *polymathic* lines; unique epistemic demands are placed on the theologian as intellectual; the sheer corpus of knowledge to be mastered remains daunting. But more than this is required. Our time requires thinkers who are not only polymaths, but also moralists, persons with a finely tuned sense of the ethical, and poets, people with active imagination who may create innovative avenues. And our time needs 'God thinkers', individuals who can turn their gaze consistently to the Ultimate Mystery. The danger in our time is closure; a frame of mind that strives for certainty, for a deductive logic that inhibits new paths. The question could be raised about the theological response to the COVID crisis, and the extent to which the church, through its intellectuals, did contribute to a public sense-making.

Theo-logy is intrinsically a practice of relating *theos* to *logos*, that is, a particular horizon of intelligibility (Tracy 1994:37). How do we speak the inexhaustible in a polyonymous time, so that the impression is not one of evoking the 'Ancient of Days' (Dan 7)? This may be the fundamental question for theology. My conviction is that the *naming of God* would have to be *trinitarian*; that is, in terms of this fourth-century symbol of the Christian faith. If this confession cannot be translated in vibrant speaking, the faith would lose its capacity for resilience. One may hesitantly ask whether this does not lie at the root of secularisation – the eclipse of signifying power. My suggestion is that trinitarian theology should attend to a range of motifs such as hiddenness, faithfulness, justice, life, vulnerability, and love, and reconfigure them to construct a profile that speaks to the heart of the present. Turning to *Africa,* the challenge is acute. Much has been done in terms of Christology, but the construal of a profile that incorporates both social/liberative and traditional categories remains elusive.

The formation of a particular *self* is obviously complex and does not take place in a short period of time. Helpful surveys do exist (see for example, Elliott 2020). Maybe a certain triangulation is at stake here, considering horizon, divine, and self. Or put differently: the self is the performative outcome of a reading of the time and the naming of the Divine. Gregersen (2020:95) recently suggested the notion of 'resonant self' that stands in a fluid relationship to the environment, in contrast to the buffered self that tends to insulate itself. Maybe the resonant self would also be a resilient self.

By discerning the character of our time, by thinking the Divine anew, theologians may contribute to the human project of living resiliently.

## 4.6 Conclusion

The chapter has contributed to the discourse on religion and resilience by advancing a specific and broadened notion of resilience. The basic suggestion was that resilience should be seen in large historical terms, and moments of severe crisis should be connected with the struggles of intellectuals to rethink the central religious symbol - God - to enable sense-making and ultimately the revitalization of the religion as such. In a genealogical overview four such trajectories were explored in the Hebraic-Christian tradition. In the scholarship on these historical complexes sufficient reasons have been found to justify the basic proposal for a re-envisioned version of resilience. At the same time, it has pointed to a crucial task in the present: the challenge to discern the character of the contemporary horizon and to engage in creative re-imagining of the Divine. This may be the task awaiting theologians.

## BIBLIOGRAPHY

Albertz, R. (1994). A history of Israelite religion in the Old Testament period. Vol 2. Louisville, KY: Westminster John Knox.

Anatolios, K. (2007). Discourse on the Trinity. In: A. Casidy & F.W. Norris (eds), The Cambridge history of Christianity. Vol 2: Constantine to c. 600 (Cambridge: Cambridge University Press), pp. 431-459.

Armstrong, K. (1993). A history of God. London: Mandarin.

Assmann, J. (2010). The price of monotheism. Stanford, CA: Stanford University Press.

Ayres, L. (2004). Nicaea and its legacy: An approach to fourth-century trinitarian theology. Oxford: Oxford University Press.

Ayres, L. & Ward, H.C. (eds) (2020). The rise of the early Christian intellectual. Berlin: W de Gruyter.

Barnes, M.R. (1998). The fourth century as trinitarian canon. In: L. Ayres & G. Jones (eds), Christian origins: Theology, rhetoric, and community (London: Routledge), pp. 47-67.

Bauman, Z. (1987). Legislators and interpreters: On modernity, postmodernity, and intellectuals. Oxford: Polity.

Bellah, R.N. (2011). Religion in human evolution: From the paleolithic to the axial age. Cambridge, MA: Belknap Press.

Blenkinsopp, J. (1995). Sage, priest, prophet: Religious and intellectual leadership in ancient Israel. Louisville, KY: Westminster John Knox.

Boff, L. (1988). Trinity and society. Kent: Burns & Oates.

Capes, D.B. (2019). New Testament Christology. In: S. McKnight & N.K. Gupta (eds), The state of New Testament studies (Grand Rapids, MI: Baker Academic), pp. 161-181.

Caputo, J.D. (2006). The weakness of God: A theology of the event. Bloomington, IN: Indiana University Press.

Carr, D.M. (2014). Holy resilience: The Bible's traumatic origins. New Haven, CT: Yale University Press.

Christian, D. (2018). Origin story: A big history of everything. London: Allan Lane.

Eggemeier, M.T. (2012). Lévinas and Ricoeur on the possibility of God after the end of theodicy. Philosophy and Theology 24(1):23-48.

Elliott, A. (2020). Concepts of the self. 4th edition. Cambridge: Polity.

Fernández-Armesto, F. (2019). Out of our minds: What we think and how we came to think it. London: OneWorld.

Garland, D. (2014). What is a "history of the present"? On Foucault's genealogies and their critical preconditions. Punishment and Society 16(4):365-384.

Gregersen, N.H. (2020). Resilient selves: A theology of resonance and secularity. Dialog 59:93-102.

Grenz, S.J. (2001). The social God and the relational self: A Trinitarian theology of the Imago Dei. Louisville, KY: Westminster John Knox.

Gschwandtner, C.M. (2013). Postmodern apologetics? Arguments for God in contemporary philosophy. New York: Fordham University Press.

Harari, Y.N. (2011). Sapiens: A brief history of humankind. London: Harvill Secker.

Henriksen, J-O & Repstad, P. (2022). God after the church lost control: Sociological analysis and critical-constructive theology. London: Routledge.

Hermans, C.A.M. (2019). God as pure possibility and the wonder of possibilisation. Acta Theologica 39(2):9-30.

(2022a). Human experiences of heart-breaking adversity, Chapter 1 in this volume (pp.13-30).

(2022b). Processes of resilience, Chapter 2 in this volume (pp.31-46).

(2022c). Resilient religion, Chapter 3 in this volume (pp.47-66).

Holmes, S.R. (2012). The quest for the Trinity: The doctrine of God in Scripture, history and modernity. Downers Grove, ILL: InterVarsity.

Hurtado, L.W. (2016). Destroyer of the gods: Early Christian distinctiveness in the Roman world. Waco, TX: Baylor University Press.

Janicaud, D. (ed.) (2000). Phenomenology and the 'theological turn': The French debate. New York: Fordham University Press.

Jonas, H. (1987). The concept of God after Auschwitz: A Jewish voice. The Journal of Religion 67(1):1-13.

Kärkkäinen, V-M. (2009). The trajectories of the contemporary 'Trinitarian renaissance' indifferent contexts. Journal of Reformed Theology 3:7-21. https://doi.org/0.1163/156973109X403697.

Kearney, R. (2001). The God who may be: A hermeneutics of religion. Bloomington, IN: Indiana University Press.

(2009). Returning to God after God: Levinas, Derrida, Ricoeur. Research in Phenomenology 39:167-183. https://doi.org/10.1163/156916 409X 448157.

Kim, Y.R. (2021). The Cambridge companion to the Council of Nicaea. Cambridge: Cambridge University Press.

Korpel, M. & De Moor, J. (2012). The silent God. Leiden: Brill.

MacIntyre, A. (1985). After virtue: A study in moral theory. London: Duckworth.
    (1989). Epistemological crises, dramatic narrative, and the philosophy of
    science. In: S. Hauerwas & L.G. Jones (eds), Why narrative? Readings
    in narrative theology (Grand Rapids, MI: Wm B. Eerdmans), pp. 139-
    157.
MacMullen, R. (2006). Voting about God in the Early Church councils. New Ha-
    ven, CT: Yale University Press.
Marion, J-L. (1991). God without being. Chicago: Chicago University Press.
Markl, D. (2020). The Babylonian exile as the birth trauma of monotheism. Bib-
    lica 101(1):1-25.
Moltmann, J. (1981). The Trinity and the kingdom of God. London: SCM.
Ponzanesi, S. (2021). Postcolonial intellectuals: New paradigms. Postcolonial
    Studies 24(4):433-447. DOI: 10.1080/13688790.2021.1985232.
Rieger, J. (2007). Christ and empire: From Paul to postcolonial times. Minneap-
    olis, MN: Fortress.
Römer, T. (2015). The invention of God. Cambridge, MA: Harvard University
    Press.
Sanders, F. (2012). The Trinity. In: K.M. Kapic & B.L. McCormack (eds), Map-
    ping modern theology (Grand Rapids, MI: Baker), pp. 21-45.
Schnelle, U. (2020). The first one hundred years of Christianity. Grand Rapids,
    MI: Baker Academic.
Shults, F.L. (2003). Reforming theological anthropology. Grand Rapids, MI: Wm
    B. Eerdmans.
Smart, N. (1996). Dimensions of the sacred: An anatomy of the world's religions.
    London: HarperCollins.
Smith, M.S. (2001). The origins of biblical monotheism. Oxford: Oxford Univer-
    sity Press.
Thompson, T.R. (1997). Trinitarianism today: Doctrinal renaissance, ethical rel-
    evance, social redolence. Calvin Theological Journal 32:9-42.
Torrey, E.F. (2017). Evolving brains, emerging Gods: Early humans and the ori-
    gins of religion. New York, NY: Columbia University Press.
Tracy, D. (1994). The return of God in contemporary theology. Concilium
    6/1994:37-46.
    (2011). Approaching the Christian understanding of God. In: F. Schüssler
    Fiorenza & J. Galvin (eds), Systematic theology: Roman Catholic perspec-
    tives (Minneapolis, MN: Fortress), pp. 109-129.
Van Oorschot, J. & Witte, M. (eds) (2019). The origins of Yahwism. Berlin: W
    de Gruyter.
Williams, A.N. (2009). The divine sense: The intellect in Patristic theology. Cam-
    bridge: Cambridge University Press.
Wright, R. (2009). The evolution of God: The origins of our beliefs. London:
    Abacus.

Young, F.M. (2006). Towards a Christian paideia. In: M.M. Mitchell & F.M. Young (eds), The Cambridge history of Christianity. Vol 1: Origins to Constantine (Cambridge: Cambridge University Press), pp. 485-500.

Zizioulas, J.D. (1995). The doctrine of the Holy Trinity: The significance of the Cappadocian contribution. In: C. Schwöbel (ed.), Trinitarian theology today (Edinburgh: T&T Clark), pp. 44-60.

# Chapter 5

# African realities and resilient religion
# An invitation to Africanize the conversation

## *D A Forster[1]*

### 5.1 Introduction

Beliefs and faith practices play a very important role in helping individuals and communities to create meaning in the midst of hardship, adversity, change and uncertainty. This project on resilient religion is important since it invites critical reflection on the role that religion plays in fostering human, perhaps even non-human, resilience at a precarious time in history.

This chapter will engage the topic of resilient religion at a meta-theoretical level. I will argue that for belief and faith practices to have anything more than a generalized, relativized, impact upon resilience for religious persons and communities in (South) Africa it is necessary to take some of the unique aspects of (South) African reality, identity, and sense-making into consideration. Of course this is not a dialectical claim – that African contributions should be universalized, as Western thought systems often are. Rather, it is theoretical commitment to an existential context and the hermeneutic systems that foster meaning within that context for the sake of religious persons (in this case Christians) whose faith and faith practices can serve to nurture resilience.

I must also name that this is not the contribution of a critical outsider, but that of dialogical insider. I am not an outsider looking in on a conversation that others are having without me. Rather, I am very gratefully a conversation partner within a rich conversation that is taking place among colleagues who are themselves seeking to make sense of this important topic. In this regard, some of what is shared in this chapter is a chronicle of my own struggle for African theological authenticity and responsible scholarship within our context.

As noted, this is a meta-theoretical contribution. What it aims to do is highlight that Western theological contributions to the discourse on resilient religion are not to be uncritically presented as the de-facto norm on this topic. It is important to acknowledge that western metaphysics, and the accompanying cannons of knowledge, emerged from particular contexts and experiences. Thus, they cannot be uncritically presented as normative or universally applicable to all

---

[1] His e-mail address is: dionforster@sun.ac.za

persons, in all places, at all times. To do so would constitute a form of ideological totalitarianism. Of course, it is also true that we need to guard against ever narrower representations of identity and experience that might create the impression that there are no meaningful points of connection between human persons across history and throughout the world. I will attempt to hold this dialectic tension throughout the chapter.

Yet, this contribution will seek to center the importance of an aspect of (southern) African identity and religiosity, namely African lived realities, within the broader conversation on resilient religion that this book invites. Hence, this chapter will not discuss resilience as such. Others have done a fine job of this. Rather it wishes to begin a step earlier than the discussion by asking who and what should responsibly constitute a discussion on a topic such as resilient religion that is hosted in (South) Africa, and that is largely taking place among (South) Africans?

## 5.2 Two ways of thinking about context and theology

The first claim that we need to consider is that all theologies are inherently contextual. This stands to reason since all theologies stem from particular contexts. The concerns, sources, traditions, and participants in theological discourses are what give content and shape to the discourse itself. In this regard, I take my lead from various African theologians, who claim that the work of theology is frequently constituted in the telling of stories, the stories that we tell about ourselves and our lives, and the stories that we tell about others and their lives.

In some sense, all theologies are narratives. They are sense-making stories that stem from a complex set of histories, friendships, commitments, and discourses. This is particularly so for African Christians. Mercy Amba Oduyoye writes that "African women", and I would also venture many African men, prioritise "story as a source of theology" (Oduyoye, 2001: 10). The stories that we tell about ourselves, our world, and our relation to the world, are the acknowledged, and at times unacknowledged, sources of our beliefs and practices. Of course, some theologies are expressly narrative in nature (dialogical and perspectival), while others are more discursive (analytical and apologetic). Stephen Garner names this as "inherently contextual" theology (Garner, 2015: 21).

Of course, the storied nature of theology is not only true of Africans. In his book, *A History of the Expansion of Christianity* Kenneth Latourette suggests the stories of Christianity can be accounted for through the spreading of the religion across varied geographies (i.e. the socio-historical reality that Christians faced at different times and in different places), varied expressions of Christianity in different ages (i.e. the theological and philosophical content the ideas that informed the establishment of beliefs, practices and movements), and then how Christianity impacted upon history, nature and humankind and vice versa (i.e. the sociological, political, anthropological, economic, ecological understanding of the ways in which religious communities were engaged by, and engaged with, humanity and all of creation) (Latourette, 1971: 417–418). This accounts for the "inherently contextual" nature of all theological thought.

In addition to this, there is another way in which theologies are contextual. Contextual theology of the second type, according to Garner, can be described as "explicitly contextual" in intent and nature (Garner, 2015: 21). Explicitly contextual theologies emphasise the experiences, concerns, approaches, and sources of particular groups, locations, and histories in their theological contributions (Pears, 2009: 7–9).

As is frequently the case with projects such as this one, and perhaps even more so when the project is hosted by a South African cohort, there was some rich and lively discussion of resilient religion within various contexts. Moreover, my understanding of the nature of contextuality developed and grew through interaction, conversation, and further research.

My initial concern was that the conversation was somewhat reliant upon western epistemologies and resources. This concern proved to be only partly true. The introductory chapters written by Chris Hermans and Kobus Schoeman drew largely upon understandings of resilience that emerged from western epistemologies framed within the concepts and contributions of western scholars (please see the introduction ##).[2] Moreover, the conception of the notion of religion which is presented in the volume is itself a construction of a particular tradition. The notion of religion is not defined in the introduction, rather it is assumed. What becomes clear is that the editors conceive of religion in ways that have become commonplace among those who are influenced by the scientific tradition of religious studies that is characteristic of post-enlightenment and modernity thinking among western scholars. The conception of religious community as a matter of belonging (i.e. being able to 'opt in' or 'opt out') is clearly influenced by what Tomuko Masuzawa describes as a form of self-description that emerged among scholars or religion from European secularisation theories (Masuzawa, 2005: 5). In this conception, religion functions as additional aspect to regular life – it is something that one does, a community that one joins, it has practices that take place outside of, or in addition to, regular life, and thus has the expectation of utility (Gerle in Forster, Gunner & Gerle, 2019: 42–44). Of course, this is not true for much of African religiosity

---

[2] It is interesting to note that a literature survey was supplied on resilience in South Africa. This was extremely helpful. Yet, it did not present much information from African theologians or religious scholars. Of course that was not the focus of the literature study. Moreover, a review of the literature that was presented also tended to rely on almost exclusively Western academic epistemologies and methodologies (see VanBreda, 2001).

where the lines between religion and life, the private and the public, the sacred
and secular, the individual and communal, do not function as they do in parts of
Europe and the United States of America (Forster, 2022: 471–480). In this regard
I concur with a critique of such approaches to religion which comes from Judith
Butler who says that,

> … any generalizations we make about "religion" in "public
> life" are suspect from the start if we do not think about which
> religions are being presupposed in the conceptual apparatus
> itself, especially if that conceptual apparatus, including the
> notion of the public, is not understood in light of its own
> genealogy and secularization projects (Butler, 2013: 10).

Of course, it may well be the case that I was invited to participate in this project
precisely to add this critical perspective. My abstract and proposal may well have
been accepted since the editors sought to include the kinds of questions that I am
raising here, and hoped to invite further critical reflection on the meta-theoretical
aspects that underpin this project on resilient religion. So, when I came to write
this chapter, I realized that my concerns (expressed earlier), while valid, must be
reconsidered as the concerns of an insider to the conversation. Moreover, during
the colloquium that took place on 24 February 2022, my own binary view of
African / European epistemologies was rightly challenged. In particular, I found
that Prof Rian Venter, Dr Junita Meyer and Prof Chris Hermans's engagements
helped me to see that I too was operating with a subtle presupposition that
somehow an 'African' contribution is overly particular, perhaps even exotic. Of
course, all of the African (indeed the South African) participants are arguably
making an "inherently contextual" contribution (by virtue of our geographies,
histories, identities, cultures etc.). In addition to this, many of the participants (as
we see in this volume) are making "explicitly contextual" contributions to our
reflection on resilient religion. Finally, on this point, the editors do seek to engage
the critical perspectives of persons who can rightly be considered "contextual"
theologians (doing African theology, Black Theology, Liberation Theology etc.),
they include Tinyiko Maluleke, Rothney Tshaka and Gerald West.

Yet, I realise that I, like many of my colleagues participating in this
project, cannot claim to be doing African theology. I am a white, male,
heterosexual, Protestant Christian, theologian, who belongs to a predominantly
Black mainline Christian denomination with a colonial history, and I work in a
South African University. My history, education, social location, epistemology,
methodology, and primary conversation partners, shape how I think, and of
course also make me vulnerable to not understanding or seeing many important
aspects of the broader context of which I am a part.

Hence, I felt that it was important that this chapter invites the reader, and
of course also the author, to understand that what is presented as "theology"
(without any qualifier, such as African, Asian, Black, Feminist, or Liberation etc.)

must be subjected to critical scrutiny. The reason for this is that its unnuanced presentation could create the impression that what is presented in this volume it is not "inherently contextual" (in origin, presentation, and construction), but somehow normative and universal. Moreover, this chapter argues that for religion to be a responsible and appropriate source of fostering resilience for (South) Africans, it will also need to be "explicitly contextual". It must centre the experiences, identities, and realities of its intended audience in the discussion. In short, it must be coherent to "our story", and not merely the presentation of "a story" or "someone else's story".

## 5.3 What might it mean to 'un-think the West' – towards centering African reality

The late South African theologian, Vuyani Vellem, named the project described in the previous section as one of "un-thinking the West" (Vellem, 2017: 1). Vellem's terminology sought to explicate what the French philosopher, Michel Foucault, described as an epistemic break in the continuity of knowledge between one period and another, when the theories and predictions of the previous era can no longer hold (Foucault, 2002: 4–5).

Sabelo Ndlovu-Gatsheni suggests that we are facing an epistemic break in many majority world settings at present, since many scholars around the world are awakening to the "crisis of Euro-American epistemologies" (Ndlovu-Gatsheni, 2013: 7). These scholars are challenging the overt, and often covert, claims of Euro-American epistemologies to be "to be universal, neutral, objective, disembodied, as well as being the only mode of knowing" (Ndlovu-Gatsheni, 2013: 7). Vellem suggests that Euro-American epistemologies have opted for forms of "strong thought"; these are concepts and ideas that propose to offer overarching narratives of meaning, large scale explanations for events and experiences, and universal and objective presentations of truth (Vellem, 2017: 2). These strong thought approaches are actually forms of "weak thought" (i.e. not universal, not normative, not entirely objective, not entirely explanatory for all events and experiences). Yet, they seek to dominate contributions of others, re-presenting them within their structures and categories of meaning and thought. Such a process is ultimately doomed to fail since it is not self-critical enough, indeed conscious enough, to be able to see what it is perpetuating in its dominance of the discourse. Simply stated, Vellem affirms that the "West is not our creator" (Vellem, 2017: 8). He affirms that,

> … [in] unthinking the West, our position is that Western civilisation can be overcome; it is crumbling as we speak. The poor and the marginalised, not Western civilisation, constitute our future for the development of life-affirming alternatives of civilisation and knowledge (Vellem, 2017: 2)

As I reflected on this contribution, in light of the theme of this volume on resilient religion, I wondered a great deal about some of what has caused our current need for resilience. Globalization is contributing towards increasing North / South economic inequalities. The pollution of the planet's atmosphere is disproportionally skewed towards Northern countries. The extraction of the resources of Africa (both mineral and human) by Western corporations and countries continues unabated. During the recent Covid-19 health crisis the West's abandonment of global justice and global human rights was on blatant display as European and North American nations hoarded vaccine supplies and Personal Protective Equipment.

If I think about the congregations that I have served in my ministry, and the students that I currently train for ministry, I realise that so much of their suffering continues to emerge from the ongoing hegemony of tacit forms of Western supremacy, white supremacy, Afro-pessimism, and Afro-phobia. These systems continue to privilege Western economies, Western political systems, and the bodies Western nations.[3] Puleng LenkaBula summarises this paradox so clearly when she writes that,

> ... [m]ainstream discourses on poverty and wealth in Africa, especially by multilateral and international institutions such as the World Bank and the International Monetary Fund (IMF) often define Africa as poor, yet Africa and African peoples are endowed with numerous gifts, talents, biodiversity, knowledge systems, and natural resources (LenkaBula, 2008: 241).

If we have these riches, then why do we remain poor? Of course, we have some obvious political, economic and social problems on the continent. However, we cannot discount what colonialism, imperialism, and the ongoing economic and political exploitation of Africa and Africans has done to damage generations of our people.

In this regard, I continue to maintain that before we turn to the pragmatic and utilitarian application of religion to foster resilience, we need to question the colonial and imperial commitments that continue to lie behind the suffering that so many of our siblings face every day. I feel all the more strongly that we, particularly those of us who are participating in this debate in (South) Africa, need to prioritise and process of "un-thinking the West". Before his untimely death, Bantu Steve Biko wrote these very poignant words:

> [While members of western societies] seem to be very concerned with perfecting their technological know-how while losing out on their spiritual dimension. We believe that in the long run the special contribution to the world by Africa will be

---

[3] Consider for a moment the difference in treatment that Ukrainian refugees have received in European nations in comparison to how Syrian and African refugees were treated.

in this field of human relationship. The great powers of the
world may have done wonders in giving the world an industrial
and military look, but the great gift still has to come from Africa
– giving the world a more human face (Biko, 2002: 46).

In light of this quote, what is the "special contribution to the world by Africa"?
In the section that follows we shall consider what it might mean for us to prioritise
our experiences, stories, identities, and traditions in the discourse on resilient
religion. As we shall see, the process of "un-thinking the West" presents some
significant considerations for *how* we think about resilient religion, but also for
*who* we choose as the sources that inform our thinking on this topic.

## 5.4 What might 'decolonization' and 'Africanization' mean in relation to this discussion?

When we speak of "Africa", what do we mean?[4] One could answer this question
in many ways. Africa is both a place and a people in popular though. Of course,
that is partly true, but Africa is in fact many different people and many varied
places. The differences between the arid north and lush centre of the continent,
between light skinned persons of Arab descent and the Bantu of Southern Africa,
between farmers and traders, are all obvious to observe. However, there is another
important aspect to consider in answering this question. How Africans, and
Africa, are viewed by 'outsiders' differs radically from how many Africans think
of themselves. A cursory study of African history in relation to the histories of
many Western nations exposes the "gaze" to which Africans have been subjected
throughout history – racism, Afro-phobia, Afro-pessimism and xenophobia are
ongoing realities in the cultural imagination of many Westerners and their
nations. As Achille Mbembe rightly claims, speaking "rationally about Africa is
not something that has every come naturally" (Mbembe, 2001: 1).

That Africa and Africans exist without question. Mbembe speaks of our
existence as a form of *facticity* (Mbembe, 2001: 3). Simply stated, Africans, and
Africa, have no need to justify our existence or identity to outside observes such
as Western powers and academics, "since things and institutions have always
been there, there is no need to seek any other ground for them than the *fact of
their being there*" (Mbembe, 2001: 3–4). Why is it necessary to state this? There
is tendency that when Africans speak or write ourselves, our location and our
reality, we have to contend with prejudices, untruths, and myths who and what
we are. The dominance of western economies, political systems, and intellectual
systems in the academy, does not entail that are more desirable, moral, or
sophisticated. As I have argued elsewhere, these systems came to dominate the

---

[4] For more on this topic please see, *The Invention of Africa: Gnosis, Philosophy, and the
Order of Knowledge* (Mudimbe, 2020).

world by means of a series of historical events that are often fraught with violence, prejudice, and self-protection (Forster, 2018: 1–4).

African decolonial discourses claim that the patterns of thought, and the concomitant structures of power, that emerged during the colonial era have determined the image that both those in Africa, and those elsewhere in the world, have of Africa and Africans (Vorster, 2021: 47). This in turn has led to a 'state of being' that is known as "coloniality". The, "long-standing patterns of power that emerged as a result of colonialism, but that define culture, labour, intersubjective relation and knowledge production beyond the strict limitations of colonial administrations", continue to operate (Maldonado-Torres, 2007: 243). African decolonial discourses seek to re-imagine, liberate, and transform communities that were previously under colonial power. Here the "ultimate goal is to reorganize the global matrixes of power and rid African societies from all forms of 'coloniality'" (Vorster, 2021: 48).

As has already been argued, so much of the ongoing hardship and suffering that Africans face are because of the historical injustices perpetrated against them by Western nations throughout history. Many of these injustices continue to operate in a globalized world because of the ways in which colonial thinking, forms of imperialism, and a lack of Western self-critique centre Western experience, knowledge, priorities, and objectives. While religion can certainly serve as a powerful source to foster resilience among African persons in the face of ongoing injustice, it can also help to question the systems of power and dominance that lead to a need for some forms of resilient religion at present.

I have argued elsewhere that there are two primary problems with some dominant Western discourses on contemporary religion. The first relates to *identity* – a great deal of Western religion is shaped by the ontological supposition of psychosocial individualism and anthropological exceptionalism (Forster, 2010: 243–253, 2021: 1–10). Notions such as personal salvation, self-fulfilment, and the telos of extreme forms of individual rights, seem to have placed the individual human person at odds with other human persons and the rest of creation. The second relates to *secularisation* – much of contemporary Western discourses on religion present an uncritical supplanting the decline of certain forms of religiosity in the West onto the rest of the world. Religion in Africa has tended to defy popular and scholarly notions of the decline of religion that arose in the late 19th and early 20th centuries. Max Weber, Auguste Comte, Emile Durkheim, Herbert Spencer, and Karl Marx argued, in various forms, that religiosity and religion would decline and vanish in both private and public life (Kotze, 2019: 3). Of course, this has not happened among Africans. The geographic and social location of these commentators is worth noting. As Hennie Kotze notes, an important critique related to the misrecognition of religious growth and decline is because most research in this field "generally emphasized trends in church attendance by Protestants and Catholics in Europe" (Taylor, 2009: 1; cf., Norris & Inglehart, 2011: 7; Kotze, 2019: 4). These studies did not include data from Latin America, Asia or Africa (Kotze, 2019: 4). More recent research by Norris and Inglehart's shows that adherence to formalized religion, and religious sentiments, "persists most strongly among vulnerable populations, especially those living in poorer nations, facing personal survival-threatening risks" (Norris & Inglehart, 2011: 4).[5]

This means that we must remain critically engaged in a robust and authentic conversation about the ways in which Western scholarship characterises religious identity and narratives around religious decline. We need to decolonize our understandings of the conception of religion and religiosity if our conversation around resilient religion is to be accurate and authentic. This is seldom a straightforward process as Andreotti de Oliveira, et.al., point out, "decolonisation is a messy, dynamic, and contradictory process" (Andreotti et al., 2015: 22). This is both because coloniality continues to have an impact on multiple aspects of our being. Moreover, we also need to acknowledge that "decolonisation has multiple meanings, and the desires and investments that animate it are diverse, contested, and at times, at odds with one another" (Andreotti et al., 2015: 22).

In our conversation on resilient religion we will have to take into "consideration how indigenous people lost their freedom to exist as indigenous people in almost every single sphere of existence" (Andreotti et al., 2015: 24). In this regard Tinyiko Maluleke argues that African theologians, "cannot proceed without taking seriously the continued and historic influence of African religions and traditions as past and present hosts of Christianity in Africa" (Maluleke, 2021: 313). Nokuzula Mndende, a scholar of African Indigenous Religion, explains the importance of this, since when Christian missionaries came to Southern Africa, "Religion, Christianity, and Western culture were incorrectly implied to be synonymous with one another" (Mndende, 2019: 158). One result of this was that, "the new imposed religion brought by missionaries displaced the indigenous forms of [African] spirituality and relegated them to exclusive and supposedly outdated cultural practices of the Black population of South Africa" (Mndende, 2019: 158).

In order to address these concerns, I propose that three movements are necessary.

### 5.4.1   Dealing with the perverse logic of coloniality

First, we need to have the courage to identify, name, and address the manner in which the "perverse logic" of colonialism has created pathologies that have injured the psychological and social realities of Africans (Mignolo, 2007: 450). Here the work of Frantz Fanon, an Algerian political philosopher and psychiatrist,

---

[5] For a detailed discussion of these notions please see *Religiosity in South Africa and Sweden: A comparison,* (Kotze, 2019), and *Public Theology and Africa,* (Forster, 2022).

as well as the work of Phumla Gobodo-Madikizela, a South African social psychologist and philosopher, are both instructive and important. Gobodo-Madikizela advocates for a process of rehumanization to undo the dehumanizing objectives that colonialism and apartheid enacted upon Black South Africans (Gobodo-Madikizela, 2002: 7–32, 2016: 43–61). Whereas, Fanon argued for a form of African liberation that was about more than just a liberation from colonial rule, but rather liberation from the pathologies of colonialism (Fanon, 2008: 35). Fanon (2008:35) noted that some approaches to "Africanisation" could inadvertently become forms of colonial "retrogression". Retrogression is not true liberation, rather it is a form of retrogression back into subjugation. The principles of division, subjugation and dehumanization (which are characteristic of coloniality) continue to operate as the "nation is passed over for the race, the tribe is preferred to the state" (in Mbembe, 2016). Fanon described such retrogression as Africanising colonisation – the names, faces, and races of the colonisers may be different, but the abusive tactics remain the same. We have seen "retrogression" in nationalist rhetoric that underpins contemporary xenophobic movements such as 'Operation Dudula'. Such movements are built on the foundations of racism, negrophobia and chauvinism (Mbembe, 2016: 34).

In the debate on resilient religion, we shall need to remain vigilant that we do not merely perpetuate the pathologies of colonialism, either in the outright rejection of the West or in the uncritical adoption of what is described as African.

### 5.4.2   Dealing with the 'soft power' of epistemology, methodology and language

Second, we will need to pay attention to the decolonization of epistemology, methodology, and language. According to the Kenyan novelist Ngũgĩ wa Thiong'o the colonial powers not only sought to dehumanize and divide persons through the exercising of violence and political power (as discussed above), they also used "soft power" to dominate (Vorster, 2021: 50). In order to achieve the aims of domination and dehumanization they malformed culture, language, the arts, and education (Ngũgĩ wa Thiong'o, 1992: 5). By means of privileging the languages, educational systems, and religions of the West they presented Europe as the centre of the cultural, educational, and 'civilized' universe. These practices continue in both overt and more subtle ways in geo-politics, academia, and of course religion.

The supposition that the experience of the Euro-American person is normative to the world is deeply problematic. As Ngũgĩ wa Thiong'o notes, the African is "now being exposed exclusively to a culture that was a product of a world external to himself. He [is] being made to stand outside of himself and look at himself" (Ngũgĩ wa Thiong'o, 1992: 17). When the self is presented as lesser in comparison to the identity, experience, and expectations of the coloniser, the consequences are dehumanization and devastation. What is needed is a "search for a liberating perspective within which to see ourselves clearly in relation to ourselves and to other selves in the universe" (Ngũgĩ wa Thiong'o, 1992: 87). An antidote to the violence of cultural, linguistic, educational, and religious colonisation is to decentre the power of the West in African thought and research. This will require that the languages, cultures, experiences, and realities of Africans are privileged in research related to our lives. Moreover, we shall also need to critically evaluate the epistemologies and methodologies of knowledge that are presented as normative in both Western and African academic settings. As mentioned earlier, this will require not only re-thinking how we engage in our research, but sometimes even "un-thinking" what we regard as normative. Immanuel Wallerstein says the following about the epistemic break that this reality describes:

> When important new evidence undermines old theories and predictions do not hold, we are pressed to rethink our premises. In that sense, much of nineteenth-century social science, in the form of specific hypothesis, is constantly being rethought. But, in addition to rethinking, which is 'normal', I think we need to 'unthink' nineteenth-century social science, because many of its presumptions – which, in my view, are misleading and constrictive – still have far too strong a hold on our mentalities. These presumptions, once considered liberating of the spirit, serve today as the central intellectual barrier to useful analysis of the social world (Wallerstein, 2001: 1).

In relation to our project on resilient religion, my invitation is that we consider our work with a necessary and healthy measure of self-critique. What are our unquestioned suppositions about what constitutes religion? What do we uncritically present as the pinnacle of academic excellence, epistemic truth, or methodological rigour? Where do we turn to, in order to learn from and inform our ideas and contributions on resilient religion?

In my own work in the last decades I have been challenged not only to cite African academics, but also to critically evaluate whether the African scholars that I cite are not themselves subtly perpetuating Western epistemologies in their research. I ask how do they undertake their research? Who are their primary conversation partners? For whom are they undertaking their research? Who are the gatekeepers that shape their work by deciding what is valuable, which locations are more desirable to present one's work, whose funding determines what gets researched, presented, and how it gets presented?

Gerald West rightly notes that "the choice of 'interlocutors', the perception of God, social analysis, the choice of theological tools, and the relationship between theory and practice", all play a crucial role in the shaping of our research, and the eventual contributions that we make from our research (West, 2009: 165). I am grateful to say that in recent decades, under the supervision of one of the editors of this book – Prof Chris Hermans – my conversation partners, and way of doing theology, has changed significantly. Prof Hermans helped me to understand the importance of listening to the voices, experiences, and beliefs of South African Christians. Moreover, he helped me to develop a research methodology that would lead to the development of a "people's theology" in which "ordinary readers" of the Bible were able to share their understandings of the political implications of forgiveness with justice among black and white South African Christians (Forster, 2019: 19, 142–146). The commitment to accessing, and listening to, the voices of "ordinary readers" transformed and enriched this theological research journey and textured and deepened the findings and contributions.

### 5.4.3   Deliberately centering African reality and experience

This leads to the third aspect that we shall need to consider in this process – that is a deliberate commitment towards the Africanisation of our contributions. As both Mndende and Maluleke noted earlier, we "cannot proceed without taking seriously the continued and historic influence of African religions and traditions as past and present hosts of Christianity in Africa" (see Mndende, 2019: 158; Maluleke, 2021: 313). The simple truth, as John Mbiti rightly notes in *Concepts of God in Africa,* is that "African peoples are not religiously illiterate" (Mbiti, 1970: xiii). Long before the missionaries arrived on Southern African shores, Africans had religious beliefs, a moral philosophy, culture, art, technologies, and law.

The neutralization of Euro-American hegemony is not enough to facilitate a truly contextually relevant and applicable form of resilient religion in (South) Africa. What we need is a deliberate commitment towards the Africanisation of our beliefs and practices. We do not simply want to "repeat Western doctrines in African guises", rather we must seek a "difference in both substance and form" in African Christian theologies (Vorster, 2021: 51). In this regard persons such as Steve Biko and Dibanga wa Said serve as examples of advocates for truly indigenous theologies. It would be disingenuous, if in this project, we cited the work of Black and African theologians, yet we unknowingly or carelessly perpetuated the dominance of Euro-American hegemony (such as whiteness, a "white God", a "white Theology", or normalise the existential and theological positions of white Europeans and Americans) in our work (Said, 1971: 503). Many of our contemporary South African theological colleagues, such as Vuyani Vellem, Tinyiko Maluleke, Rothney Tshaka, and Fundiswa Kobo draw upon the formative work of Steve Biko which centres the daily pain and experiences of Black South Africans (Biko, 2002: 59).

What the project of Africanisation invites us to do is to re-centre our location, our lives, and our experiences in our work. This does not mean an outright rejection of the contributions of our siblings from other contexts. Our task is not a reactionary one – as if the West is the powerbroker of all knowledge and our only option is to respond to that power. Africa is not a mere extension of the West. Africanisation is an ideological project to expel knowledge from the West, or other contexts. Rather, our aim is to clearly define what our centre is (Mbembe, 2016: 35). Re-centering African reality and experience indicates that we recognise that various perspectives on life and reality exist. Some perspectives have, rightly, are more appropriate to our context. What we want to do is identify and dismantle a worldview that has been placed upon us from outside of our lived reality. Then, we wish to clarify who we are, what we believe and understand of our lives and our context, and place that in the centre of our reflection. This is a humbling process that enables us to recognise in both critical and appreciative terms who we are. It does not mean negating the perspective of the 'other', but simply placing our perspectives within their rightful place. Central to this task is the recognition of relationality in place of individuality, and a desire to avoid competition and hierarchical subjugation between the self and the other (Vázquez, 2015: 99).

As I mentioned earlier, I am an ordained minister in a largely Black South African denomination – the Methodist Church of Southern Africa. However, as so much of my research shows, we continue to struggle with the subtle, yet powerful, presence of our colonial history and dominance of European thinking, traditions, and whiteness, in our beliefs and practices. For a Church such as the one that I belong to, to be able to meet its members at the point of their daily struggles and hopes, we will need to centre them and their existence, if our hope is to discover a truly authentic form of resilient religion.

## 5.5 Some tentative implications for religion and resilience in South Africa

In the previous of the chapter, it was argued that we need at least three forms of decolonisation and Africanisation for a project such as ours on resilient religion. The first deals with the psychological and social wounds of colonial domination; the second deals with epistemologies, methods, and approaches to meaning making; while the third centres African experience and reality.

These commitments present some implications for our project on resilient religion. As mentioned in the introduction to this chapter, this discussion is largely meta-theoretical in nature. It invites us to think about how we do what we hope to achieve.

First, the invitation to decolonize and Africanize our project will require that we are courageous and honest enough to maintain a healthy measure of self-critique in our research. Who are the persons that are hosting this conversation? Where is it taking place? Who are the participants in this conversation? What is the nature of the inquiry that is taking place? Who is not present? What are we not studying? All of these are important questions to consider as we move forward.

Second, we shall need to interrogate our unquestioned assumptions about what we believe to be true, right, and necessary in our research. In this instance, we shall need to carefully consider how we conceive of resilience and religion. In what ways do we conceptualise each of these topics? Whose voices, experiences, and realities inform what we tentatively name as resilience? Which forms of belief and practice do we consider forming the core of a religion or expressions religiosity? Are these appropriate to our population and context?

Third, there may be some instances in which we confess our blindness and inadequacy by virtue of our social locations, histories, and identities (for example, I am a white, male, English speaking, academic theologian, who belongs to a historically colonial Christian tradition). The recognition of my own inadequacy may just open some space for the voices of those who are not centered in my life to speak. This will require that I am willing to listen and to learn.

Fourth, there may be some very important things that I will need to un-learn and un-think as the process unfolds. I confess that this is not easy. I have invested my whole career, indeed my whole life, in developing the skills and capabilities that I have for academic research of a particular kind. It is scary to think that some of what I have been doing may need to be un-learnt. But, if the intention is to work towards truthful and responsible academic contribution that is relevant to our South African context, then I will need to muster the courage to do so.

## 5.6 Conclusion

This chapter invites the reader to consider the importance of (South) African identities and experiences in the conversation around resilient religion. In some senses, this chapter presents something of a personal struggle and a personal journey as the author sought to undertake the task of theological reflection in a manner that is responsible and authentic to his context.

In this regard it is important that we maintain a healthy tension between "inherently contextual" theological development and "explicitly contextual" theological development. In large measure, this contribution leans towards the latter, while acknowledging some of the problematic ways in which the former can malform theological research. This task will require a commitment towards "un-thinking" the ongoing hegemony Euro-American influence in (South) African theologies and theological research. Three forms of decolonisation and Africanisation are proposed as a means towards developing a more authentically (South) African conversation on resilient religion. Acknowledging, and engaging, with the wounds and dehumanization of African persons as a result of colonialism. Reconsidering epistemologies, methodologies, and conversation partners in theological research. And finally, re-centering African experiences and contributions in the conversation around resilient religion. I am grateful to my colleagues who have so patiently served as companions and conversation partners in this journey. I have great hopes for what lies ahead.

## BIBLIOGRAPHY

Andreotti, V. de O., Stein, S., Ahenakew, C. & Hunt, D. (2015). Mapping interpretations of decolonization in the context of higher education. Decolonization: Indigeneity, Education & Society. 4(1):21–40.

Biko, S. (2002). I Write What I Like: Selected Writings. Chicago, Il: University of Chicago Press.

Butler, J. (2013). Parting Ways: Jewishness and the Critique of Zionism. New York, NY: Columbia University Press.

Fanon, F. 2008. Black Skin, White Masks. New York, NY: Grove Press.

Forster, D.A., Gunner, G. & Gerle, E. Eds. (2019). Freedom of Religion at Stake: Competing claims among Faith Traditions, Sates and Persons. (Church of Sweden Research Series no. 18). Eugene, OR: Wipf & Stock Publishers. Available: https://www.amazon.com/Freedom-Religion-Stake-Competing-Traditions/dp/1532660561.

Forster, D.A. (2010). African relational ontology, individual identity, and Christian theology An African theological contribution towards an integrated relational ontological identity. Theology. 113(874):243–253. DOI: https://doi.org/10.1177/0040571X1011300402.

Forster, D.A. (2018). Democracy and Social Justice in Glocal Contexts. International Journal of Public Theology. 12(1):1–4. DOI: 10.1163/15697320-12341530.

Forster, D.A. (2019). The (Im)possibility of Forgiveness: An Empirical Intercultural Bible Reading of Matthew 18.15-35. Eugene, OR: Wipf and Stock Publishers.

Forster, D.A. (2021). Post-foundational theology and the contribution of African approaches to consciousness and identity. Verbum et Ecclesia. 42(2):10. DOI: 10.4102/ve.v42i2.2363.

Forster, D.A. (2022). Public Theology in Africa. In T&T Clark Handbook of Public Theology. C. Hübenthal, Ed. New York, NY: Bloomsbury Academic. 469–488.

Foucault, M. (2002). Archaeology of Knowledge. London: Routledge.

Garner, S. (2015). Contextual and Public Theology: Passing fads or theological imperatives? Stimulus: The New Zealand Journal of Christian Thought and Practice. 22(1):21–28.

Gobodo-Madikizela, P. 2002. Remorse, forgiveness, and rehumanization: Stories from South Africa. Journal of humanistic psychology. 42(1):7–32.

Gobodo-Madikizela, P. (2016). What Does It Mean to Be Human in the After-math of Mass Trauma and Violence?: Toward the Horizon of an Ethics of Care. Journal of the Society of Christian Ethics. 36(2):43–61. DOI: 10.1353/sce.2016.0030.

Kotze, H. (2019). Religiosity in South Africa and Sweden: A comparison. In Freedom of Religion at Stake: Competing claims among Faith Traditions, Sates and Persons. D.A. Forster, E. Gerle, & G. Gunner, Eds. (Church of Sweden Research Series no. 18). Eugene, OR: Pickwick Publications. 3–17.

Latourette, K.S. (1971). A History of the Expansion of Christianity. V. 7. New York, NY: Harper & Row.

LenkaBula, P. (2008). Poverty, wealth and wellbeing and African feminist Christian ethics : poverty and well-being. Practical Theology in South Africa = Praktiese Teologie in Suid-Afrika. 23(1):239–260.

Maldonado-Torres, N. (2007). On the Coloniality of Being. Cultural Studies. 21(2–3):240–270. DOI: 10.1080/09502380601162548.

Maluleke, T. (2021). Why I Am Not a Public Theologian. The Ecumenical Review. 73(2):297–315. DOI: 10.1111/erev.12602.

Masuzawa, T. (2005). The Invention of World Religions: Or, How European Universalism Was Preserved in the Language of Pluralism. Chicago, Il: University of Chicago Press.

Mbembe, A. (2001). On the Postcolony. Los Angeles, CA: University of California Press.

Mbembe, A.J. (2016). Decolonizing the university: New directions. Arts and Humanities in Higher Education. 15(1):29–45. DOI: 10.1177/1474022215618513.

Mbiti, J.S. (1970). Concepts of God in Africa. Santa Barbara, CA: Praeger Publishers.

Mignolo, W.D. (2007). Delinking. Cultural Studies. 21(2–3):449–514. DOI: 10.1080/09502380601162647.

Mndende, N. (2019). African Traditional Religion and Freedom of Religion in South Africa. In Freedom of Religion at Stake: Competing claims among Faith Traditions, Sates and Persons. D.A. Forster, G. Gunner, & E. Gerle, Eds. Eugene, OR: Wipf & Stock Publishers. 157–174.

Mudimbe, V.Y. (2020). The Invention of Africa: Gnosis, Philosophy, and the Order of Knowledge. Bloomington, IN: Indiana University Press.

Ndlovu-Gatsheni, S.J. (2013). Perhaps Decoloniality is the Answer? Critical Reflections on. Africanus: Journal of Development Studies. 43(2):1–12.

Ngũgĩ wa Thiong'o. (1992). Decolonising the mind: the politics of language in African literature. Nairobi: East African Publishers.

Norris, P. & Inglehart, R. (2011). Sacred and Secular: Religion and Politics Worldwide. Cambridge: Cambridge University Press.

Oduyoye, M.A. (2001). Introductions in feminist theology: Introducing African Women's Theology. Sheffield: Sheffield Academic Press.

Pears, A. 2009. Doing Contextual Theology. London: Routledge.

Said, D.W. (1971). An African Theology of Decolonization. The Harvard Theological Review. 64(4):501–524.

Taylor, C. (2009). A Secular Age. Cambridge, MA: Harvard University Press.

VanBreda, A.D. (2001). Resilience Theory: A Literature Review. South African Military Health Service, Military Psychological Institute, Social Work Research & Development. (October):334.

Vázquez, R. (2015). Decolonial Practices of Learning. In going glocal in higher education: the theory, teaching and measurement of global citizenship. Netherlands: de Drvkkery. 94–102. Available: http://www.ucr.nl/about-ucr/Faculty-and-Staff/Social-Science/Documents/GoingGlocal_DEF_02.pdf#page=94.

Vellem, V.S. (in press). Un-thinking the West: The spirit of doing Black Theology of Liberation in decolonial times. HTS Teologiese Studies / Theological Studies. 73(3):9 pages. DOI: 10.4102/hts.v73i3.4737.

Vorster, N. (2021). African Decolonization and Reformed Theology. In Reformed Public Theology: A Global Vision for Life in the World. M. Kaemingk, Ed. Grand Rapids, MI: Baker Academic. 47–59.

Wallerstein, I.M. (2001). Unthinking Social Science: The Limits of Nineteenth-century Paradigms. Philadelphia, PA: Temple University Press.

West, G.O. 1956-. (2009). Human flourishing and social transformation: bringing embodied theology into the public realm. Reformed World. 59(3):163–180.

# Chapter 6

# Resilient preaching
## A critical appraisal of Johan Cilliers' trilogy on "grace"

*M Laubscher*[1]


## 6.1 Introduction

In an introduction to a collection of Karl Barth's early sermons (key in the origins of Barth's "theology of crisis" and eventual *Church Dogmatics*), Will Willimon, the well-known North American homiletician and self-described *accidental preacher*[2] mentions that "[a] preacher, unlike an academic theologian, cannot forever postpone a verdict, cannot avoid a weekly, public declaration of God. A preacher must preach even if the preacher feels (as Barth felt) that it is impossible for him to preach" (Willimon 2009:xii-xiii).

Willimon's insight may sound so obvious and self-evident, but in some way, I think that there is something profound within it. Preachers who experience this sense of urgency, constant immanent crisis, listeners with serious needs and high expectations, leaving one with no room to shift the ever-recurring deadline of Sunday morning is coming, surely assumes some first-hand experience and knowledge of what is meant by becoming and being resilient. If there ever was a theological act and practice that offers us some glimpse into the actual meaning of "heartbreaking adversity" (Hermans 2022a) and the possibility of "new beginnings" (Hermans 2022b), then I believe that preaching could be one of the main contenders.

Preaching may represent the idea of resilience in more than one sense. On the one hand, there are the specific experiences and cases of dealing with heartbreaking adversity, but so too might it be important to take another step back and explore the idea of preaching *per se* being an embodiment of resilience itself. Besides the challenge to relate resilient religion and preaching to particular issues and scenarios, it might be even more helpful to re-imagine preaching as such a resilient endeavour. In other words, mere showing up, even before we say a

---

[1] His e-mail address is: laubscherm@ufs.ac.za
[2] See Willimon's memoirs (2019).

single word, might "possess" within itself the gift of seeing things differently (anew).

However, before you object, let me also state that I am well aware that preaching often limits and endangers resilience. There are many listeners and critical observers who will protest, but also preachers (if they are honest) who will confess that, in preaching, we often struggle to breathe ourselves in the so-called Word event. Preaching may easily be weaponised to suffocate and narcotise so that people neither can neither breathe nor stay awake "cometh the hour, cometh the person, *and* cometh the word". In other words, instead of dealing with adversity, preaching can also cause it. It is also important to reckon with the idea that preaching might not only consequentially generate the possibility of a new beginning but being that within itself. Resilience is what preaching assumes and craves, but often fails to deliver. In short, "resilient preaching" is no given or guarantee, but that does not mean that I, as a homiletician and preacher, is not resilient enough to continue to hope, dream, and work towards exploring the loaded idea of "resilient preaching".

## 6.2 "Introducing" Johan Cilliers

One possible way to get this going is to highlight fellow colleague Johan Cilliers' work and see how it, and especially his latest trilogy on "grace" (caused by various forms of crisis, among others the COVID-19 pandemic) might help in defining religion. However, before I get to it, let me first "introduce" his oeuvre, as it sets the stage for why we need to take note of his work, and frame it in this particular manner.

Cilliers, who formally retired in Stellenbosch in 2019, and is currently (since early 2022) only one of a few A1-rated scholars in theology in South Africa, is indeed a well-known and highly respected voice in various international homiletic circles (a former president of *Societas Homiletica*, often a leading voice at these and other national conferences, and delivering guest lectures in Germany). As the recent rating indicates, there is probably much more significance and potential to his work than simply being heard in these often limited and closed spaces in academia. There is a growing awareness that his critical insights, over many decades, into the state of "emergency" within especially White Dutch Reformed circles in South Africa is still awaiting the necessary recognition by the people implicitly implied in his writings over many decades (see Laubscher 2022a). I mention this not in order to postpone and limit the scope of exploring his latest accidental trilogy on "grace", but rather to take note of the key insight that there is already, from early on, a general characteristic knack of reading and responding – and often in trilogies (of which I will ultimately get to their significance) – to these imminent forms of crisis we need to face, whether we like it or not. The (homiletical) struggle is real, intense, and needs to be taken up for real.

For instance, in his PhD thesis (1982), he studied the sermons of Drs Andries Treurnicht (leader of the Conservative Party and opposition in parliament, and editor of [then still] *Die Kerkbode*) and Allan Boesak (leading voice in the struggle against apartheid and author of influential texts such as his PhD study, entitled *Farewell to innocence – A social-ethical study of black theology and black power* [1976], and *Die vinger van God – Preke oor geloof en politiek* [1979]). His findings in this work caused such a stir that the Conservative Party threatened with court action, but nothing came of it ultimately. It was, however, Cilliers' first published academic monograph a decade later (1994) that showed some signs of severe resilience, namely *God vir ons – 'n Analise en beoordeling van Nederduitse Gereformeerde volksprediking (1960-1980)*. In fact, in 2006, this work was translated into English; it is now a prescribed text at many overseas universities in contexts and societies where people grapple with populism and various forms of nationalisms in an age of identity politics. His first trilogy also appeared between 1994 and 2006, when he responded to the crisis of moralistic preaching in a collection of sermons heard and studied on national radio during the early-to-mid 1990s (years of rapid change and transition in South Africa). The titles of the monographs in the trilogy are extremely revealing: *Die uitwissing van God op die kansel. Ontstellende bevindinge oor Suid-Afrikaanse prediking* (1996); *Die uitwysing van God op die kansel. Inspirerende perspektiewe op die prediking – om God te sien en ander te láát sien* (1998), and *Die genade van gehoorsaamheid. Hoe evangelies is die etiese preke wat ons in Suid-Afrika hoor?* (2000). Other academic monographs followed such as *The living voice of the gospel – Revisiting the basic principles of preaching* (2004), which one could view as a culmination and summary of all the previous works.[3]

It is important to add that Cilliers not only focused exclusively on preaching-and-homiletics *per se* over the years, but also that liturgy-and-worship, and for that matter also practical theology as such, was also integral to this work. There is a profound liturgical intelligence within and throughout all his "homiletical" work, and of course also the other way around. The differentiation and distinction between disciplines and questions are important, as it helps grasp more fully the problems confronted with, but they cannot be separated if we want to address them in profound ways. For instance, his *Dancing with deity: Re-imagining the beauty of worship* (2012) continues to address the apartheid legacy he exposed in his previous works, but now simply in terms of its static, dull, ugly, boring remnants still present in (often White Reformed) liturgical settings (see Cilliers 2012:118-119, 174, 185, 217). In fact, this work in a sense provides an

---

[3] This is not the only major work in Cilliers' oeuvre during this time that fits our description above. Another and perhaps even more (internationally) noteworthy book is the one he co-authored in 2012 with Charles L. Campbell, *Preaching fools: The Gospel as a rhetoric of folly*.

important hinge or even crossover into a new phase in Cilliers' work, as the earlier ethical concerns are now introduced and viewed through an aesthetical imagination of the crisis resilient preachers and liturgist were facing.

Against this background, Cilliers planned to write his "last" two major books, namely *A space for grace – Towards an aesthetics of preaching* (2016) and *Timing grace – Reflections on the temporality of preaching* (2019) before retiring in 2019. In both these texts, references to the other are heard, such as for example:

> This is not a Do-It-Yourself handbook for preaching. Readers looking for ten (easy) steps to prepare their sermons will in all probability be disappointed. The book does, however, hopefully grapple with some of the most fundamental issues related to preaching as an event in space and time. More precisely: It strives to develop homiletics from an aesthetical-theological point of view, of which time and space are decisive constituents (Cilliers 2016:iii).

> I believe we indeed need both time and space, but linked together in a meaningful manner. If space reigns, we fall prey to exclusivist ideologies, becoming strapped down in our settings; if time reigns, we lose sight of our bodies and our physicality. But when time and space coincide meaningfully, *kairos* is born. Time and space, and their *kairotic coincidence*, signify the gift of time to enter the space of grace – a gift of grace granted by God. *I reiterate: God, not needing time or space, moves in time through space, moving time and space – towards the telos of time and space* (Cilliers 2016:160-161).

> As I argued elsewhere, time cannot be understood without space, and vice versa. A presence can only be experienced in a space; and this space is always linked to a time. A 'space for grace' always calls for, and always is constituted by, the 'timing of grace, i.e. the *pre-sencing* of a Presence in the present' (Cilliers 2019:24).

References, or even a slight expectation or hint of a possible third book to produce yet another trilogy is nowhere to be found in these two texts. However, in retrospect, its advent during the first few months of retirement, and into the unknown of the pandemic (where grace is "to know that you do not know, fully", and "to know that you will know, fully", as well as "to know that you are known, fully") could perhaps be anticipated if you read between the lines of the above. Its characteristic sound, and dare I say "resilience", is clear from the get-go, when the opening lines state:

> This book wrote itself. The impulse(s), to write this book, often appeared in the most curious places ad times … The point is, I could not resist the voice(s) of this book calling out to me. The impulses [were] too persistent. She was not to be denied. … [& towards the end of the preface] This book has not finished writing itself. Neither have I. For that, the topic is too broad and wide and deep. Too 'human'. The finger(s) keep on writing, keep on moving on (Cilliers 2020:xi-xii).

In short, reading these three texts together seems to be important. The one comments and complements the other as one single movement of threefold grace in the "here" and "now". We need to read and listen closely to all three of them individually and together before we can determine to what degree Cilliers makes a valuable contribution to the question of resilient preaching. As is already clear, "resilience" is not its theme, question, or keyword, but its take on such threefold grace might simply unlock certain mysteries in grasping what is yet to be discovered in resilient preaching.

## 6.3 A space for grace – Towards an aesthetics of preaching (2016)

Much of what is heard in the early parts of this work reminds us of what was stated in *Dancing with deity* (2012) on the issue of *kitsch* liturgy and preaching. If we cannot fathom the ugly beauty of the cross, we shall struggle to sense this exploration of an aesthetics of preaching. Already early in the text, we hear Cilliers (2016) articulating the following:

> The relationship between the proportion of order and the disproportion of chaos is important for our understanding of beauty. … The link between these two realities could be described as beauty. Beauty exists in the tentative space between proportionate order and disproportionate chaos (6).

> This holy space – where God's face is revealed – is constituted by the faces of the marginalized; as a matter of fact, God's face cannot be seen without the faces of the marginalized (14).

> To enter the space before God's face does not primarily indicate accessing a physical space, but the potential and mystery of encounters (15).

Apartheid's "lokasie" is early on once again exposed as a serious "dislocation" (read: "dislokasie") in this context as actual places of forced migration and bitter sour irony (8).

Bearing in mind what was said in *Preaching fools* (2012) – for instance, referring to this "iron theology" with its "wagons", "laagers", "bunkers", "castles", "fortresses", "ivory towers", "enemies", and language of "us" and "them"

– it is now even further critiqued in a profound series of formulations such as the following:

> God's 'presence' is not set in stone, not cast in concrete, not immortalized in marble; rather, it is epitomized in fluidity and movement, revealed in flux and flow (18).

> This space cannot and should not be fixated and monumentalized. … [T]he empty tomb of Christ is the greatest statue of history! The movement of Christ from death to life transforms all statues into stones that are rolled away from their fixed places. The resurrected Christ now moves through life (21).

> In this 'tent of transit,' in this space-time tabernacle, time and space are not eternalized or postulated as cyclical and fixed, but experienced as a space-time event, constituted by the interplay of relationships. Here we find no finalities frozen in time and space, but foam floating in and with time and space; no perfection, but play; no monument, but movement (25).

> Home 'happens' through encounters, through seeing the faces of others and the Other (34).

Reading these words in the South African context, and especially against the backdrop of Cilliers' earlier work and oeuvre, is to my mind a profound way of continuing with the struggle for a just and more humane South Africa. This depiction of a real space for grace exposes the ideology of apartheid's closed and endangered spaces of fear, being apart, and filled with hatred. Or, stated more positively, as it is actually formulated, it seeks and voices an open, moving, dynamic, and relational space called "home" where we can discover "others" and "the Other".

It is important to note that this spacious movement does not consist of nor assume mere repetitive or predictable (and boring) movements. There is (again!) emphasis on playfulness, creativity, newness, and (of course, the importance of "constant") reframing occurring within preaching and worship. These are all very familiar ideas in various earlier works of Cilliers (2004; 2012; Campbell & Cilliers 2012). Again – and this is important – although it is familiar, there is even a creativity, newness, playfulness, in short, an originality and authenticity in how it is phrased with new nuance and a different subtlety.

> In view of preaching, in my opinion, reframing implies a theological reconfiguration of the existing in such a way that something distinctly new is born, but never without the existing (100).

> Reframing is not equal to mere repetition or re-gurgitation. On the contrary, reframing implies dynamic processes such as 're-naming' ('re-labelling'), 're-visioning', 're-aligning' and 're-

imagining'. Instead of 'more of the same', reframing entails al-
ternatives, even paradoxes, that challenge the existing to attain
new meaning, thereby evoking behavioural change. Reframing
is not a harmless event (110).

I do not necessarily want to get ahead of myself, but Cilliers' subtle but potent
critique on how "prophetic preaching", for example, is understood by many colleagues in the field, especially since the post-1994 dispensation in South Africa,
is profound. He himself does not use this term (read: label), and I think that it is
a deliberate and conscious move, which does not mean that he is not aware of the
discourse or withholding a meaningful contribution. Again, we need to read between the lines, or at least the footnotes and indexes to see how "resilient" preaching could operate without even falling into the temptation of claiming nor pro-
jecting such façade or label. Or, to put it "in other words" that tries to stay "real"
and "embodied" in a different kind of "being with it", I highlight the following
formulation:

It is my opinion that whenever our 'body-liness' is not taken
seriously in our preaching we tend to 'spiritualise', which ends
up with our offering no more than meaningless trivialities and
religious clichés, even soothing and sentimental kitsch. ... that
kitsch 'spiritualises' par excellence (123).

Prophetic (and thereby assumingly "resilient") preachers cannot continue to refer
to "I can't breathe" in such a way that it continues to suffocate and narcotise and
inevitably "transform" into "I can't stay awake". Slogans can easily become clichés; blunt and dangerous. Discerning and naming the present, "pre-sensing Presence" (as we shall shortly see), or being truly "with it" in an exciting and creative
(meaning theological-homiletical) manner, is what is at stake for the – and if I
may – "resilient (prophetic) preacher":

The role of the prophets has always been to conquer space that
has become institutionalized as eternal. They point towards
something new. ... Destructive myths always tend to change
history into nature. Time is arrested and fixed in space. The
clock has stopped for the sake of solidification. Flow becomes
finality" (153-154).

## 6.4 Timing grace – Reflections on the temporality of preaching (2019)

A first glance at the title of this book might create the idea that it is only a mere
logical follow-up from the previous work where he clearly indicated "when I will
be speaking about space, the notion of time will always be lingering in the background" (Cilliers 2016:3). They do indeed belong together, but Cilliers' antenna
for timing preaching as such, does stretch a long way back into his oeuvre. It is
"about time" that Cilliers had to write timely (again – time after time) about the

timing of the Gospel, especially within the South African context. This work shows that the struggle in South Africa can easily also be called a struggle to time the proclamation of the Gospel as such (and with that said, also expose and counter the serious mistiming thereof).

Continuing with the discussion on prophetic preaching referred to earlier, it is noteworthy how Cilliers deliberately goes against the grain of portraying such kind of preaching in terms of mere relevance, social political commentary on the day, and thus being seemingly "with it". For Cilliers, the creative, interruptive, even disruptive element of preaching is now at the fore. For preaching – and I may add, for "resilient preaching" – it is not simply a question of truth as such, and even whether we speak it to power as such, or even with power, but it is timing. In short, it is about the sense for the hour of truth. We might know that *truth* speaks, but do we also *now* know that the truth *speaks* anew (for itself – or not)? In other words, careful with the truth, especially that which we so easily brand as eternal truths, as they are simultaneously timely and temporal truths. Cilliers articulates the matter eloquently as follows:

> Preaching might sound even spectacular or popular ... but it could still be false. The right content, delivered to the 'right' people, but it does not fit into the 'right' time. Indeed, preaching might sound 'correct', but still be 'wrong'; in fact, it can be 'so' correct, that it is 'so' wrong ... The what, whom, and when in preaching need to be in sync, and perhaps timing (the when) is the most important 'homiletical synchroniser' (23).

Whereas Cilliers' earlier work was about exposing particular forms of homiletical escapism (read: the mistiming of the Gospel) in fabricating forms of "'antiprophecy' that does not dare to jump ahead, but rather arrests time and reproduces history" (46), he constructively now emphasises the significance of being in agreement with the "now". It is the quality of the "now", this layered notion of time, in which the present links and connects with past and future for the present to be more than present, and the now more than simply "now" (10). Against a superficial reading of the present which solidifies the present into "presentism" (10), he calls for "the lenses of the Christ-event", meaning a sense for "the deeper meaning of the present moment – as a moment being filled with Christ Himself" (91). The hopeful tenor of all preaching is thus, according to Cilliers, "about timing as pre-sencing the Presence of Christ in the present" (91).

Grace is, in this sense, "already", without Cilliers "already" saying it, "grace upon grace". Spacious and layered grace is also textured and timed grace. There is a familiar yet surprising element to it. There is a new, fresh, creative element to it. In short, especially when thinking about resilient religion and preaching, there is a nuance to grace. The eternal truths become audible in the form of being simultaneously timely and temporal. There is a present giftedness to the present time as such. What we mention "for now" is indeed "for now". "The present is the present is the present" (91).

What makes this line of thinking so attractive is that preaching essentially becomes neither stuck nor predictable, but rather in a multi-sensory way ever present on the move. This is a "moving homiletics" with a very dynamic "touch and go" element to it. Thus, for Cilliers, grace "cannot be scheduled, manipulated, or choreographed – homiletically, or otherwise. Grace happens – therefore it is called 'grace'" (24). I recognise a surprising continuity in his thought when he states anew that this grace cannot be "monumentalized" (10), nor "pillarised" (25), nor be a certain "enclave of rigidity" (29).

How space and time graciously intersect in this kind of homiletics, is well articulated in the following formulation:

> Preachers have the calling to pre-sense the Presence of the mov-
> ing God in the present, in the 'now' – knowing all the time (!)
> that they cannot fast-freeze this God according to a patented
> image (58).

Such timing of grace thus ensures that any form of a static, closed, predictable, boring, linear, and even cyclical experience of time is infused and contrasted with a fluid spiral movement (9). Besides the mere theoretical merits, a timely engagement with other new contemporary challenges preachers face "today" makes Cilliers' work, in this sense, so interesting. There are sides to "wasting time" and "breaking the silence" in which truth speaks within and towards the current South African and global context. Besides the critical notes on some forms and advocacy of prophetic preaching (23), there is, for instance, also a critical note on the buzz surrounding the current discussion on missional ecclesiology and preaching. Stated differently, the timing of grace wants the pendulum to sway creatively in the tension between the centrifugal and centripetal centres of movement (142). Again, the crucial point, in this instance, is not to mistake mere relevance and actuality as being necessarily relevant and actual. In essence, it stimulates and grooms one to be very suspicious – or at least cautious; well-nuanced, articulated, and qualified – in just hopping on the (seemingly moving) bandwagon, joining mere talk of the town. In short, it shows resilience in seeing right through it – and seeing it through, anew.

The movement within this kind of homiletics often calls "time-out" – not to be associated here with any form of escapism; in fact, the exact opposite – meaning to unmask, ground, re-root, and re-connect in God's "now". "Time-out" reveals what it means to re-member Christ and be re-membered within His body. "Time-out" reveals that we are somebody (instead of nobody); with not only raced bodies, but also graced bodies; who should not be erased, because we are "now" all raised in Him. Such agreement with the timing of the Gospel calls for truly being attentive in the moment, experiencing flow, and riding the wave it provides (and the words it speaks).

In short: now is movement, not a monument being erected in
the centre of the ocean, trying its best to resist the force of the
waves, standing fixed and firm against the gale. Preaching is,
in my opinion, the art of riding the waves of now; more than
constructing a monument that must withstand the movement of
these waves (210-211).

## 6.5 Grace upon grace – Reflections on the meaning of life (2020)

Against the above background, it is perhaps not surprising to note Cilliers'
(2020:xi) statement in the preface: "[t]his book wrote itself. ... I could not resist
the voice(s) of this book calling out to me". As it is his first year into retirement,
on the back of the series of the two former monographs, and the first few months
into the pandemic, it is a telling remark about living into and through the "now".
There is within this form of (resilient) preaching indeed grace upon grace. This
triangular spiral spirals forth as a threefold grace simultaneously confessing "that
you do know, fully", "you will know, fully", and "you are being known, fully".
Thus, a trilogy appears out of the blue, is new, and yet it represents an apt conclusion that is neither closed nor set in stone.

The artistic playfulness in his work is, in a sense, well captured in his
refection on this ever-maturing aesthetic shift during the latter years of his career.

[A]esthetics would be one of the most helpful spaces to enter in
any endeavour to link grace with the quest for the meaning of
life. Why? Because aesthetics constitutes the exact opposite of
moralism, of rigid knowledge, of cause-and-effect structures.
While moralism, for instance, clamps down on immovable
'laws', aesthetics says: what if? While cause-and-effect structures know about one, inescapable outcome, aesthetics is not
impressed by cul-de-sacs. (4).

In fact, this existential meditative take on life is framed by acknowledging up
front that such a "search for meaning could not be undertaken without aesthetic
expression" (xii); only to reiterate at the end – once he has shown his sense(s) for
the question – that "it is by way of aesthetics that we can juggle interpretations"
(79). Cilliers now calls the beauty of this threefold grace "bricolage", meaning to
"tinker around" and "play with possibilities, continuously asking: what if?" (27).
There is grace in "not knowing", meaning "an openness, a stance of expectancy,
an embracement of being led into the mystery" (27). To my mind, resilience resonates with this idea of preachers being "bricoleurs" who love "playing with perspectives" – instead of being trapped as "security guards, patrolling along the
borders of ecclesial dogma" (30). The all too familiar tinkering around with ideas
such as "creativity", "improvisation", "imagination", "interruption", "preaching
as play", or "liturgy as dancing with deity", thickens in an ever more dimensional
image of the "preaching fool" who now knows the grace of not knowing fully.

In the second section, "grace: to know that you will know, fully", Cilliers takes the familiar distinction between "future" and "advent" and renames it with a new illuminative concept of "intology", meaning "eternity does not bypass time and space, but simultaneously penetrates and transcends them – 'as' eternity" (46). "Intology" is thus about "the infinite instant(s) of being taken 'into' Christ, of being 'in' Christ" (46). Whereas "bricolage" explores the art of interpretation – guarding against the temptation to succumb into nihilism or activism (being mere wind-chasers) – "intology" pulls us into the art of expectation – guarding against temptations of futurism or escapism (being mere cloud-watchers) (79). Again, eternal grace resonates in a timely yet temporal manner as the living Word moves us.

Therefore, in the third and final section, we now know that we are also being known, fully. Although we move, we are neither drifting nor fading. This movement generates space and time, and there is destiny and certainty within the kairos of being underway. Besides the arts of interpretation and expectancy, there is also now the art of healing – guarding against the temptations of quietism or pietism (being mere bench-sitters) (79). We know in this movement where to ever side and take a stand.

For Cilliers, such threefold grace spells the beginning of poetic new meaning-making possibilities such as:

> The Black Swan of unexpected events might indeed be the dis-
> guise of the White Dove of Pentecost. The wind that snuffs out
> the candle, and extinguishes the last glimmerings of the dying
> light, might be the wind that kindles a new Light, might be the
> wind that carries us 'into' life (61).

Again, by the grace of God, we "now" know in Christ that we are being known (fully), and thus we cannot but continuously create *and* dismantle our God im-ages. This, in short, with so much more still between the pages, is what Cilliers' fully embodied witness of grace upon grace is about.

## 6.6 Moving towards a preliminary conclusion?

Before I conclude with a preliminary conclusion, let me also be honest and self-critical in the way I seem to name and frame my reading of Cilliers' work. Much of the emphases in this portrayal reminds me of ideas I also came across and explored more thoroughly in Barth's work (Laubscher 2022b). This threefold grace and many other triads are often characteristic "patterns" in the architecture of Barth's thought. The sheer beauty of it in Barth's work (as in full flow in his Doctrine of Reconciliation, *CD* IV/1-3) does cause one to recognise some resem-blance in Cilliers' knack of witnessing to the threefold grace in the one particular form of the Word of God, namely preaching. As Willimon rightly notes concern-ing the time and space of Barth's early sermons, preachers do not have the luxury to postpone the verdict and proclamation of God's word. Behind Barth's resilience in producing his (unfinished!) *magnum opus* "Church Dogmatics", lies the pulpit in Safenwill. The crisis of preaching does offer the possibility of becoming a resilient preacher – and a theologian for preachers. Resilient preaching is thus first and foremost in engaging with the act and practice of preaching itself, before necessarily responding with, and embodying particular resilience in the face of certain kinds of adversities. In short, in making such a first move, I am surely influenced by this background in reading Cilliers' work.

However, back to the latter's work, and now in summary. It is perhaps still an open question as to whether "resilient religion" is adequately and thoroughly addressed in this discussion. I do know and truly appreciate from his work that there is, for the preacher (and her/his fellow witnesses), a layered, "ever moving" and "always timed" eventful Word of grace here and now at work. As Craddock (2011:117-136) used to say, there is a simultaneous "'nod' and 'shock' of recognition" in being encountered by this Word (of threefold grace). It is serious, yet playful; recognisable, yet new and surprising. In short, it is resilient in terms of language that is often "in other words" (*met ander woorde*).

Secondly, this hesitation, even careful reservation, and qualification in "using" labels (and "buying" into genitive theologies) such as, for instance, "prophetic preaching", or even for that matter "resilient preaching", is of great importance.[4] These terms and terminology are of great importance, and we should not be arrogant nor ignorant in not being "with it", but careful in mere (eager and opportunistic) claims and usage of them. Those who often are eager to claim and use these (fashionable and favourable) phrases and labels are often – and I am sorry to say – tempted into contradicting the very idea they so dearly are pursuing. Somehow Cilliers (and Barth) continues to sensitize my own thought and work in this regard. Any talk of "movements" (!) and/or "border control" (with in- and outsiders on a bandwagon) just does not fit well in this manner of theologising and preaching (and doing homiletics).

Thus, for "now", let me "close" with some (other) words often uttered by Cilliers: (resilient) "preachers know Monday morning is too late to start, and Sunday morning too early to stop" your preparations in order to proclaim the news of the Word week after week … and crafting a response to a theme/question such as mine/ours.

---

[4] For argument's sake and thoroughness, this reference to "prophetic preaching" is only one of many examples to cite in this regard. Terms such as "decolonial", "African", "missional", or even "Reformed" could easily be deployed in the same fashion/manner in this regard.

# BIBLIOGRAPHY

Barth, K. (1956-1975). Church Dogmatics. Edited by G.W. Bromiley and T.F. Torrance. Translated by G.W. Bromiley and others. Four volumes in 13 parts. Edinburgh: T&T Clark.

Boesak, A.A. (1976). Farewell to innocence – A social-ethical study of black theology and black power. New York: Orbis.

(1979). Die vinger van God – Preke oor geloof en die politiek. Johannesburg: Ravan Press.

Campbell, C. & Cilliers, J. (2012). Preaching fools. The gospel as a rhetoric of folly. Waco, TX: Baylor University Press.

Cilliers, J. (1982). Soos woorde van God. Ontwerp van 'n preekanalitiese model. Unpublished PhD dissertation. Stellenbosch: University of Stellenbosch.

(1994). God vir ons. 'n Analise en beoordeling van Nederduitse Gereformeerde volksprediking (1960-1980). Kaapstad: Lux Verbi.

(1996). Die uitwissing van God op die kansel. Ontstellende bevindinge oor Suid-Afrikaanse prediking. Kaapstad: Lux Verbi.

(1998). Die uitwysing van God op die kansel. Inspirerende perspektiewe op die prediking – Om God te sien en ander te láát sien. Kaapstad: Lux Verbi.

(2000). Die genade van gehoorsaamheid. Hoe evangelies is die etiese preke wat ons in Suid-Afrika hoor? Wellington: Lux Verbi. Bm.

(2004). The living voice of the gospel. Revisiting the basic principles of preaching. Stellenbosch: Sun Press.

(2006). God for us? An analysis and assessment of Dutch Reformed preaching during the apartheid years. Stellenbosch: Sun Press.

(2012). Dancing with Deity. Re-imagining the beauty of worship. Wellington: Bible Media.

(2016). A space for grace. Towards an aesthetics of preaching. Stellenbosch: Sun Press.

(2019). Timing grace. Reflections on the temporality of preaching. Stellenbosch: Sun Press.

(2020). Grace upon grace. Reflections on the meaning of life. Stellenbosch: African Sun Media.

Craddock, F. (2011). Craddock on the craft of preaching. St. Louis, MO: Chalice Press.

Hermans, C.A.M. (2022a). Human experiences of heartbreaking adversity. In: C.A.M. Hermans & J.W. Schoeman (eds), Resilient religion (Münster: Lit-Verlag), pp. 31-46.

Processes of resilience. In: C.A.M. Hermans & J.W. Schoeman (eds.), Resilient religion (Münster: Lit-Verlag), pp. 31-46.

Laubscher, M. (2022a). Wit issie 'n colour nie (it is a 'sermon'!)? After preaching, faith formation, and whiteness in South Africa today. Paper delivered at the annual Society for Practical Theology in South Africa, 11 February 2022, Bloemfontein, and currently under review).

(2022b). Publieke teologie as profetiese teologie? 'n Kritiese beskouing van die sosio-ekklesiologiese implikasies van die drieërlei amp in die teologie van Karl Barth. Stellenbosch: African Sun Media.

Willimon, W.H. (2009). The early preaching of Karl Barth. Fourteen sermons with commentary by William H. Willimon. Louisville, KY: Westminster John Knox Press.

(2019). Accidental preacher. A memoir. Grand Rapids, MI: Wm B. Eerdmans.

# Chapter 7

# Becoming a Resilient Christian Community: A narrative approach

*E Baron[1]*

## 7.1 Introduction

What are the ways in which we communicate and articulate the *missio Dei* as a story of resilience? It is about God's people challenged by adversity since the opening of the God's story, and God's involvement in such adversity experienced and lived by congregants in the present millieu. This involvement of the triune God in the lives of congregants is the expression of the *missio Dei*, God's mission on earth, as well as the "suppressed" environment. The role of the preacher within congregations, and the liturgical space, and communicating God's care and involvement in various forms of adversity is sufficiently documented. Nevertheless, it is often left in the hands of the pastor, or the Minister of the Word to anticipate the "kind" of adversities that people are struggling with, and through their sermons, address and facilitate a moment of "revelation" (cf. Stroup 1981:59-68).[2] On the other hand, it is the same pastors that also uses "reason", exegeting the biblical texts as a way of communicating such adversities within a *missio Dei* perspective.

In this chapter it will be argued that following a narrative approach within congregations, including personal storytelling would permit some vulnerable stories to enter the "sacred" spaces of churches, that would contribute to a "resilient religion". This would make the church, and members to bounce back after experiencing adversities from *all* sorts. However, the challenge of reflecting on the *missio Dei* within a modernist paradigm, has not evaded academia, but also not the churches, in particular Reformed churches, which still allow the modernist paradigm to frame congregational life and liturgical spaces. This seals Bosch's (1991:352) prediction, that the experiential religions will exponentially grow and expand while others that only narrows and restrict themselves within the modernist paradigm will die out.

---

[1] His e-mail address is: barone@ufs.ac.za

[2] See George Stroup's (1981:59-68) discussion on Niebuhr's argument on how "revelation" takes place, which for him is the integration of the "external history" into one's "internal history".

There is still largely a dependence of certain churches on propositional, and foundational approaches. Nevertheless, it promotes the role that narrative can play as "form" and "approach"[3] to epistemological construction for congregations in becoming a resilient Christian community. Hermans argues that a "resilient religion" incorporates the values of the community, and the "ethos" of a community, which serves as an invaluable part, and not only what people would "know" about the doctrines of the church, or religion.[4]

There has, even the move towards a "postmodern paradigm" in theology, been an evasiveness of a narrative approach and story forms in some Christian traditions, as well as to demonstrate, how such an approach might be utilised in congregations. Therefore, this chapter will discuss how narrative does facilitate resilience within a Christian community. The church should facilitate a meta-narrative (not oppressive), the story of the *missio Dei* in which the faith community is able to find ultimate meaning by providing space for the dialogical interaction between the 'personal', the mundane, and the sacred story (cf. Stephen Crites 1971). It is because of such dialogue that Christian communities and its members become more resilient in the face of adversity. Hermans defines a "resilient religion" as one that interacts with other "systems" in society (individuals, families, and communities).[5] This is what a narrative approach facilitates, and integrates, which would forster resilient churches, and congregations.

## 7.2 The narrative quality of the Christian Church

The Christian church is not only a "confessional" church, or a "doctrinally" constructed one either, though many denominations would like us to belief this to be the basis of the construction of a religious community. It is also a community that shares and identifies with the same story, the story of Jesus Christ. The early church was built on the story, as it unfolded in history; the life, death, and resurrection of Jesus Christ. We see this often in the various responses of Paul to the churches and believers, and Christian communities that he wrote and addressed.

Bosch (1991) would argue that Western Christianity and mission was deeply influenced by the Enlightenment and the project of modernity. This meant that often "missionary churches" became one that would also base their faith mostly on reason. The way faith would be explained, was to provide reasons and to give account to one's faith, and in such a way such a faith was able to maintain its credibility within the broader part of society, and for it to be taken seriously.

---

[3] Ganzevoort distinguishes between two ways in which narrative is used, as an approach, and as form. The author therefore uses both, in the sequence of narrative form within a narrative approach paradigm.

[4] See his discussion in Chapter 3 of the book on "Resilient Religion", pp.31-46.

[5] See his introduction to the chapter, "Resilient Religion", pp.1-12.

However, to give account of one's faith meant to provide good theological arguments. This explains why the role of apologetics was taken seriously in defending
one's faith against adverse religions, faiths, and "false teachings". Other indigenous knowledge systems were not regarded as "scientific" and factual
knowledge, and therefore was repudiated as a source of reality and truth for in-
forming one's faith.

Therefore, those that link their origins with the Western Missionary
Church, became "rational" religious communities. Rational in this sense meant
to primarily base their faith on abstract reason and propositions as fundamental
to explain their faith. Newbigin (1996) in his chapter *Dogma and Doubt* argues
that why certain Christian communities moved within the private sphere because
they are made to believe that their faith is not "truth" (within a modernistic paradigm) and therefore not anything to go by unless it is expressed and explained
through reason. Reason here, meant the western "factual" knowledge system. In
Africa, and other instances, including experiential religions where such an approach to knowledge were not ascribed to, for example other means to access an
understanding of God in the world, experiential knowledge were not deemed
credible and valid but merely subjective and emotional.

In Bosch's (1991:352-353) conceptualisation of a new emerging missionary paradigm, he suggests the deconstruction of the influence of the modernistic, enlightenment paradigm that has made "reason" the only way to access the
truth about God. Nevertheless, he emphasises the salience of myth, symbols, and
narrative. This chapter focus on embracing and arguing for narrative as a means
of building a resilient religious community. The proposal of Hermans (2022a:6)
that a resilient religion has three dimensions, namely "thinking, acting, feeling"
is important for all religious communities. It is mostly an either/or in terms of
"thinking" and "feeling" when it comes to Christian traditions, Reformed (emphasis on reason) and Pentecostal (emphasis on experience).

In reflecting on this challenge, I will mostly discuss my own experience
within the Reformed tradition, in which it has become important to focus on the
Bible (*Sola Scriptura*), and its truth to be affirmed within congregational worship.
It was a tradition that broke away from the Catholic Church during the time of
the Reformation, critiquing their perspectives on indulgences, and a move towards the centrality of the Bible with the mantra *Sola Scriptura* as means to affirm the eternal truth found only in the Bible. The way to find truth in the bible
was mostly through "critical-historical" methods that often lead to "allegorical
meaning" away from the benefits that the literal meaning of the Biblical text
might have offered for its readers (cf. Hans Frei, *The eclipse of Biblical narrative*). Hence, "meaning" for their everyday lives was often obscured. The key to
"truth:" was based, within theological schools, as well as universities that promotes "scientific knowledge", and its apparatus as the only way to arrive at the
truth about God. Though such a paradigm was debunked by theologians such as

Friedrich Schleiermacher (truth is subjective), and Bosch,[6] this has not necessarily translated into a different approach in praxis of congregational life. In fact,
Bosch was proposing an "expansion of rationality", in which he argues for the
inclusion of narrative, and where both reason and narrative would be equated,
and both affirmed as avenues to "faith knowledge". In fact, Bosch argued that
the exponential growth that we witnessed in the Global South (as well as within
Western countries through increasing migration of people). For instance the Pentecostal movements, is an example because of their appropriation of "experience"
as a valid category to affirm their faith.

The following section will now deal in short with the questions why the inclusion
of a narrative approach is crucial for developing and sustaining "resilience" in
religious communities.

## 7.3 Resilience, narrative, religious community: interconnectedness

What does narrative has to do with "resilience" and Christian Reformed communities? Narrative provides the religious communities significance experiences,
and "handles to cope" with the stressors of life. The author of the biblical book
of Hebrews would refer to a "cloud of witnesses". The enumenrated list provides
by the author of Hebrews include certain historical figures and in a narrative manner reflect on their experiences of adversity as people of faith. The author of Hebrews is therefore using such narratives to provide substance to the kind of adversities that his audience is facing. Of course, this is dealt with and informed by
the doctrines, and confessions of the churches, and all the propositions that the
church affirms and communicates. There are indeed also other parts in which the
author of the book of Hebrews also uses propositions, and tradition. Therefore,
the author is in no way juxtaposing the two epistemologies, but affirming that
these two can naturally affirm, confirm, or even create new knowledge and understanding of the faith. Conradie (2008:18) confirms that "stories" do contribute
to questions concerning suffering: "How can I cope with the many demands of
life? How can I cope with myself? Why am I in pain? Why does the innocent
have to suffer so much (a question once described as 'the rock of atheism')?
Where does evil come from? How can we overcome evil?" Therefore Klaasen
(2020) would argue that narratives is equally assisting countries, and the existential crisis of migrants. This he does by drawing from the narrative theology of
Hauerwas (1989), Stroup (1981), Muller (2004; 2011; 2012) and others. He argues that in such crisis, narrative could provide those migrants with a sense of
identity, and to foster a sense of belonging. It is also true of those within the walls

---

[6] I specifically refer here to his argument that theology, or mission should do away with
the "object-subject" scheme.

of congregations, that experience adversity, who equally find themselves at the margins of society.

## 7.4 The relationship between the "mundane" and "sacred" stories

A further conceptual discussion is that of the relationship between sacred and mundane stories". It is in the bringing together of both, that the conversation on "fostering a resilient religious community" lies. The work of Stephen Crites (*The Narrative Quality of Experience*) is important because it assist us in reflecting on how people come to develop their "meta-narrative" or, their Christian Story. For Crites, each human being lives in a "story". He or she gathers fragments of what they "think" and "experience" bodily and this is then linked-up with their "mundane" and "sacred" story that they internalized. This is further shaped by the community that they are part of, and that gives meaning towards the construction of their personal story. However, reading through the work of Crites, it is not linear but circular, or beter said, dialogical – a movement between the "sacred" and the "mundane". Here is where the author thinks personal stories and testimonies can play a role in congregational life and building the resilience of members and making the congregation one that become resilient. The following two sections will be mainly autobiographical in nature, both reflective on my personal experiences within "experiential" movements and "reasoned" Christian communities.

## 7.5 An autobiographical reflection on "experiential" and "reason" Christian congregations

### 7.5.1   Mundane Stories in Pentecostal (experiential) Movements

Personal testimonies are one of the central features within Pentecostal movements in South Africa. I recall a time when I visited a "tent-campaign" of a Pentecostal church in the Northern Cape province of South Africa. The service was within a large tent-structure that could accommodate at least a thousand people. There was no proper "floor", and on top of it, they will dance so that the dust from the ground will blur the attendees' view from being able to even see the "pulpit" and the stage in front. But congregants were overwhelmed by the singing and dancing of choruses, with often the same refrain sung countless times, as if it was needed to allow people to shun themselves up from their struggles of life, and then to become more mindful, and conscious of the God of the Bible. These services were often unstructured, it was not your formal liturgy that you would find in your Reformed congregations, where you would be interrupted by some unstructured, too informal single contributions to the service, but it was open for the "spirit"[7]

---

[7] Here "spirit" is referred loosely, as it is understood within these churches, as a feeling, or an urge from the inside that compels you to act.

to guide. But what indeed caught my attention, is when often the "liturgist" would open-up a church service for testimonies. During such a moment the testomonies would not necessarily, often not, refer to a biblical text, but only tell their story – how they experienced God's acts of salvation and redemption in their life. It is in these mundane stories that people during the service could make the connection between God's involvement, and even non-involvement[8] in their everyday life, but also the person itself rendering the testimony that was constantly making the connection between the mundane, and the sacred during the week, the specific day, and then share it with the congregation. For these people, all the acts (cf. MacIntyre, 1989) occur not as "fragments" but as part of a bigger story, their story as part of God's story and involvement in the world (*missio Dei*).

In his critique on rationalism within the church van Engen (1996:218) states,

> Are we willing to consider ways of knowing the truth about God other than and complementary with rational proposi-tions? Maybe we could learn more from the traditional Pen-tecostal movement and the more recent charismatic move-ment in terms of images, stories, praise, music, metaphor – right-brain reflections as well as left-brain logical proposi-tions…Maybe we need to create more space for a "hermeneu-tical spiral" that offers us ways of knowing Jesus Christ, the way, the truth, and the life, through narrative, poetry, wisdom literature, prophecy, and parable….

What is strange is that this comes from an Evangelical that is more often, than not, amused by the "lively" or "unstructured" ways in which Pentecostal churches functions. They would often argue that their actions are obstructing the focus, that should be on the main item of the agenda, God speaking through his Word – which for them only meant the preaching of the pastor during the church services. This brings us to the discussion on how God is more often than not, "revealed" in Reformed Churches.

## 7.6 Mundane Stories in (reason) Reformed Churches

We do not have the same form and shape within the Reformed tradition,[9] without being more "structured" in terms of planning and scheduling of the format of the liturgical services, it has also not an "open-session" for personal testimonies. However, this is not the problem, because you might not have such an item biut

---

[8] However, I must admit that this is a rare occurrence. If people would refer to God's absence, it would just be to affirm and conclude that at the end God did show-up.

[9] I am a member of the Uniting Reformed Church in Southern Africa (URCSA). I am brought up in the Reformed tradition, and this often informs my theological thinking. However, I have been challenged during ecumenical gatherings, especially when our church was invited with Pentecostal churches as hosts.

still allow for personal testimonies. However the issue is rather that congregants in these Reformed Churches are less exposed to the "vulnerable" stories of people of the congregation, and the closest that you might be to "vulnerable stories" is when the preacher would venture into those biblical characters, or perhaps personal stories that fits the "categories", but would not always be close, explicit, or vulnerable to the extent that it exposes the "social location" in which members find themselves.

Nevertheless, the preaching moment cannot be ignored, as this is a moment in which the theory of Ricoeur (1984) will makes sense in terms of the congregant seeing themselves as part of the "Story of God". However, the question is however how skillfully, is this being done, as well as the approach of the preacher to the text, as a book of "doctrine", a moment of sharing "propositions" or a moment of sharing God's story, through human, mundane stories. It is the role of the preacher in this instance to allow the congregant to make a connection with their own story to that of the Bible. Lee assist preachers in religious communities on how they could facilitate this and allow people to image them as part of God's narrative that will help them to cope with their adversities. Lee states (2015:25),

> Therefore, considering the previous attempts of those in the congregation to narrate their lives based on other narratives, the task of narrative preaching is to engage the pre-figured narratives of the listeners with the larger narratives of Christian Scripture. In the sermon the preacher not only preaches a biblical "story," but also through the narrative engages in an imaginative enterprise to open-up the possibility of a new way of life and then invites the congregation to allow these stories to shape the way they perceive themselves in the world.

The issue of engaging in "pre-narrative" for preachers is perhaps the crucial point here for our discussion. It is personal, mundane stories that allows this. This might be gathered through "house-visitation" of members of the church, but still does not guarantee its inclusion in the most "sacred" moments of the congregation; the Sunday morning service. For Stroup (1991:431-432), it is not only the story of the community that assist in the process of identity formation, but also biblical stories. He argues, "When the biblical narrative falls silent, the people of God have nothing to remember, and with nothing to remember, they soon forget who they are. Their untutored imaginations turn to other narratives and other gods".

Therefore, the challenge often within Reformed and protestant churches is the function of statements of faiths. In most cases the churches are building and structuring their life around "confessional documents", which is not entirely problematic, but how it functions in the congregation and the church, as propositional. For instance, as a case in point we can assess the function of the Belhar Confession in the Uniting Reformed Church in Southern Africa (URCSA) and its struggle for unification with the sister churches in the Dutch Reformed Church Family. Baron (2017) laments that it has often become a "stick to punish" [*stok om mee te slaan*] than to appreciate its existential value, which lies in the "meaning-making" and the stories of "struggle for liberation" of the members of the "mission churches" within the DRC family. Therefore, for Baron, the Belhar Confession is made-up of countless personal stories, if it is dealt with in narrative form than merely functioning as a "propositional document". Müller (2012) also laments that the reason for the Belhar Confession becoming a "stumbling block" among other things, could also include the fact that it is no longer being embraced as a "story" and has become a propositional document. It has become a way to share "The Truth" which Muller does not deny, but it does not become "truth" that opens-up spaces for including more "stories". His arguments stem from a workshop on the Confession of Belhar that he was facilitating in a small rural town of Orighstad. During the conference one of the delegates of URCSA, a minister of the Word, during all debates, said that for most of his people Belhar was just a document, and therefore should not stand between them (URCSA and the sister churches). It became a "heart" "embodied" matter instead of a (propositional) "document".

Therefore, historically the issue was that URCSA asked that the "document" should be accepted as a "confession" alongside all other confessions. This is the same stance that James Buys took during his discussion at a workshop in Belhar. Müller (2012:22) asserts that he "wonder and imagine how different things can be if Belhar [confession] is not defended or attacked as if it is about the absolute truth or not; if it is not made powerless because of the idea that there are many perspectives and interpretations possible; but if all participants can be drawn into the creation of a new story". Therefore, unlike James Buys (as mentioned above) Allan Boesak, that was and still is a staunch proponent of the acceptance of the Belhar Confession by the Dutch Reformed Church, he conceded that if they are living Belhar, the "acceptance" of the "document" is secondary (see Baron & Botha, 2020:48). Is this than the signs of Boesak opting for a "narrative" approach, constructing a new story? The epistemological category of "experience" links us to one another, links us with each other's histories and stories. This is often what, treating confessions as "documents", "propositions" and "truth" statements fails to achieve. However, this should indeed not be used as a case in point that church confessions, like the Belhar Confession, Belgic Confession et cetera should not be made an obligatory document in the church, but rather to re-imagine the paradigm in which those confession would function in future in churches. Not only confession, but also other documents, statements, or oders (e.g., Church Order & Polity), that would demand a narrative approach, instead of a "propositional" approach.

The ministry of the sacraments, the Baptism, as well as the Holy Communion within Reformed Church are both moments of social identity, moments in which the church share the story of the identity of Christians. It is through the story of God, and that of Jesus Christ that the Christian members understand where they are coming from. However, this could also become moments in which it becomes easy to focus on the "propositions" related to these sacraments, whether it is about the "doctrine of election" at the Baptism, or the "doctrine of atonement" during the ministering of the Holy Communion – these are abstraction of the moment that plays itself off before members of the congregation. The question is: should this not be a time to share the story of God's inclusion of all his creation in the salvation history, and the table of which the Lord shared with sinners and tax collectors, and all those he loves? It could become moments that draws the congregants into God's story, and stories of embrace and inclusion. Linking those sacraments with God's involvement in the "history" of the world, invites, and links ordinary members to identify with such a story through their own experiences of adversity. But it also allows people to tell and reflect on their own personal, mundane stories of salvation, of god's provision, but also of God's absence, which the story of the crucifixtion of Jesus might so aptly reflect, in Jesus' words, "My Father, why has thou forsaken me?" Therefore, Stroup argues that people's identity and memory is kept alive by narratives and traditions. He aptly states,

> ...the theme of narrative touches an exposed, raw nerve in the life of Christian communities, and in the life of the larger culture. Not only do the traditions and the narratives that they embody provide a sense of personal and community identity, but it is also true that we remember by means of stories. And when we are no longer a part of a community that is struggling to appropriate its stories and traditions, we run the risks of losing that memory that binds us to others, both in the present and in the previous generations. Those people who do not understand themselves to be a part of a larger narrative have neither anything to remember not how to remember. The fascination with narrative in North American culture suggest crisis of memory.

### 7.7 The imperative of personal stories of adversity in the life of congregations

Van der Borght (2008) focuses on the role that "storytelling" can play withinhave in European churches, where the membership of churches constitutes less of the local nationals, but foreign nationals. However, people decide not to tell their stories to each other and therefore has not a "shared story". He argues that the inclusion of the sharing of stories in the congregation might remove the sense of vulnerability among members and lead to the sustainability of the future church in Europe. Interestingly so is van der Beek's (2008) focus on a "shared story" between "victims and perpetrators" after colonialism, apartheid, independence et cetera. He also refers to the TRC processes in different countries and that the "exchange" of stories (between victim and perpetrator) that would enhance reconciliation in such countries. Further he argues that through the sharing the "story" of Jesus Christ those "victim and perpetrator" stories can find meaning in the "sacred" story. He argues that the perpetrator is dealt with in terms of his guilt by the death of Christ, and the victim is dealt with in terms of his suffering by the death of Christ. What better symbol (eucharist) – story of the cross being shared during the celebration of the eucharist – where our own stories can make way for a shared story.

## 7.8 Preliminary reflections

The experience that I have in visiting some Pentecostal churches is not without critique. Jacobs (2003:6) for instance lodges his own critique against "personal" stories that in these Pentecostal churches is often reserved to "conversion stories". Jacobs (2003:10) states the err in testimonies that have made the church urge people to only look at the Christian story than individual testimonies,

> It's this kind of Christian "testimony"—the airbrushed past and the sugarcoated future—that causes Christian "testimonies" to set people's teeth on edge. We may therefore find ourselves tempted to neglect or even abandon the practice of testimony, absorbing all individual differences of vocation and experience into the one great story of the Church—and to some degree that is just what recent narrative theology has done. Embarrassed by the presumption, the triumphalism, and the sentimental self-absorption of the testimonies that have arisen especially from the evangelical movement, narrative theologians have drawn our attention back to the great narrative arc of God's work among His people in the world. Yet Christians are commanded to be "prepared to make a defence to anyone who asks you for a reason for the hope that is in you" (1 Peter 3:15), and unless one is determined to do no more than mutely wave people towards the nearest church, this can only be achieved by giving some account of the coherence (not perfection) and development (not fulfilment) one discerns in one's own life". However, similarly Augustine, also follow his understanding of God through narrating his own experiences in which he finds God. This could be found in his book *Confessions*.

Furthermore, the fact that Pentecostal churches has "stories" through personal testimonies, does not mean that they follow a "storied" or narrative approach, as in many cases they are also modernistic in their approach in being only influence by their own Pentecostal theologies and story. Their story might also be told as a "truth" that is not "open-ended".

Furthermore, the Reformed tradition, and the confession could not only be seen as "propositional" but as Baron (2017:185-198) refers to in his chapter *"Belhar as a Therapeutic Resource"* that the confession contains "meaning" and that it could assist in the existential crises that various South Africans experience, and the church experience in post-apartheid society. The work of Richard Kearney assists with explaining how this *storying* takes place. For instance, he argues that "plotting" (*mythos*) is always taking place when we experience an event. However, the next step would be to "verbalise" the story. In the explanation of Kearney (2002:131-132) "confessional statements" is such documents, where is indeed the "verbalization" of a particular "story" in the live of the church and its members. He refers to the process of mimesis by Ricoeur, in which what is "already our story" is plotted, than "presented" through confessional documents and statements. The problem here would lie in terms of the linking between the document and the "meaning" behind it – which is less made in Reformed Churches, with a confessional basis.

## BIBLIOGRAPHY

Baron, E. (2017). Belhar as a Therapeutic Resource to the Dutch Reformed Church Family. In, Plaatjies, MA & Modise, L. (eds). 2017. Belhar Confession. The Embracing Confession of Faith for Church and Society. Stellenbosch: Sun Media.

Baron, E. & Botha, N.A. (2020). Obedience and Servant Leadership. Apollis, Appies, Buti, Buys. Bloemfontein: Sunbonani.

Bosch, D.J. (1991). Transforming Mission. Paradigm Shifts in Theology of Mission. Maryknoll, New York: Orbis Books.

Conradie, E.M. (2008). The Earth in God's Economy: Reflections on the Narrative of God's Work. Scriptura, 97: 13-36.

Crites, S. (1971). The Narrative Quality of Experience. Journal of the American Academy of Religion, Vol. 39 (3): 291-311.

Hermans, C.A.M. (2022c). Resilient religion, Chapter 3 in this volume (pp.47-66).

Kearney, R. 2002. On Stories. London: Routledge.

Klaasen, J.S. (2020). Church, narrative, community and Identity in times of Migration. In die Skriflig, 54 (1): 1-7.

Lee, M. (2015). A Ricoeurian Vision. Reading the Biblical Text for the Narrative Sermon. Restoration Quarterly, 57 (1): 19-37

MacIntyre, A. (1989). Epistemological Crises, Dramatic Narrative, and the Philosophy of Science. In, Hauerwas, S & Jones, LG. 1989. Why Narrative? Readings in Narrative Theology. Grand Rapids, Michigan: WB Eerdmans.

Müller, J.C. (2011). Postfoundational Practical Theology for a time of transition. HTS Theological Studies, 67 (1): 1-5

Müller, J.C. (2011). '(Outo)biografie as teologie', HTS Teologiese Studies/Theological Studies 67(3), 1-7.

Müller, J.C. (2012). '(Practical) theology: A story of doubt and imagination', 8th lecture in the UP expert lecture series, University of Pretoria, Pretoria, 05 September, viewed 12 June 2013, from http://repository.up.ac.za/handle/2263/20311

Müller, J.C. (2004). HIV/AIDS, narrative practical theology, and postfoundationalism: The emergence of a new story. HTS Theological Studies, 60 (1/2): 293-304

Niebuhr, R.H. (1989). The Story of Our Life. In, Hauerwas, S & Jones, LG. 1989. Why Narrative? Readings in Narrative Theology. Grand Rapids, Michigan: WB Eerdmans.

Ricoeur, P. (1984). Time and Narrative. Volume 1. Translated by Kathleen McLauglin & David Pellauer. Chicago: University of Chicago Press

Stroup, G.W. (1991). Theology of Narrative, or Narrative Theology? Response to Why Narrative. Critic's corner. Theology Today, 47 (4): 424-440

Stroup, G.W. (1981). The promise of Narrative Theology. London: SCM Press.

Van de Beek, A. (2008). A Shared story for reconciliation – Which Story? Conclusive Reflections. Journal of Reformed Theology, 2 (0): 17-27.

Van der Borght, E.A.J.G. (2008). The Church as the Community of a Shared Story. Journal of Reformed Theology, 2 (0): 5-16.

Van Engen, C.E (1996). Mission on the Way. Issues in Mission Theology. Grand Rapids, Michigan: Baker Books.

# Chapter 8

# The congregation as a community of discernment and practice – enhancing resilient religion

*WJ (Kobus) Schoeman[1]*

## 8.1 Introduction: The congregation and adversity

South African communities experienced different challenges and, to a certain extent, hardship due to a variety of factors in the last few years. A report of the World Bank on the situation in Southern Africa stated that these countries " … have been severely affected by the COVID-19 pandemic, as both lockdowns and health risks left people unable to work for long periods. Given the context of high inequality, poverty, and unemployment even before the pandemic, the adverse consequences of the pandemic are likely to be substantial." (Sulla, Zikali & Cuevas 2022:109). Adverse events like the COVID-pandemic, poverty and public unrest made life in the South African society and communities difficult. Adversity may include a host of events that also may be traumatic (Dreyer 2015:653). Adversity refers to difficult or unpleasant times, and the past few years in South Africa could be described as a time of adversity or even trauma due to difficult circumstances.

What do the church and congregations do in times of tragedy and trauma? An article was published in the City Press on 9 April 2022 under the heading "The dead faith of Christian churches" by Dikeledi Molatoli. He reflects on the call of the general secretary of the SACC for the victims of the floods in KwaZulu-Natal: "As the country celebrates Easter this weekend, the council encourages members of the Christian faith to set aside a moment of prayer on Good Friday to pray for KwaZulu-Natal and the victims of the floods." He continues and makes the following disturbing comments: "I remarked with shock: Really? Was that it? Was that all the council could say and offer on behalf of Christians in the midst of such a devastating tragedy and disaster? Couldn't the council have at least set up a bank account and encouraged its member churches and Christians across the country, not just in KwaZulu-Natal, to make financial contributions during Easter? Or contributions of blankets, non-perishable food, water and clothing, and collect

---

[1] His e-mail address is: schoemanw@ufs.ac.za

them from all the churches to be sent to the disaster-affected areas?" He challenges Christians and the church, in light of James 2:15, to make their faith visible by doing good works.

What happened with congregational life during the time of lockdown? Worship services and congregational activities came to a halt and a slow restart as lockdown levels changed. Typical community and congregational life were not possible during the lockdown. The church became distanced and may be absent during the pandemic (see Campbell 2020:3-6), and the church as congregations are currently in the process of rediscovering their role and responsibility within a changed environment living with the effects and consequences of the pandemic.

The human experience of heart-breaking adversity could be described as being separated from the good life and others (Hermans 2022a:5). The Covid-19 pandemic is probably the best example of a recent time of adversity. The different levels of lockdown social distancing to trauma and death all contributed to an experience of heart-breaking adversity on different levels for individuals and communities. This includes congregations and their membership.

The most direct and visible consequence of the pandemic on congregational life was the effect of the lockdown on the congregation's worship services. The use of online platforms became the norm. Small groups, catechism classes and youth groups were negatively affected. The ministry and activities of the congregation were put on hold and may even have affected their service in the community.

Against this background of adversity, the main research focus of this chapter is formulated in the following question: *How does a congregation develop and enhance resilience in response to adversity in the community or society?*

The first section of this chapter will focus on discussing a theoretical framework for the congregation's response to adversity. What is the role of a congregation in a situation of adversity, or to put it in another way, could a congregation be a source of hope and meaning-making in challenging times? Individuals experience adversity on a personal level, but could a congregation be a network of support in a situation of adversity? On the other hand, resilience allows one to experience a meaningful life and handle situations of tragedy. Dreyer defines resilience as "... the ability to 'bounce back' from adversity and trauma." (2015:653). Could this be true for congregations, and how would they react or respond to adversity? Resilience is a characteristic of individuals and can also be found in communities, institutions, and societies (Dreyer 2015:651). The challenge is to develop a theoretical framework for a resilient response for congregations.

The second section of this chapter focuses on a quantitative empirical survey amongst congregational ministers during the lockdown. The empirical section aims to describe and understand what happened in congregations during the lockdown, focusing on the role of congregations and the role of the leadership in the development of resilience during adversity.

## 8.2 The congregation as a community of discernment and practice

In looking for a response to adversity, resilience could be seen as an outcome and a process; resilience could be a good outcome in the face of adversity, or resilience may be seen as supportive of relationships and hope for the future. Van Breda defines *resilience* as "…the multilevel processes that systems engage in to obtain better-than-expected outcomes in the face or wake of adversity "(2018:4). Resilient processes locate not only within individuals but also within networks of social relationships like families, schools and neighbourhoods (Van Breda 2018:8).

This would also include congregations, which could facilitate a process with unique outcomes in facing adversity like the pandemic. What would be the description of the congregation as a resilient community?

The World Evangelical Alliance (WEA) developed in 2016 a report on "Building Resilient Communities: A Guide to Faith Community Partnerships" as part of a United Nations World Humanitarian Summit reflecting on world development. The summit's focus was on disaster risk reduction within the context of climate change. However, this guide could also be used in a broader context not only by referring to the effects of climate change but as part of a broader theoretical framework. The WEA guide place the following emphasis on the local faith community: "The local faith community is a central part of the local community, and working with the community cannot succeed without all members of the community. Further, local faith communities have expert local knowledge. They know who are vulnerable, they are connected to different groups in the community, and they will be present in the community for the future." (Boan 2016:3). The local faith community's value and contribution should not be undervalued.

In building the congregation as a resilient community, the congregation need to be described as a community of discernment, on the one hand and, on the other hand, to see the congregation as a community of practice. These two aspects, discernment and practice, may enhance the development of a resilient faith and response in the congregation and the community as part of a theoretical framework.

### 8.2.1   The congregation as a community of discernment

The congregation, as first part of a theoretical framework in building resilience, should be seen as a community of discernment. The collective and communal discernment process refers to the decision-making and hermeneutical process in the congregation, especially amongst the leadership, to understand her identity and calling (see Marais 2019). The congregation is called to listen and interpret her mission within a local context and may as such be described as a community of interpretation. "Any reader in any context and time can be part of the ongoing process of interpretation. This also implies to get into dialogue with other interpretations of the text by the community of interpretation and in dialogue with other texts and the community of interpretation of these texts" (Hermans 2022a:27). The congregation is in a sense also a community of interpretation.

As part of the hermeneutical process of doing theology, the congregation should read their text and context. The reading of the text could be seen as reinterpreting the tradition by the congregation (the Bible and the confession) as, for example, described by de Gruchy: "Traditions only stay alive and remain transformative because those who share them are in conversation with the past – above all, for Christians, in conversation with Scripture – and debate with each other about their meaning for the present." (2014:46). The incarnation of the gospel is an essential task of the congregation.

The reading of the context is part of the ecology of the congregation. The ecology of a congregation describes how a congregation "… interacts with other units in society, people, organisations and cultures, even other churches and congregations." (Hendriks 2004:70). It would be very difficult or even impossible for a congregation to close her eyes to her surrounding environment. The question should be: what is happening around us, and how should we faithfully respond?

South Africa is, for various reasons, an unequal society and congregations are part of this reality. "A disparity is an extreme difference between people in the same community along the same dimension. We often hear about disparities in wealth, which is an extreme difference between people in terms of personal income and wealth. Disparities also occur in health status." (Boan 2016:10). Attending and listening to the local context is an essential capacity for the congregation to identify disparities and needs.

The pandemic highlighted the inequalities of South African society in a very profound way. The more affluent communities had the ability to navigate the restrictions of lockdown, keep safe distances, work from home and buying from time to time the necessary from a local mall or shop. This is not possible in poorer settlements "…where lockdown is physically impossible because of time and space constraints, as in these neighbourhoods the 1.5-m or 2-m rule no longer makes sense, and cannot apply to individuals as it does not even apply to the distance between dwellings. In these settlements, nobody can stock up on essential food items, either for lack of space or, more importantly, for lack of cash. Washing hands from a running tap is not possible as there is no running water in every home, but only communal taps where social distance again is problematic. They cannot work from home and continue to earn their salary, as their income, if any, came from being day labourers who are now prevented from working and therefore also prevented from earning an income." (Meylahn 2020). Congregations should be sensitive to and identify these inequalities in their community as part of contextual analysis.

The congregation, as a community of interpretation, need to develop a capacity for <u>critical thinking</u>. Critical thinking is the ability to think analytically about information to come to an opinion or form a judgment (Boan 2016:12). It is the assessment and discernment of critical information from the text and context that a congregation needs to do. Critically discerning processes of resilience would not only be in accommodating or handling adversity but also in challenging adversity. This would be in terms of agency and structure (Van Breda 2018:10). "Agency reflects the power that individuals exercise over their lives and social environment, while structure reflects the macro systems that constrain the choices and opportunities of individuals." (Van Breda 2018:10).

Adversity challenges a congregation to listen very carefully. The invisible and unjust may become apparent in a time of crisis. "When you get down to root causes, you begin to see that injustice is often at the root of a disaster. You also see that the poor, the disabled, the children, and the powerless suffer the most from injustice. This is one of the basic missions of the local faith community, to speak out against injustice and speak for the vulnerable. A local faith community engages in disaster ministry in part to serve those in need, but it also engages because disasters reveal the injustice that exists in the community." (Boan 2016:10). Challenging adversity places unjust actions and systems on the congregation's agenda. There is a need, according to van Breda, to research social justice and its contribution to human flourishing (Van Breda 2018:13). The prophetic voice of the congregation should be heard as an outcome of a process of discernment but also to enhance resilience.

Listening, critical discerning, challenging adversity and a relevant prophetic response are necessary discernment capacities for the congregation to develop in discerning the text and context and developing a resilient framework. The congregational leadership should be aware, especially within the South African context, to respond to inequalities as part of a process of discernment in traumatic times.

### 8.2.2  The congregation as a community of practice

The second section of the theoretical framework describes the congregation as a community of practice. A congregation's ministry includes the activities and practices of the faith community in line with its understanding of the congregational calling. The congregation may therefore also be described as a community of practice. Boan describes a community of practice as a group with a shared concern and professional or scientific interests who come together to learn and apply what they learn (Boan 2016:7). A congregation could fit into this description and be valued as a community of practice to contribute to developing resilience. As a community of practice, the congregation needs specific capacities to develop to function as a resilient community, and this entails at least the following capacities: leadership skills, engagement with the community and learning practices (see Boan 2016:14-17).

Leadership play a central role in the functioning and growth of the congregation and her ministry. Leadership has the vital task of describing and interpreting reality, and the circumstances need to be interpreted before a responsible and appropriate response is possible. Situations may be viewed in different ways, and realities may equally limit the choices a leader can make (see Shuster 2009:17-18). Complex leadership skills are needed for a congregation to have the capacity to grow and develop as a community of practice (see Niemandt 2015). This would include the ability to be a facilitator or a servant leader (Boan 2016;14). A congregation and its leadership need to develop resiliency in ministry "... a toughness combined with elasticity that enables them to endure without breaking when facing tough challenges and difficult tasks that come from trying to follow in Jesus' way." (Carrol 2006:206). Reflective leadership enables the leadership to respond innovatively and appropriately to every changing world (Carrol 2006:208). Carrol (2011: e-source) defines reflective leadership as: "The authority of the reflective leader resides in her or his ability to assist patterns in ministry from a vision of Christian life and construct responses that are both faithful to that vision and appropriate within the complex, messy situations that we face today, individually and collectively." Complex and reflective leadership skills play a distinctive role in the development of resilient ministry practices of a congregation.

The congregation's engagement or interaction and environment is an important focus of the congregational ministry. The congregation and the local community have a symbiotic relationship because the members of the congregation live, work and play in the community, and it is therefore almost impossible for a congregation to isolate itself from the local community. Some congregations might exist as enclaves and focus primarily on their maintenance and inward ministry (see Cilliers 2012, Schoeman 2020), but a missional orientation would encourage congregations to engage with the community and the surrounding environment (see Hendriks 2007; Nel 2015:106). A missional ecclesiology assists a congregation in interacting with the community and connecting with and understanding the community's values (Boan 2016:14). The establishment of ecumenical and other networks is also enhanced through the development of a missional ecclesiology. "In South Africa, a broad consensus has grown amongst churches of diverse backgrounds that the church should be involved with those who suffer, people who are poor, oppressed, HIV patients, vulnerable children, gender issues, combatting crime and corruption, the destruction of the ecology – to work towards a healthy and sustainable society, beginning in the local community." (Van Niekerk 2014). A missional ecclesiology and an ecumenical network would help the congregation with a meaningful engagement with the community.

A healthy congregation is, thirdly, a <u>learning</u> community that reflects on and evaluates current ministerial practices. "A learning organisation is able to transform itself through continuous learning." (Watkins & Kim 2018:18). Continuous learning happens across an organisation where the leadership support and creates favourable conditions for learning, including a connection with the external environment. Strategic leadership practices focus on a shared intention to create a culture of learning and change within the organisation (Grandy 2013:616). An essential aspect of a learning organisation is team learning that starts with a dialogue between the members of a team that transcends their own assumptions and begin with thinking together and " ... a free-flowing of meaning through a group, allowing the group to discover insights not attainable individually." (Senge 1990:10). A learning congregation focuses on its capacity to be innovative and to create new possibilities in the future founded on a shared vision and leadership (see Marlow 1995:74-75).

Adversity or a crisis ask a congregation a response, and part of the reaction lies in lessons learned from past experiences, in other words the ability of the congregation to adhere to the characteristics of a learning community. Boan (2016:17) place the following aspects on the table: Understanding the root causes of the problem; vulnerabilities – Who suffers from the problem or is most at risk to suffer. Resources – What is available to help with the problem? Stakeholders – Who is interested in fixing the problem or who will be impacted if the problem were fixed ?, Congregations as learning communities should reflect on good practices as part of the normative task of interpretation (see Osmer 2008: 152). These good practices offer a past and present model to reform the congregation's current ministry, and it may generate a new understanding of God, Christian life and social values.

The process of discerning the congregation's calling should inform the congregation's holistic ministry and practices in the development of a theoretical framework to foster resilience as an outcome in reaction to adversity.

## 8.3 The response of the leadership – an empirical lens

As discussed in the previous section, the leadership of a congregation plays a significant role in response to adversity and the development of resilience in congregations. This section focuses on an empirical study that was done during lockdown amongst ministers of the Dutch Reformed Church (DRC), called the Pastoral Panel[2] (P.P.). A simple random sample was selected from all the DRC ministers serving full- and part-time in DRC congregations. The findings from

---

[2] Afrikaans: Predikante Paneel (PP)

the three surveys are there for a representative voice of the DRC ministers. South Africa started with Level 5 of the lockdown on 27 March 2020 and was on Level 2 in September 2021. The three quantitative online surveys were done, during these lockdown levels, between May 2020 and September 2021[3].

The biographical background (Tables 1, 2 and 3) describes the sampling population's characteristics. The majority of the ministers are male, but the female component of the ministers is steadily increasing, indicating a shift in the gender composition of the ministerial population of the DRC ministers. Most ministers are between 40 and 59 years old, although those younger than 40 are also increasing. The ministers of the DRC are older, but the increasing number of younger ministers is a promising sign. The current voice of the P.P.'s is that of older males. The congregations are evenly divided between rural and urban, although the urban congregations are slightly in the majority.

**Pastoral Panel tables**

| Table 1: Gender | | | | | | |
|---|---|---|---|---|---|---|
| | PP1 | | PP2 | | PP3 | |
| | N | % | N | % | N | % |
| Male | 69 | 85.2 | 55 | 88,7 | 135 | 82,8 |
| Female | 12 | 14.8 | 7 | 11,3 | 28 | 17,2 |
| Total | 81 | 100.0 | 62 | 100,0 | 163 | 100,0 |

| Table 2: Age | | | | | | |
|---|---|---|---|---|---|---|
| | PP1 | | PP2 | | PP3 | |
| | N | % | N | % | N | % |
| Younger than 40 years | 17 | 20.7 | 12 | 18.8 | 49 | 30,1 |
| 40 to 59 years | 44 | 53.7 | 37 | 57.8 | 82 | 50,4 |
| 60 years and older | 21 | 25.6 | 15 | 23.4 | 32 | 21,5 |
| Total | 82 | 100.0 | 64 | 100.0 | 163 | 100,0 |

---

[3] PP 1 (May 2020) Response 64,5% (82 ministers) from 10% random sample.
PP 2 (October 2020) Response 52,7% (64 ministers) from 10% random sample.
PP 3 (September 2021) Response 67,9% (163 ministers) 20% random sample.

| Table 3: Region | | | | | | |
|---|---|---|---|---|---|---|
| | PP1 | | PP2 | | PP3 | |
| | N | % | N | % | N | % |
| Urban | 36 | 43.9 | 28 | 43,75 | 80 | 49,4 |
| Rural | 46 | 56.1 | 36 | 56,25 | 82 | 50,6 |
| Total | 82 | 100.0 | 64 | 100,0 | 163 | 100,0 |

The aim of Table 4 is to report on the opinion of the respondents regarding their experiences of certain aspects during the lockdown. The ten statements and the response on a Likert-scale that were chosen are relevant in answering the main question under discussion in this chapter.

**Table 4: Opinion during lockdown**

| Do you agree with the following statements or not? (as a percentage) | Strongly agree | Agree | Neutral or uncertain | Disagree | Strongly disagree |
|---|---|---|---|---|---|
| 1. I experience that our larger community has been making progress towards reconciliation since the beginning of the pandemic. (PP1) | 3.7 | 39.0 | 28.0 | 24.4 | 4.9 |
| 2. I feel traumatized by the extent and intensity of illness and death in my congregation. (PP3) | 22,22 | 40,12 | 14,81 | 19,75 | 3,09 |
| 3. The pandemic makes me more aware of the economic inequalities in our society. (PP1) | 19.5 | 63.4 | 7.3 | 7.3 | 2.4 |
| 4. The pandemic makes me realize that I am economically advantaged due to our country's past. (PP1) | 15.9 | 45.1 | 9.8 | 20.7 | 8.5 |
| 5. Technology can replace the personal contact of the faith community. (PP1) | 0.0 | 4.9 | 3.7 | 51.2 | 40.2 |

| | | | | | |
|---|---|---|---|---|---|
| 6. There was an accelerated movement from a self-directed congregation to spontaneous, service-orientated networks. (PP1) | 8.6 | 54.3 | 27.2 | 9.9 | 0.0 |
| 7. I feel part of a network of partners that transcends different boundaries. (PP1) | 15.9 | 56.1 | 18.3 | 9.8 | 0.0 |
| 8. I, as a leader, need to develop spaces within which reconciliation can take place. (PP2) | 23,44 | 45,31 | 15,63 | 14,06 | 1,56 |
| 9. Our local community worked very well together during the lockdown. (PP2) | 26,56 | 53,13 | 17,19 | 3,13 | 0.00 |
| 10. Our congregation works well together in partnerships that span across racial boundaries. (PP2) | 9,38 | 46,88 | 23,44 | 18,75 | 1,56 |

The emotional impact of the pandemic, as an adverse event, cannot be underestimated. The ministers should experience the trauma in the congregation on a personal level. Illness and death lead to a traumatic experience for the minister in the congregation (statement 2 – 22% strongly agree, and 40% agree). This response asks for a process of reflection and discernment on a personal level for the minister. However, the membership would also be struggling with existential questions regarding the effect and consequences of the pandemic.

Adverse events bring the context and current state of affairs in a particular way to the foreground. Adversity compels the leadership to read and reflect on their context. The pandemic highlighted the inequalities of the South African society on different levels: economic inequalities and the differences in access to health facilities and relief, to name but two. The ministers became more aware of the economic inequalities in our society (63.4% agree, statement 3). The pandemic, on a personal level, made them to the taken notice of their own position of privilege due to the past of the country (45.1% agree, statement 4).

The longstanding need for reconciliation in South African society cannot be underestimated. As a consequence of the pandemic, Ministers realised the need for reconciliation in the larger community (39.0% agree, statement 1) and the need for the leadership to develop a space where reconciliation may occur (23.44% strongly agree and 45.31% agree, statement 8). This strong positive response asks the congregational leadership to be actively involved in creating spaces for reconciliation.

Developing resilience in a community depends on the <u>cooperation and networks</u> within the community. Congregations are not islands, and they are in interaction with the community therefore the need for cooperation and networks in the community as part of communal formation processes. DRC congregations are mostly Afrikaans-speaking and more privileged than most other congregations. They could be seen as living and ministering mainly in cultural enclaves (see ). The pandemic may have an influence on this position of privilege. The ministers feel they are part of a network that transcends different boundaries (56.1% agree, statement 7). This response may indicate that some boundaries were crossed due to the pandemic. The ministers also indicated that the community worked well during the lockdown 53.13% agree, statement 9) and that partnerships were formed across racial boundaries (46.88% agree, statement 10). The responses of the ministers regarding these three statements may indicate a positive development in the formation of more networks in the local community and the positive role that the leadership of the DRC congregations might have played in this regard.

The most visible and direct impact of the pandemic and lockdown on congregational life was most probably on the <u>worship services</u>. The migration from face-to-face worship to online platforms during the different lockdown levels definitely impacted relationships within the congregation. Online worship services ask questions about the koinonia and the personal interaction amongst the membership in a faith community. Could this be sustainable to replace personal contact with different forms of online communication? The ministers disagree that technology could replace personal contact (51.2% disagree and 40.2% strongly disagree, statement 5). There is a very strong response from the side of the ministers that technology would replace personal contact in the congregation in the long term. The strategy to navigate between face-to-face and personal contact and ask significant questions about the quantity and quality of building processes of discernment in the congregation.

Congregations in the DRC had pre-pandemic a strong intent to focus on the maintenance of the congregation (more than two-thirds in 2018 were busy with maintenance). Could the pandemic have influenced on <u>missional intent and practices of the congregation</u>? The ministers indicate that there was an accelerated movement from a self-directed congregation to spontaneous and service-orientated networks (5437% agree, statement 6). This missional intent led to a more active engagement of the congregation in the community. Covid-19 gave in almost 50% of the congregation's momentum to developing missional practices (table 5).

| Table 5: Missional practices (as a percentage) | Yes | Uncer-tain | No |
|---|---|---|---|
| Covid-19 gave momentum to the missional practices of the congregation (PP3) | 48,47 | 26,99 | 24,54 |

One outcome of this movement was that all the congregations, in one way or the other, were involved with projects within the community (table 6). The adversity of the pandemic leads to a better engagement of the congregation with the community.

| Table 6: Community engagement (as a percentage) | Yes | No |
|---|---|---|
| Our congregation is involved in projects in the community (PP1) | 97.6 | 2.4 |

**8.4 Conclusion – the congregation enhancing resilience?**

"Poor people's growing vulnerability to natural disasters and economic shocks also exacerbates the inequality challenge, largely because they tend to have few strategies to cope with shocks." (Sulla, Zikali & Cuevas 2022:117). The Covid-19 pandemic challenged in a very specific way congregations as contributors towards resilience amongst their members and their communities. "Resilience allows people to experience the good in life events (here and now). And this experience gives meaning life, offers unlimited happiness and to handle situations of tragedy." (Hermans 2022b:31).

Congregations in developing the capacities of discernment and good practices may enhance the formation of a more resilient community and offer happiness and purpose in response to adversity. The empirical results indicated a movement in that direction, but the process and outcome need a critical reliction. Meylahn (2020) makes the following critical remark: "The church's response, specifically taking the various posts on social media into consideration, could be interpreted as a typically state church response: do as the government says but add a little mercy and charity, and that would be your Christian responsibility. Stay at home, do not go to church, but reach out via social media or financially to those in greater need than yourself.". The church and congregational leaders should look beyond the local and challenge adversity. The prophetic voice of the church and congregations needs to be heard in situations of inequality and suffering.

Religion keeps a sense of the 'human measure' alive in society through the awareness of the unlimited purpose (telos); the focus on human dignity and the common good, and the demand for fulfilling happiness, peace and love. (Hermans 2022c:3:63). A congregation as a community of discernment and good practice may develop and enhance resilience in response to adversity in the community and society. Congregational leadership play in this process a significant role.

## BIBLIOGRAPHY

Boan, D. (2016). Building Resilient Communities: A Guide to Faith Community Partnerships. Wheaton: World Evangelical Alliance

Campbell, H.A. (2020). The Distanced Church: Reflections on Doing Church Online. Texas: Digital Religion Publications, 2020.

Carroll, J.W. (2006). God's Potters. Pastoral leadership and the shaping of congregations. Grand Rapids, Michigan: Wm. B. Eerdmans Publishing Co.

Carroll, J.W. (2011). As one with authority. Reflective leadership in ministry. Second edition. Eugene, Oregon: Cascade Books.

Cilliers, J. (2012). 'Between Enclavement and Embracement: Perspectives on the Role of Religion in Reconciliation in South Africa', Scriptura, 111(3), pp. 499–508.

De Gruchy, J.W. (2011). "Transforming Traditions. Doing Theology in South Africa Today." Journal of Theology for Southern Africa, 139, no. March: 7–17.

Dreyer, Y. (2015). 'Community Resilience and Spirituality: Keys to Hope for a Post-Apartheid South Africa', Pastoral Psychology, 64(5), pp. 651–662. doi:10.1007/s11089-014-0632-2.

Grandy, G. (2013). 'An exploratory study of strategic leadership in churches', Leadership and Organization Development Journal, 34(7), pp. 616–638. doi:10.1108/LODJ-08-2011-0081.

Hendriks, H.J. (2004). Studying congregations in Africa. Wellington: Lux Verbi.BM.

Hendriks, H.J. (2007). 'Missional theology and social development', HTS Teologiese Studies / Theological Studies, 63(3), pp. 999–1016.
(2022a). Human experiences of heart-breaking adversity, Chapter 1 in this volume (pp.13-30).
(2022b). Processes of resilience, Chapter 2 in this volume (pp.31-46).
(2022c). Resilient religion, Chapter 3 in this volume (pp.47-66).

Marais, F. (2019). "Discernment as Generative Dialogue. A Constructive Proposal for the Challenges of Missional Corporate Discernment in an Age of Contingency." In Theology in an Age of Contingency, edited by Chris A. M. Hermans and Kobus Schoeman, 99–116. Zurich: Lit Verlag.

Marlow, J.D. (1995). 'Beyond teaching: The congregation as a learning community', Christian Education Journal, XVI(I), pp. 63–78.

Meylahn, J.-A. (2020). 'Being human in the time of Covid-19', HTS Teologiese Studies / Theological Studies, 76(1), pp. 1–6.

Nel, M. (2015). Identity-driven churches. Who are we, and where are we going? Wellington: Biblecor.

Niemandt, C.J.P. (2015). 'Complex leadership as a way forward for transformational missional leadership in a denominational structure', HTS Teologiese Studies / Theological Studies, 71(3), pp. 1–9. doi:10.4102/hts.v71i3.2951.

Osmer, R.R. (2008). Practical Theology. An Introduction. Grand Rapids, Michigan: Wm. B. Eerdmans Publishing Co.

Schoeman, W.J. 2020. 'Re-imagining the congregation's calling – moving from isolation to involvement', Acta Theologica, 40(2), pp. 321–341. doi:10.18820/23099089/actat.v40i2.17.

Senge, P.M., 1990. The fifth discipline: The art and practice of the learning organization, Doubleday, New York.

Shuster, M. (2009) 'Leadership as interpreting reality', in Jacobsen, E.O. (ed.) The three tasks of leadership. Wordly wisdom for pastoral leaders. Grand Rapids, Michigan: Wm. B. Eerdmans Publishing Co., pp. 17–23.

Sulla, V., Zikhali, P. and Cuevas, F. (2022). Inequality in Southern Africa: An assessment of the Southern African Customs Union. Washington: World Bank.

Van Breda, A.D. (2018). A critical review of resilience-theory and its relevance for social work. Social Work/Maatskaplike Werk 54(1)1, pp.1-18

Watkins, K.E. and Kim, K. (2018). 'Current status and promising directions for research on the learning organization', Human Resource Development Quarterly, 29(1), pp. 15–29. doi:10.1002/hrdq.21293.

# Chapter 9

# Resilience and resistance in the Book of Job: An African socio-economic hermeneutical reading in a pandemic context

*F Olojede*[1]

## 9.1 Preliminary considerations

Scholars, including Christian Hermans in his forthcoming monograph (2022), have acknowledged the transdisciplinary character of resilience theory. In theology, it is shown that resilience theory, which is said to have its roots in studies of adversity, also cuts across different aspects of theology. The connection between resilience and a biblical hermeneutics, which takes its point of departure from Black theology, has also been documented. However, it is difficult to talk of resilience in biblical hermeneutics without reference to resistance because studies in other areas of theology, specifically in pastoral care, have shown a connection between the two concepts (Carlin *et al.* 2015:549-551). The question is: When considered from the perspective of both resistance and resilience theories, can the Book of Job be read in relation to the pandemonic context of recent pandemics in Africa in a way that offers hope and respite to the afflicted?

The outline of this chapter begins with a preliminary discussion of the connection between resistance and resilience. The second part shows that, like the bulk of the Old Testament text itself, African Biblical Hermeneutics, under whose rubric this chapter falls, is a methodology steeped in both resistance and resilience. Then, specifically, the chapter attempts a hermeneutical reading of the Book of Job in the context of the major pandemics that have ravaged the globe and, in this case, the African continent.

On a methodological level, the discussion engages with an aspect of Hermans' present volume, which employs the theory of resilience as its framework. Hermans describes heart-breaking adversity as a focus of religion and notes that "[o]ne cannot reflect on adversity or resilience without the concept of experience". Thus, "In experiences of heart-breaking adversity, the experience of the good (and God) in certain life events is lost. The ground on which one stands, has fallen away from under someone's feet" (Hermans 2022a, Chapter 1). Hermans (2022a, Chapter 1) further explains that it is the awareness of the absence or loss

---

[1] His e-mail address is: funlola@sun.ac.za.

of the good that results in heart-breaking adversity. Resilience, therefore, enables people to handle situations of heart-breaking adversity and "to experience the good in life events" (Hermans 2022b:31). Taking resilience theory as the point of departure, therefore, I will argue that resistance goes hand in glove with resilience in the Book of Job and that situations of heart-breaking adversity call not only for resilience, but also for resistance. It will be helpful at this point to consider the relationship between resilience and resistance.

## 9.2 Resilience or/and resistance?

According to the American Psychiatric Association, resilience is "the process of adapting well in the face of adversity, trauma, tragedy, threats, and even significant sources of stress such as family and relationship problems, serious health problems, or workplace and financial stressors. It means 'bouncing back' from difficult experiences."

*Collins Dictionary* defines resistance as the act or an instance of resisting; the capacity to withstand something, especially the body's natural capacity to withstand disease. Writing from the perspective of female resistance, Allen (1999:125) defines resistance similarly as "the capacity of an agent to act in spite of or in response to the power wielded over her by others ... Resistance seems fundamentally to involve asserting one's capacity to act in the face of the domination of another agent."

Although Hermans writes from a practical theological/religious perspective, his understanding of resilience as a response to heart-breaking adversity has, I would say, hermeneutical significance and finds resonance, in particular, with the task of African Biblical Hermeneutics (ABH). Hermans' emphasis on experience as a central point of reflection on adversity or resilience is particularly noteworthy in relation to a hermeneutical framework (ABH), which not only places a premium on context, but also acknowledges the diversity of both human experiences and social realities. Furthermore, the notion of resilience in the context of heart-breaking adversity resonates with the African context which is, by and large, characterised by heart-breaking experiences of adversity brought about and reinforced, in this case, by serial pandemics including COVID-19, which was preceded by Ebola and Human Immunodeficiency Virus (HIV) cum Acquired Immune Deficiency Syndrome (AIDS), respectively. Even though these pandemics are considered global crises, the death rates of HIV/AIDs and Ebola in sub-Saharan Africa were significantly higher than on other continents compared to deaths due to COVID-19, which were much lower than on other continents. Sub-Saharan Africa was described as the world's epicentre of HIV/AIDs, reportedly being home to 64% of all people living with HIV/AIDS in 2006 (UNAIDS 2006:15).

It is within this milieu – and among a resilient people – that ABH operates and plies its brand of hermeneutical trade. Thus, a resilient context such as the African context calls for a resilient hermeneutics.

However, ABH was also forged out of the crucible of pain and persistent suffering brought about by the oppressive powers of slavery, colonialism, apartheid, imperialism, exile, neo-colonialism, and so forth as well as by the forces of poverty, disease, illiteracy, corruption, and perennial internecine wars and violence that have characterised the African context. Thus, ABH has become unavoidably the product of a resistant theology – a radically resistant post-slavery, postcolonial and post-apartheid hermeneutics that takes a swipe at traditional or conventional Eurocentric interpretations of the biblical text and of Western indoctrination and their imperialising realities and tendencies and that resists their relics and memories. The approach is found in the continuum of other liberation theologies such as Black theology, which developed as a resistant theology to apartheid ideology, African liberation theology or postcolonial theology. For postcolonial and decolonial biblical interpreters such as Dube (1996:38), to 'decolonise' means "awareness of imperialism's exploitative forces and its various strategies of domination, the conscious adoption of strategies for *resisting* imperial domination, as well as the search for alternative ways of liberating interdependence between nations, races, genders, economies, and cultures" (italics added). Segovia (2006:41) explains that, in postcolonial contexts, "there is always – sooner or later, major or minor, explicit or implicit – *resistance* to the center on the part of the politically, economically, culturally, and religiously subordinated margins, even when such *resistance* brings about, as it inevitably does, further measures of control on the part of the center, designed to instil fear into the minds and hearts of the margins" (italics added).

No doubt, ABH's exponents recognise this as a resistant enterprise. Presenting Adamo's brand of ABH as a resistant hermeneutics, Ramantswana (2021:376) notes that, among other things, it "is a form of resistance in that it seeks to dismantle Euro-Western hegemony in biblical scholarship by both distancing itself from Euro-Western hermeneutics and promoting African identity and culture". In the words of Ramantswana (2021:379), Adamo regards ABH as a process of 'blackening' the Bible, which in itself "is an act of resistance against hermeneutical practices which marginalise Africa and Africans".

In conceptualising ABH as both a resistant and a resilient hermeneutical approach, in this instance, it can be inferred that the approach not only resists the dictates of and domination by Euro-American methodologies, which use biblical criticism as a tool of control and repression of other interpretive voices and experiences, but it also musters resilience in the face of academic discrimination, rejection, and unwarranted criticism. More importantly, it problematises and addresses the persistent challenges and heart-breaking adversities experienced daily in their communities by the resilient people of Africa. Thus, ABH calls for a socially engaged scholarship that is cognisant of the social justice and socio-economic issues in its domain. In South Africa, for example, the struggles of the poor working class, (which invariably implies the struggles of people of colour), has been at the centre of a resistant Black theology, which grapples with issues of racism, classism, sexism, etcetera.

Hermans (2022b:31) affirms that "[r]esilience processes take place in multiple domains or levels of the social ecology of which people live." If we follow this claim, it is safe to regard ABH as one of those multiple systems that help individuals or groups handle heart-breaking adversities, to the extent that it offers hermeneutical strategies and solidarity to the afflicted in ways that can cause the process of resilience to produce positive outcomes. If the biblical text is viewed as a spiritual capital, as Hermans (2022c:56) points out, then, like other hermeneutical approaches, part of what ABH does is to tease out or draw from that spiritual capital to help not only build resilience but also overcome heart-breaking adversities. At this point, I will turn to the biblical text, specifically, the Book of Job, to draw from the spiritual capital that it offers.

### 9.3 Resistance and resilience – The Book of Job

First, the text of the Old Testament itself has been viewed as mainly a resistant text. Scholars have argued that most of the books of the Old Testament were written or revised in the exilic/post-exilic period and were calibrated in response to the trauma caused by the Assyrian-Babylonian captivity of the sixth century BCE. Significant portions of the Old Testament are said to be polemic expressions of Israel's resistance of imperial domination by both Assyria and Babylon. Specifically, large corpuses of the Old Testament text such as many of the individual and communal laments psalms, the P writer of the Pentateuch, the Prophets, and so forth were produced in a period of great national trauma that witnessed the loss of Temple, land, throne, and people. For example, Stulman and Kim view prophetic literature as resistance literature. Of the Book of Ezekiel, they state: "Ezekiel is a manifesto for war-torn refugees, a survival strategy for the crushed and conquered; or put more modestly, this diasporic text is literature of resistance in the struggle for communal survival" (Stulman & Kim 2010:145). These authors also note that, in the Book of Jeremiah, hope is buoyed by resistance, that is, "[r]esistance and hope are partners in meaning-making" (Stulman & Kim 2010:8). Similarly, wisdom literature has been described as a site of conflict where the "sages disagreed with each other, and they disagreed with the larger Israelite society" (Penchansky 2012:7).

For their part, some feminist biblical interpreters also read the Old Testament through the lens of female resistance, as they argue that the text presents various ways and instances in which the women of old resisted dehumanisation and oppressive male power (Lapsley 2005; Claassens 2016). Similarly, some ABH scholars identify acts of resistance in the biblical text which they then use to mirror oppression and social injustice in African contexts. For example, Mitshelsewa (2021:503-529) reads Exodus 1-15 as a resistant text which he uses to lend voice to the plight of Zimbabwean migrant workers in South Africa (Nzimande 2008:223-224, 27-28). West (2021) also engages with the works of Wittenberg, Nzimande, and Ramantswana, which locate resistance in real communities of struggle, both ancient and contemporary. According to West (2021:536-537, 538), Wittenberg claims that resistant theology in the Old Testament is located in a particular sector of society, that it was shaped by the people's historical struggles and conflicts, and that such a theology "could serve as a model for struggles of resistance and theological reflection arising out of the struggles" in the South African context (Wittenberg 2007; Nzimande 2008:223-258). West further cites Ramantswana (2017:74-75) who claims that "a decolonial reading also seeks to uncover the voices of those who have been marginalized and the suppressed voices of resistance within the same Bible".

Thus, voices of resistance clearly permeate the text of the Old Testament. However, besides the elements of resistance, processes of resilience are observed also in the text that emanated from the large-scale personal and communal tragedy experienced by the people of Israel. On the pages of the biblical text, the reader encounters a resilient people who experience again and again situations of adversity and traumatic pain.

If we view resilience as a coping mechanism for handling tragic situations, the Book of Job is a classic text that can be used to explore its processes. Despite its text-critical difficulties, the Book of Job remains a hermeneutical goldmine, especially when grappling with issues of theodicy and trying to make sense of human tragedy and pain. Using mostly the poetic genre, the Book relates the experiences of Job who, undoubtedly, has been subjected to heart-breaking adversity with the death of his ten children, the loss of his business and material substance, and the affliction of his body with disease (Job 1:13-19, 2:7-8). But Job's pain was a shared pain – his wife also lost her ten children and her property (Maier 2014:87). Thus, in light of the horrendous and unprecedented catastrophe that COVID-19 introduced to an already troubled world, it seems fitting to revisit Job's experiences of heart-breaking tragedy and his resilience in the midst of that pain.

The opening scene of Job features the divine council in session, with Satan also appearing in what can be likened to a court scene. After obtaining a court order against Job twice, God permitted Satan to destroy Job's children and his property, inflicting sore boils on him for no reason (Job 2:3). Balentine (2018:43) describes God, in this instance, as "an (indirect) agent of gratuitous suffering". When his three friends – Eliphaz, Bildad and Zophar – come to commiserate with Job over his loss, they urge him to admit his wrongdoing and make peace with God. They regard Job's ordeal as a punishment from God or a disciplinary warning for some wrongdoing on Job's part. Accordingly, Job needs to acknowledge his sins, repent, and turn to God. But Job, in an act of resilience, refuses to consider the possibility of accepting evil from God. His wife also asks him to "curse God and die" (Job 2:9), but Job would have none of that. Rather, he chooses to curse the day he was born and the night he was conceived (Job 3:1-19). He maintains his innocence and integrity, saying, "I will not agree that you are right. Until my dying day, I won't give up my integrity. My righteousness I hold fast and will not let it go: My heart shall not reproach me as long as I live" (Job 27:5-6). In Job's view, he is not guilty of any misconduct and there must have been an error somewhere. Job then goes on to accuse God of cruelty (Job 6:4, 7:19-20, 9:17, 10:16, 12:9, 16:9) and maintains that even God knows that he is not guilty. Finally, he decides to subpoena God, as his friends have no answer, explanation, or solution to his predicament.

It is important to consider the experiences of Job and his resilience in relation to his utterances at this point, since the book of Job is full of discourses. Speeches consisting of dialogues and monologues permeate the text. The narrative opens with dialogues between God and Satan (Job 1:6-12, 2:1-6). Whereas Job's monologues occur in Chapter 3 and Chapters 29-31, dialogues between him and his three friends (Chapters 4-27), dialogues between Job and God (Chapters 38-42), and the speech of Elihu to Job and the three other friends (Chapters 32-37) make up the bulk of the book. Other minor speeches also occur between Job and his servants (Job 1:14-22); between Job and his wife (Job 2:9-10), and between God and Job's three friends (Job 42:7-9). Significantly, Job's speeches – his action or expression of his thoughts – underscore his resistance and resilience. He vehemently resists his friends' attempt to classify him as a sinner who is reaping punishment for wrongdoing, while at the same time he demonstrates his resilience by expressing hope that God will still vindicate and restore him.

Job clearly expresses his feelings in words. How he feels is discernible from his speeches. His feelings and moods range from sorrow, grief, shock, frustration, betrayal, and desperation to hope, trust, and a longing for God (Job 13:15, 19:25-27, 23:3-10, 31:35). He feels wronged by God and by his friends and he openly expresses his pain. He talks about the unquantifiable weight of his grief (Job 6:1-2, 17:7); the bitterness and anguish of his soul (Job 3:20, 10:1, 23:1-2); his helplessness in the hands of a mighty God (Job 9:11-19, 13:24-28, 14:13, 19:6-13, 23:13-16, 30:15-31, 31:23); the desire to die (Job 6:8-9, 7:15-16, 10:1, 17:1); his feelings of nostalgia (Job 29), and his shame (Job 21:3, 30:1-14, 19:14-22). He also expresses some feelings of regret, not only about his life but also about his birth (Job 3:1-19, 7:7, 10:18-19).

Trauma counsellors encourage victims to articulate their feelings as a therapeutic act in the healing process. But, in the first seven days of his ordeal, Job's grief was unspeakable. Though not much is revealed about his thoughts, the first seven days of mourning indicate that he was deep in thought as his friends sat down with him on the ground for seven days and seven nights. They were all speechless. It is not too difficult to imagine the thoughts of Job during those seven days, given the bitter and heavy words that proceeded from his mouth afterwards (3:1ff.).

Thus, the dialogues with the three other interlocutors and, subsequently, with his younger friend Elihu reflect Job's resilience. In the discourse in Job 26-31, Job maintains his innocence. He refuses to succumb to his friends' unfounded accusations and pressure to make him admit that he was at fault. Earlier, in Job 13:15, Job had insisted, "Though he slay me, yet will I trust in him: but I will maintain mine own ways before him". Even God testified of Job's resilience to Satan, saying, he still retains his integrity, even though you incited Me against him to ruin him without cause" (Job 2:3, 13:18, 14:14b, 19:25, 23:10).

Unquestionably, Job exercised resilience in the face of his heart-breaking adversity and existential crisis. Despite his feelings of vulnerability, he refused to break or yield to pressure from Satan, from his friends, or from his wife. At the same time, the dialogues between him and his friends show that, besides his re-silience, Job also expressed radical resistance against the traditional wisdom of his day. Job's friends, who tried to make sense of his unprecedented personal tragedy, take recourse to traditional wisdom which assumes that Job's misfortune must have been a punishment from God for some wrongdoing, perhaps even a secret sin (Job 15:4-6, 22:2-11).

A tension develops between Job and his friends, as Job resists their argu-ments and maintains his innocence. Job argues that his personal experience of tragedy as an innocent man deconstructs their traditional ideology that is centred on the law of retribution – doing good produces reward and doing evil produces tragedy. He claims that his suffering is not punishment from God. His experience contradicts their claims. Thus, Job resists the world-view and social construct that characterise him as a sinner based on his experience of personal disaster. He re-jects the wisdom of his friends, because his experience negates their traditional understanding that punishment must be meted out to the wrongdoer and reward given to the righteous. In other words, Job resists his friends' model of right and wrong as categories for viewing God. Ultimately, God resists and rejects not only the model endorsed by Job's friends, but also Job's anthropocentric model, which assumes that "innocent suffering had to imply the injustice of God" (Newsom 2012:214).

However, one would agree that Job, in a way, also resists God – resists what God has doled out to him. Claassens (2015:149), who views "tragic laugh-ter" as a means of resistance, argues that tragic laughter offers some important insights for understanding the tragedy of Job. Claassens (2015:151) rightly notes that "a key feature in the book of Job, which has cemented its enduring value in societies later facing trauma, is the bold act of *resistance* on the part of its main character. Job's challenge to God is probably the fiercest in the Old Testament: God's role in Job's suffering is faced head-on" (italics added).

It is remarkable though that Job's is not the only resistant voice identified in the Book. Feminist interpreters point out that Job's wife also introduces a theology of protest and resistance when she calls on her husband to "curse God and die", that is, to resist the ideology of suffering and retribution (Kangwa 2020:80-83; Nadar 2006:189-203). Her brief statement that encourages Job to resist God's dealing is in itself an act of resistance. She does not see why her husband would be placid in the face of the tragedy that has befallen them, presumably from God. Job's rhetoric of "the Lord gave, the Lord has taken away" (Job 1:21) does not sit well with his wife who taunts him and dares him to curse God.

So far, I have endeavoured to show, in broad and general terms, that both resistance and resilience are attested to in the story of Job. First, we encounter a subdued Job – subdued by tragedy and grief – then, a resistant and resilient Job with a resilient faith that refuses to back down. Job not only resists the traditional wisdom of his friends and God's measure but, in an act of defiance and resilience, he bounces back from the land of sorrow. How then does this help us grapple with the existential issues of our day, especially in the African context? Job's physical and emotional trauma are often highlighted in most interpretive endeavours. The impact of Job's economic loss – the loss of his business and ground staff in one day – seems to be overlooked. He no longer has a source of livelihood. In Hermans' words, it is clear that the ground on which Job stood has practically been removed from under his feet. Job has not moved from rags to riches; he has fallen from grace to grass. Thinking of "the good old days" when he basked in affluence (Job 29:6) and his glory was fresh in him (Job 29:20), in light of his present misfortune, simply breaks his heart.

## 9.4 Job and contemporary sufferers

Newsom (2012:212) notes that Job "has been shocked out of his own previous complacency by the wholly undeserved suffering he has experienced. Gradually, he begins to see things from a different perspective, from the perspective of those who suffer." Here is a wealthy and healthy man whose situation changed overnight. Of course, he would see things differently. He would readily be able to empathise with those who suffer loss and grief. But one could turn this view around and say that those who suffer could actually be encouraged to view things through the eyes of Job. They can read Job's story and tap from his unwavering stance on resistance and resilience. In this regard, Fried (2016:164) shows that, although the tragic events narrated in the story of Job represent a personal or individual tragedy, on a corporate level, the story serves as "an ultimate metaphor for Jews looking for a way to relate to suffering in exile". Fried (2016:164) explains:

> The book of Job gives the Jew a vehicle to scream out about God's injustice, the injustice that the Rabbis certainly must have felt looking upon the children dying from starvation in the

streets of Jerusalem, or the blood running in the streets after the massacre at Beitar; the feelings that Jews throughout the centuries must have felt looking upon the Crusades, the Inquisition, or the gas chambers of the Holocaust. "We know we've sinned, God, but there is nothing, NOTHING, we could have done to deserve this".

If we follow Fried's line of argument, relating the individual tragedy of Job to broader contexts of communal or global sufferings should not be considered far-fetched, as it could also offer "a vehicle to scream" to those who, even at the present time, are hurting in deep and unprecedented ways. Concerning this point, we note Zhang's reading of the story of Job and Job's feelings of being loathed and discriminated against in light of the experiences of Asians (Chinese) in foreign spaces during the COVID-19 outbreak. Zhang notes that, like Job, who "was abhorred, mocked, and left aside by people" (Job 30:9-10), some Wuhanians, Chinese, and Asians also experienced feelings of being discriminated against and shunned because of their geographical or ethnic connection to the place of the outbreak (Zhang 2020:607-612). In short, the story of Job could offer those being shunned and loathed "a vehicle to scream".

Likewise, Job's tragic situation, which was aggravated by the reversal of his fortune, calls to mind the broader milieu of pandemics in Africa, in particular, of COVID-19. Since March 2020, individuals and communities have lost thousands of loved ones – family members, friends, neighbours, colleagues, parishioners, and so forth, to COVID-19, which has left a trail of tears and sorrow in its wake. Although the death rates from COVID-19 in Africa are much lower than those reported from other continents, especially the Americas, Asia and Europe, the economic fallout of this disaster is tremendous, as many bereaved families and individuals also lost their sources of livelihood, homes, and other property to loan sharks and bank mortgages during and after the lockdown periods. On communal levels, coping with the socio-economic and psychological consequences of the 'new normal' marked by terminologies such as self-isolation, quarantine, masking, social distancing, lockdown, COVID-19 testing, Zooming, curfews, supply chain, remote jobs (working from home), hybrid meetings, webinars, travel restrictions, vaccination (or resistance to it), boosters, etcetera, also requires a strong dose of resilience – of communal resilience.

Even though the spread of COVID-19 has abated, the ongoing war in Europe between Russia and Ukraine has exacerbated the socio-economic crisis in Africa, as in other parts of the world. The rising cost of petroleum products, grains, and other commodities implies that the poor will continue to groan under the yoke of shifting economic policies and uncontrollable inflation for a long time to come. Could Job's resilience and resistance offer coping mechanisms to individuals, families, and communities experiencing heartbreaking adversity in these times? I suppose so.

I should also stress that the hermeneutical enterprise in the African context must continue to be an effort in resilience and resistance. Its conceptions of God should relate to that of the Psalmist: "For thou hast considered my trouble; thou hast known my soul in adversities" (Ps. 31:7). A hermeneutics that is born out of pain must continue to administer healing balm to the open wounds found in its hermeneutical space. In seasons of life brought about by unforeseen circumstances such as pandemics and lockdowns, resilience is a key not only to survival, but also to human flourishing. Central to the process of resilience is hope. This demonstrates that Job's condition of adversity, his resilience, as well as his ultimate vindication and change are a testament of hope for those experiencing similar situations of tragedy and trauma. Pastoral caregivers could, therefore, consider reading the story of Job with those who suffer, in order to instil and affirm the triumph of that hope. As long as tragedies and adversity remain part of the human experience, resilience and resistance will continue to be indispensable. Their discussion should also continue.

## BIBLIOGRAPHY

Allen, A. (1999). The power of feminist theory: Domination, resistance, solidarity. Boulder, CO: Westview Press.

American Psychiatric Association (2014). The road to resilience. https://uncw.edu/studentaffairs/committees/pdc/documents/the%20road%20to%20resilience.pdf [Accessed: 20 July 2022].

Balentine, S.E. (2018). Wisdom literature. Nashville, TN: Abingdon Press. Core Biblical Studies.

Carlin, N., Capps, D. & Dykstra, R.C. (2015). Living stories of resilience, resistance, and resourcefulness. *Pastoral Psychology* 64:549-551.

Claassens, L.J. (2015). Tragic laughter: Laughter as resistance in the book of Job. *Interpretation: A Journal of Bible and Theology* 69(2):143-155.
    (2016). Claiming her dignity: Female resistance in the Old Testament. Collegeville, MN: Liturgical Press.

Hanks, P. (ed.) (1979). Collins English Dictionary. Glasgow: HarperCollins.

Dube, M. (1996). Reading for decolonisation (John 4:1-42). *Semeia* 75:37-59.

Fried, D. (2016). The book of Job as a way of relating to Jewish national suffering. *Jewish Bible Quarterly* 44(3):157-166.

Hermans, C.A.M. (2022a). Human experiences of heart-breaking adversity, Chapter 1 in this volume (pp.13-30).
    (2022b). Processes of resilience, Chapter 2 in this volume (pp.31-46).
    (2022c). Resilient religion, Chapter 3 in this volume (pp.47-66).

Kangwa, J. (2020). Women and nature in the book of Job: An African eco-feminist reading. *Feminist Theology* 29(1):75-90.

Lapsley, J. (2005). Whispering the Word: Hearing women's stories in the Old Testament. Louisville, KY: Westminster John Knox.

Maier, C.M. (2014). Good and evil women in Proverbs and Job: The emergence of cultural stereotypes. In: N. Calduch-Benages & C.M. Maier (eds), The writings and later Wisdom books (Atlanta, GA: SBL), pp. 77-92.

Mitshelsewa, N. (2021). Resistance of oppression in Exodus 1-15 and Southern Africa: An intersectional perspective. *Old Testament Essays* 34(2):503-529.

Nadar, S. (2006). "Barak God and die!" Women, HIV, and a theology of suffering. In: R.S. Sugirtharajah (ed.), Voices from the margin: Interpreting the Bible in the third world (Maryknoll, NY: Orbis Books), pp. 189-203.

Newsom, C.A. (2012). Job. In: C.A. Newsom, S.H. Ringe & J.E. Lapsley (eds), Women's Bible commentary (Louisville, KY: Westminster John Knox Press), pp. 208-215.

Nzimande, M.K. (2008). Reconfiguring Jezebel: A postcolonial imbokodo reading of the story of Naboth's vineyard (1 Kings 21:1-16). In: H. de Wit & G.O. West (eds), African and European readers of the Bible in dialogue: In quest of a shared meaning (Leiden: Brill), pp. 223-258.

Penchansky, D. (2012). Understanding wisdom literature: Conflict and dissonance in the Hebrew text. Grand Rapids, MI: Wm B. Eerdmans.

Ramantswana, H. (2017). Decolonial reflection on the landlessness of the Levites. *Journal of Theology for Southern Africa* 158:72-91.

(2021). Distinctive African readings of the Old Testament: A review of D.T. Adamo's publications in Old Testament Essays 2003-2020. *Old Testament Essays* 34(2):370-384.

Segovia, F.F. (2006). Biblical criticism and postcolonial studies: Toward a postcolonial optic. In: R.S. Sugirtharajah (ed.), Postcolonial biblical reader (Oxford: Wiley-Blackwell), pp.33-44.

Stulman, L. & Kim, H.C.P. (2010). 'You are my people': An introduction to prophetic literature. Nashville, TN: Abingdon Press.

UNAIDS (2006). Report on the global AIDS epidemic: A UNAIDS 10th anniversary special edition. https://data.unaids.org/pub/report/2006/2006_gr_en.pdf [Accessed: 15 May 2022].

West, Gerald O. (2021). A decolonial (re)turn to class in South African biblical scholarship. *Old Testament Essays* 34(2):530-553.

Wittenberg, G.H. (2007). Resistance theology in the Old Testament: Collected essays. Pietermaritzburg: Cluster Publications.

Zhang, Y. (2020). Reading the book of Job in the pandemic. *Journal of Biblical Literature* 139(3):607-612.

# Chapter 10

# "Surviving my story of trauma": A pastoral theology of resilience

*J Meyer*[1]

## 10.1 The life of trauma through story

It is often through story that the experience of trauma lives. By that is meant that trauma naturally embodies the form of story and remains *the* story until it can be owned and claimed as *my* story. *The* story becomes *my* story only through the process of courage and what may be called 'resilience'. When *the* story remains a story, unclaimed by any author or narrator other than the unconscious, it is inaccessible to consciousness and direct experiences and detached from the sense of self.

However, when the story remains *a* story, unprocessed and often denied, it has the power to become even a bigger threat – an abstract object of danger – that slowly invades any sense of reality and coherent existence. It has the power to sustain denial and the fantasy that the dreadful event did not take place. Research consistently shows that unprocessed trauma will psychosomatically manifest through uncomfortable and disturbing physiological and mental reactions. The story will, therefore, remain and linger as an unwelcome guest. It will not, however, go away.

As such, there is power in (in)articulation. What is never said, never happened. Similarly, what is said – articulated – can never be unsaid. Herein lies the ambiguity of the story of trauma. On the one hand, to speak and affirm reality, however painful, can liberate. Paradoxically, however, as soon as trauma is spoken, the 'dragon' must be faced. That is a journey that most people do not want to endure, cannot endure – a journey of telling, and retelling, until what you tell becomes your reality – a reality with which you can live or not.

Nevertheless, a story never articulated becomes a vessel of shame. Shame is the intense feeling that there is something wrong with the person,

---

[1] Her e-mail address is: meyerj@ufs.ac.za

ironically, often the victim of trauma. Shame is often experienced by the emotion of 'disgust' or finding oneself disgusting (Arel 2019:15). The experience of shame has immense power to silence a story. Shame creates a space for the 'unsayable' to operate, so that the trauma becomes seemingly invisible, deniable as if it never happened (Rogers 2007:44).

A story *articulated* breaks the silence and becomes a weapon of resilience. Narratives and the stories they consist of can survive despite the will of the psyche they embody. The articulation of the story, therefore, requires a person to accept the reality of the event and to gain the courage to take ownership of the story in such a way that the author (the owner of the story) has control over the life of the story in his/her narrative. Resilience through authoring and narrating is to be unwilling to allow the story to haphazardly live in the mind, controlling the trajectory of the narrative.

Because stories are the ingredients of our narrative identities, trauma has the power to cut to the core of the Self and destroy the coherency previously experienced in the life narrative. Although no life narrative is fully coherent, it is usually filled with meaning, purpose and structure that unifies the stories in a narrative (memory), which directs future behaviour and decisions (anticipation). The experience of a traumatic event can, therefore, corrupt memory and corrode anticipation.

Within stories, however, lies the human capacity for resilience. Although trauma lives through story, the narrator can be liberated by the same story that held [2]her captive. Human beings' ability to derive meaning from life and various events through story enables them to transform something destructive into something constructive. Not by way of denial or ignorance, nor by way of fleeing, but by courageously facing, deconstructing, reconstructing, and reframing, the narrating victim is transformed into a resilient survivor.

In this chapter, storying will be framed as an essential component of a theology of resilience. The author proposes that a theology of resilience is a collection of stories and narratives that tell us something about the character of the triune God as revealed through the stories of God in three persons with humankind throughout Scripture. Such a theology offers people an endless resource centre, from which stories can be borrowed, incorporated, and embodied to remain resilient amidst inevitable

---

[2] The author uses gender references interchangeably in acknowledging that all genders are affected by trauma and adversity, but also easing the reading experience by not continuously referring to he/she. It can thus be assumed that when a specific reference to gender is made, that other genders are implied.

experiences of suffering. A resilient religion might then entail the utilisation of spiritual practices that enhance and sustain a sense of resilience by embodying theologies of resilience.

A theology of resilience through storying is discussed in the framework of three themes borrowed from Swain's (2011) trinitarian pastoral model of care. These three narrative themes are suggested as three turning points in the trajectory of authoring and narrating the story of trauma to construct the story of *my* trauma in the coherent and stable paradigm of finding being in the triune God. It is suggested that a resilient religion offers its affiliates the opportunity to reframe their metanarrative in the framework of the Master Narrative to remain resilient in the face of inevitable suffering. The promise of a resilient religion lies in the crux of the Master Narrative that reveals God as Earth-maker (Creator), Pain-Bearer (Redeemer), and Life-Giver (Sustainer).

## 10.2 Desecrating the sacred

### 10.2.1 The sacred, annihilated

The notion of trauma, as either an event or an experience and the consequence thereof (for example, to be traumatised), is complex and difficult to capture in a single definition alone. Instead, trauma can be more clearly understood as existing on a continuum, with associated feelings moving between the polarities of experiencing a crisis, adversity, and even tragedy. Although the experience of a crisis might develop into feelings of being traumatised, the latter is not implied as a result of experiencing a crisis or adversity. Instead, the phenomenon of being traumatised is specific to the experience of desolation and despair that often lingers long after the experience of the horrific event. Cooper-White (2011:113) describes a traumatic *event* as an event characterised by horror and the feeling that human life is threatened. Psychospiritually, often post-trauma, a person will feel overwhelmed, annihilated, or defeated and lack a sense of being in control. In the face of a traumatic event, the body and psyche innately respond to the observed danger, by employing 'emerging mechanisms' such as fighting, fleeing, or freezing for survival.

Adversely, crisis can be described as a "disturbance of meaning, due to the appraisal of events as too demanding and resources as too limited, and visible in symptoms of the disruption of psychological equilibrium" (Ganzevoort 1998:261). In this sense, any life event can cause a crisis for an individual when an individual cannot successfully resolve the disturbance of meaning that he/ experiences (see also Ganzevoort 1994). In a sense, it can be expected that human beings will face a series of crises in their lifetime and that the successful resolution of each crisis will result in a sense of accomplishment and the maturation of the personality (Erikson 1968). It is thus not expected that crises will result in feelings of horror, fear, and desolation, however difficult they might be to handle or resolve.

Hermans (2022a:13-24) characterises adversity, on the other hand, as a situation that includes physical, social and/or mental suffering and causes a sense of 'brokenness' in the individual. When associated with the framework of religion, adversity is the "experience of being separated from that which gives life lustre, perfect happiness, purpose, an ultimate reason to live for". Experiencing adversity, especially when prolonged, might result in feelings of despair and desolation and might be more closely related to what is understood as experiencing a traumatic event and the impact thereof on the ability of the sufferer to live life to the fullest. As such, Hermans (2022a:13) mentions another level of adversity that causes more intense feelings of despair. He coins this type of experience as experiencing "heartbreaking adversity", which he describes as "the awareness of the feeling of the absence of the good". Accordingly, experiencing heartbreaking adversity causes a person to be unable to connect a concrete experience with the ultimate good (Hermans 2022a:16). The disconnection between the realisation of a good life causes a sense of brokenness, which

> is registered within oneself as a disproportion between one self and the other itself (idem). That is why the demand for mediation or wholeness is a demand for mediation between one itself and the other itself. It is incorrect to release the one 'self' from the other 'self', to separate the biological of the spiritual and then build the whole from the parts (Ricoeur 1986:4) (Hermans 2022a:16).

Similarly, Cooper-White (2011:114) mentions the impact of experiencing trauma on a person's sense of existence and the meaning he attains from it: "Nothing strikes more deeply at the sacredness of life and one's sense of spiritual health/wellness/holiness than trauma and violence". Wulf (2019:133) confirms that trauma affects a person's sense of identity; morality (sense of freedom and responsibility); physical and mental health; a person's relationship to space and time, and individuality that is expressed through the experience of personal dignity, where dignity relates to the notion of truth and sense of worthiness. Because a person's sense of meaning and purpose is affected, this cuts to the core of spirit and notions of transcendence, which might lead to a further search for meaning amidst continuous experiences of adversity (Wulf 2019).

One severe consequence of experiencing both trauma and adversity, however, is often the extent to which the sufferer/victim/survivor dissociates from experiences and life in general. 'Dissociation' might be circumscribed as an unconscious way to separate from the personality, while the splitting of memory is referred to as 'fragmentation' (Fischer & Riedesser 2003:116). Both 'dissociation' and 'fragmentation' indicate the inability of the traumatised to fully access experiences of the traumatic event (Wulf 2019:136). Someone may dissociate from time through the fragmentation of memory and space through the inability to position (bodily and sensory) experience in the 'here-and-now'. Instead of being the actor or the author of the story, the person becomes an observer or even totally absent. Dissociation and fragmentation cause a person to withdraw into silence (Jones 2009:29). This is experienced "as a dissolution of the death-life boundary" and is emphasised by "feelings of dissolution, of losing the world, of being destroyed, of being afraid of existence or relationships" (Rambo 2010:25).

From literature, it seems that trauma often relates to the experience of adversity (horror, pain, violence, neglect, and the like) at the hands of the other. By contrast, adversity may refer to any event that causes a sense of despair and desolation (losing a loved one through death, job loss, experiencing a terminal illness, and so on). Although small, this difference does affect how the victim relates to the world and others post-trauma differently from someone affected by adverse events (in the absence of a perpetrator). Nevertheless, both trauma and heartbreaking adversity may lead to the sense of an absence of good/God in one's life, which leaves the sufferer with a deep sense of despair and unworthiness.

It is argued that the impact of trauma inevitably affects how the story of trauma is successfully 'plotted' into the metanarrative of the individual. Unfortunately, trauma leaves an eternal psycho-emotional scar that cannot be 'erased', and all attempts to do so will result in further dissociation and disequilibrium. Alternatively, it is proposed that the framing of the story of trauma within the metanarrative (where 'metanarrative' refers to the story of the self or identity story) to maintain a sense of integrity and coherence and ultimately remain resilient in the face of resulting crises and adversity might successfully result in living a full life, despite one's scars.

## 10.2.2 The desecrated, embodied

The fact that the human body is a primary sensory source of experiences means that both spiritual/religious experiences and experiences of trauma will first manifest themselves through the body (McGuire 2008:98) before being processed by the mind. Because neither spiritual encounters nor traumatic experiences are ever entirely articulated through linguistic grammar, both tend to be expressed through the body via "drives, affects, fantasies, dreams, ecstasies [...] hope, sensations, and moods" (Ganzevoort & Sremac 2019:5). It is then proposed that, because these two antagonist experiences are processed and expressed in similar ways, trauma has an increased probability of affecting one's understanding and experiences of the 'sacred' in the form of the other, the Divine Other, and the self.

Lived religious experiences contain instances with, and perspectives of the sacred and, as such, constitute a series of symbols and narratives that attribute meaning to extraordinary experiences of the sacred or experiences of the desecrated.[3] The act of 'desecrating' is "to damage or show a lack of respect toward something holy or respected" (Ganzevoort & Sremac 2019:3-4). Trauma, in its very nature, tends to threaten the integrity of a sense of the sacred by damaging and disrespecting a sense of dignity and safety.

The 'sacred' does not necessarily point to a place or point in time, but to a specific way in which the world is perceived and how one's role in this world is understood in light of extraordinary experiences. The 'sacred' is thus not another reality but rather another way to *perceive* reality and being in this sacred reality. Therefore, the impact of trauma affects a sense of 'being', on a physical, social, and psychological level, on how that 'being' functions on the dimensions of spatiality and temporality (Ganzevoort & Sremac 2019:4). A sacred sense of being safe, being protected and thereby being able to embrace life and the world and everything it offers, is desecrated. Trauma transforms the mundane into something potentially dangerous. Living in a constant state of alertness enslaves a person with fear.

---

[3] With specific reference to traumatic experiences, but which does not necessarily imply that traumatic experiences are void from experiences of the sacred, of God's presence or the like. It simply means to describe such experiences being the opposite of pleasant experiences of the sacred.

### 10.2.3 A void of sacred meaning and relation

Hermans (2022b:42) illustrates how the experience of heartbreaking adversity (the absence of the experience of the good) ultimately results in the experience of tragedy or the absence of happiness. Accordingly, I propose that both the experience of the ultimate good and that of happiness are sacred notions of "a moral scheme in which the good should also be available for the just and innocent" (2022b:42). The experience of trauma or adversity can, therefore, strip a person from experiencing the ultimate good – the sacred – or inhibit a person from even considering the proposition that s/he is deserving of the ultimate good.

Trauma, as an experience of heartbreaking adversity, changes into the experience of tragedy as soon as the person realises that no sufficient explanation can be given as to why this event took place and why he should have experienced such an event in the first place. This realisation causes a sense of powerlessness, a lack of control or agency in preventing the event from taking place or escaping the consequences thereof. A sense of tragedy is amplified in the absence of experiencing the 'good' in his life and his ambivalent reluctance to give up on the idea that the ultimate good is meant to be experienced by all. After all, as Hermans (2022b:40) states: "The absence of the good in life is 'what should not be'". As a result, the sufferer experiences a deep sense of injustice, unfairness, and dismay but tries to make sense of the absence of the good by using a "moral scheme" to identify the cause (Hermans 2022b:40; Van Dalen *et al.* 2019:237).

The above illustrates a spiral of despair that often entraps sufferers and sheds light on the power of trauma to infiltrate the symbolised, narrative, and imaginary framework with which a person understands not only the world, but also his place in it, and God's relation to it. As such, trauma often strips a person of all sense of meaning and purpose, alienating her from a meaning system formed by a lifetime of extraordinary experiences, leaving her desolate in a reality of discrepancies, ambivalence, and uncertainty, filled with anxiety (Slattery & Park 2015:127, in Wulf 2019:132). It is not uncommon for the sufferer to feel rejected, isolated and without the comfort previously experienced through faith and a community of faith. Instead of experiencing faith as a protective factor, God is experienced ambivalently and in uncertain terms (Walker *et al.* 2015:10; Frawlei-O'Dea 2015:169ff.; Richards *et al.* 2015:85ff. in Wulf 2019:132-133).

Similarly, the basis of a person's psychological growth lies within relationships that acknowledge existence, uniqueness, and dignity. When a person's fundamental human values and rights have been violated, the image of God is ultimately violated and equated with a persecuting moral system (Wurmser 2012:119ff.), in whose presence the traumatised person experiences shame and guilt (Wulf 2019:142) instead of acceptance, comfort, and liberty. Trauma, therefore, removes a person not only from all sense of the sacred and the good, but also from a community where a sacred sense of belonging is experienced under the notion that everyone is *deserving* of the good.

The sufferer finds himself in a place where "the good they experience is simply too scarce and too transient to generate a positive attitude to a life of happiness" (Hermans2022a:19). When stripped of all sense of the good and the sacred, a person is left with relationships characterised by what Buber (1970) calls an I-it relation, where either the 'other' or both the 'other' and the 'I' are experienced as objects, subdued to the level of functionality or utility. Where one or both of these entities are not appreciated in their entirety, the result is a lack of intimacy, closeness, mutual respect, and positive regard, as well as inevitably a dissociation with the self, the other, and, ultimately, with God (Balswick *et al.* 2016:47-53).

### 10.2.4 Enslaved by shame

Shame becomes an 'antagonist' in the story of trauma, thus creating conflict that needs to be resolved between the protagonist and the antagonist of the story (Halverson *et al.* 2011:14). It is, therefore, important to deconstruct shame, its origins and impact on the construction of the story, and to reframe it in the metanarrative.

Shame is generally viewed as an affect on a continuum of experiences such as feelings, emotions, and mood (Cooper-White 2011:114). In short, *affect* refers to innate bodily reactions that result from the direct experiences of the body (Basch 1998:114), while *feeling* is a cognitive experience that results in conscious awareness of that specific feeling. *Emotion,* on the other hand, is also a cognitive experience (albeit more complex in nature) that gives meaning to the experience of a specific feeling. *Mood,* which results from biochemical processes in the brain, is the persistent experience of a specific affect (Nathanson 1994:40-43). As a result, researchers (Tomkins [n.d.]; Basch 1998; Nathanson 1994; Bradshaw 1988) have identified shame as one of nine identified affects, but an affect that is experienced as significantly negative. The difference between shame and guilt is that guilt results from something bad that has been *done*, while shame results from the feeling that the person is inherently 'bad' (Cooper-White 2011:115).

Shame is often experienced as 'being exposed' and thereby feeling unsafe. Exposure refers to the exposure of something viewed as fundamentally private (Wurmser 1981). As a result, experiencing shame increases the need for a sense of safety – to be 'covered' or protected: "The etymological root of the word *shame* itself means 'to cover'" (Cooper-White 2011:116) and supports the notion of being unsafe and the need for protection. Shame results from a threat that lingers within the mind and escape becomes quite impossible. Karen (1992:10) underscores the complexity of shame as an antagonist to dignity. Karen suggests that three types of shame have been identified. Of interest, in this instance, is what Karen (1992:10) refers to as 'situational shame', defined as feelings of shame related to experiencing humiliation, rejection, or the violation of one's personal boundaries or a social norm. This type of shame might turn into long-term emotions of disgrace or stigma (see also Cooper-White 2011:116). Arel (2019:54) affirms that feelings of shame cause a person to withdraw into the self in an attempt to conceal the shame. This results in a 'silencing' of the experiences regarding trauma and shame, thus creating fertile ground for the impact of trauma to become self-destructive (Dutra *et al.* 2008).

The relation of shame to the affect, disgust, intensifies the devastating impact of feeling shame after experiencing a traumatic event. Tomkins (2008:22, 56, 57) describes 'disgust' as a natural and evolutionary affect that warns a person of possible danger and motivates that person to avoid the object of anger/disgust. Human beings then tend to correlate the feeling of disgust with unfamiliar objects when those objects share characteristics with the initial object experienced as disgusting. The vast majority of cultures operate with a series of norms and standards and, as a result, something or someone operating outside these norms is then regarded as 'disgusting' (Nussbaum 2004:86). As a result, a victim internalises these expressions of disgust towards the self, perhaps because of experiencing a disgusting event.

Despite the irrationality inherent in internalising feelings of disgust, this theory sheds some light on the severity of the feelings of shame and its debilitating effect not only on the person's sense of worth, but also on why victims of trauma tend to retract into isolation. Because trauma as an event occurs beyond the boundaries of the normative – often viewed as an unpleasant experience feared by most – it becomes something to be

avoided. Therefore, when experiencing a traumatic event, a person becomes a victim by experiencing an event viewed with disgust by others
(and previously by the self). I propose that it is difficult for a victim to
dissociate herself from the event of disgust and the subject to which disgusting acts were done. Being the subject that experienced a disgusting
event, the event is internalised as shame. The person feels embarrassed,
humiliated, or objectified by experiencing an event of disgust. Often these
feelings are revealed through the language used by the sufferer post-
trauma to describe the self: 'bad', 'broken', 'damaged', and 'used'.

### 10.2.5 Isolated with the Unsayable

A person who experienced trauma often finds it difficult to utter these experiences or to narrate even the most significant aspects of the event, caus-
ing a retreat into silence regarding the event. The inability of the traumatised person to articulate and describe the event creates a space that Rogers
(2007:44) calls "the unsayable". The Unsayable [deliberately capitalised,
in this instance] becomes a space that encapsulates the dissociation of the
traumatised person with the trauma event. In this perceived 'safe' space,
the reality or *actuality* of the traumatic event is escaped (Herman 2011:5).
In this wordless, speechless space, the trauma becomes invisible (Rogers
2007:44) and eludes the person: What is never said, never happened.

       The illusion held forth by the Unsayable is that it is sustained by
constant feelings of shame. In the 'world' of the Unsayable, the actuality
of the event assumes "a coded form in the body, in human action, and
speech", and in this manner, the Unsayable becomes a space of danger,
where "silence becomes a weapon of destruction" (Arel 2019:56; Rogers
2007:44). Unknowable to the victim, silence and the growing sense of
shame are the driving forces of power, control, and domination that the
(perpetrator of the) trauma continues to exert.

### 10.3 Life as narrative

When studying theology, meaning *Theos* and *logos* – discourses on God –
we cannot exclude the importance of narrative and story. God is known
through the stories of the Bible and the witnesses of people. The stories
people tell and retell about their experiences of God, life, and the intersec-
tion thereof, form the foundation of the belief system. It is, therefore, not
strange to view human experiences such as trauma in the framework of

narrative and to comprehend that the impact of trauma can likewise be addressed through the same avenues.

In the same way that beliefs and convictions are understood, studied, and practised through narrative, people tend to understand themselves likewise through narrative. McAdams (2001:101) suggests that identity development occurs alongside story development, where one's past, present, and future are continuously reconstructed through an internalised and developing narrative of the self, which he calls, the 'self-story'. Understanding the operations inherent in story and narrative is, therefore, important to understand the development, functioning, and impact of trauma on the story of self and the story of self in relation to the divine Other.

To gain a better understanding of the intricacies of story, narrative, and discourse, insights from narratology are investigated. Accordingly, a story is understood as a particular event or a sequence of events situated within a larger narrative, often narrated to convey a specific meaning, ideology, or rhetorical account. The event (or a series of events) inherent in stories often includes various actors or entities that relate to each other in some way or the other (Halverson *et al.* 2011:14). The act of storytelling is humankind's ability to make sense of their experiences, using words and phrases and often solving conflicts that drive and direct the trajectory of story-form (Halverson *et al.* 2011:12). As such, Halverson *et al.* (2011:14) propose that "[t]hese conflicts … play out through the actions of protagonists and antagonists in the narrative".

All stories are directional in time. They move forward from a beginning and end at a certain point in time. The telling of the story through the timeline is referred to as 'narration'. A story unnarrated exists on its own with the possibility of being narrated in a variety of ways (Abbott 2007:39). To a certain extent, a story has no meaning if it is not plotted and narrated. Abbott (2007:40) proposes that, as a story exists separate from its narration and its interpretation, plotting an event in a story and plotting a story in a narrative takes place through the linking of a sequence of events as they are interconnected relationally. The events in a story or the stories in a narrative relate to each other through a trajectory that results in either resolution or reconciliation (Richardson 2005:167; Abbott 2007:43).

Story, plot, and narration are then the three primary components of a narrative and, as a whole, are referred to as 'narrative discourse'. Of these three, Ricoeur (in Abbott 2007:43) suggests that plotting is the creative exposé of story, where the gaps between the stories are artfully opened or closed. The so-called 'gaps' between the stories or events contain a myriad of possibilities that can either be actualised through 'plotting' or left as possibilities (Abbott 2007:40, 50).

Not all narrative discourse, according to Robinson and Hawpe (1986), contains narrative structure. Narrative structure relates specifically to the act of *interpretation*. Through interpretation, the author (and not yet 'narrator') aims to make sense of his experience (Ganzevoort 1998b:3). Sense-making results in understanding or developing an appreciation for specific experiences, albeit unpleasant. This sense of appreciation and insightful comprehension shapes relationships with the self, the other, and the ultimate Other, thereby aspiring toward teleological significance.

Ganzevoort (1998b:3) proposes four distinct features of narrative discourse that are aimed at narrative structure, namely the author, the audience, the purpose, and the story itself.

### 10.4 The author(s)

Every narrative or story within a narrative has an author or collaborating authors. As with a master narrative of religion, the author might be an abstract entity. In the case of a cultural master narrative, a community/ies might be collaborating authors throughout history. A 'narrative' is defined as "a system of stories", or a *collection* of *systematic* stories that relate to each other *thematically*, where the whole is "greater than the sum of its parts" (Halverson *et al.* 2011:1). A master narrative is culturally embedded and transhistorical. This type of narrative has gained the status of 'transhistorical' because a particular culture, community, or group of people reverberated and revered the narrative (or a collection of stories) over time (Halverson *et al.* 2011:14). Halverson *et al.* (2011:15) emphasise that master narratives have the function of creating a sense of coherence and consistency, providing a clear course of action and events that, in turn, inspire people to hope that their desires would be satisfied through the course of action they are inspired to take.

McAdams (2006:118-119) warns against pushing narrative into a coherent role without acknowledging the incoherence inherent in most of the life narratives. It is important to note two influences on understanding narrative and its power accurately: storying and narrative take place within the boundaries of culture, community, and collaboration; due to the complexity of life and living, narrative and storying might contain some form of incoherence; thus, coherence should not necessarily be the main goal of narrating trauma.

Actors take actions and authors make interpretations. Although an actor and an author might be the same person, in story, they embody different roles. The actor engages in actions that relate to the factual events of the story, whereas the author has the freedom to restructure, reframe, and reinterpret facts by the wilful use of fiction, abstraction, and/or imagination. Other characters might also be actors in a story and play a significant role in (re)authoring (Ganzevoort 1998b:2-3).

## 10.5 The audience

The audience, who listens or reads the story, is important in that they legitimise the story as (re)authored and the probability that the authored story will be narrated. The audience, even if only in the author's mind, actively judges the plausibility of the story and gives the impression that the story, eventually narrated, will be morally acceptable, albeit not. Finally, the fact that there *is* always an audience indirectly initiates and ignites the urge of the author to make sense of a story, its events, and how the spaces in between are plotted into a coherent narrative. This may be because an audience might include significant people who are active listeners and concerned about the well-being of the author and actor of the story; because the author might feel the need to gain acceptance from the audience, or because the audience might be imaginary, but nevertheless important figures who are actively included as a significant secondary audience that contributes to the plotting of the story in one way or another. When religion and beliefs are important themes in a narrative, God becomes one of these significant members of the audience (Ganzevoort 1998b:3; Day 1991; Gergen 1994; Ricoeur 1995; Shotter 1993).

## 10.6 The purpose

The purpose of the story or narrative is better understood by using the notion of significance (Pargament 1997), because 'significance' can have both a positive or a negative connotation and is purely a matter of subjective interpretation. Ganzevoort (1998b:3) suggests that the 'significance' of the story can only have two purposes. I suggest that these two purposes are directed respectively to either the private or the public audience of the story. Ganzevoort (1998b:3) refers to the first purpose as 'structure', which aims to support a coherent and significant personal identity. By contrast, the latter notion of purpose refers to finding purpose in context and sustaining social identity. It is suggested that both types of purpose (significance) of story construction are present in all stories but that one would generally dominate and direct the narrative. 'Structure' is the need to maintain a coherent and evocative trajectory in the story, while 'acceptance' determines how an author will construct the actor's role, in order to receive acceptance from the audience. I propose that the audience might be public, which includes both significant others or the other, or private, which may include the Self or the existential Other.

These features dynamically interact to plot the story within a framework with a series of stories, which collaboratively contribute to a central storyline that constitutes the notion of a personal or metanarrative (Ganzevoort 1998b:2-3).

## 10.7 The story: Temporality and spatiality

With specific reference to the processing of trauma, Bridgeman (2007:52) postulates that, in the same manner that fictional narratives are positioned within notions of temporality and spatiality, metanarratives are also subjected to this positioning. Metanarratives comprise a series of stories, that respectively develop in a timeline – past, present, and future – which illuminates the actors' actions and affects the author's (and the audience's) interpretation of the actions or the possible motives behind the actions.

Similarly, the movement and positioning of the actors in different spaces and settings localise and contextualise their actions, thereby providing insight into possible motives. The temporality and spatiality of the actual events of each story within the narrative prevent both antagonist and protagonist from intervening in factual events, irrelevant of time or space. The result is that, although the author cannot alter actual events, he can reframe, reconstruct, or reinterpret these events in both space and time, in order to construct a trajectory of meaning that is in line with the central storyline of the narrative, aimed at sustaining structure and acceptance (the two ultimate purposes of narrative).

Temporality in narrative differentiates between 'story', which generally relates to the sequence of events (the time in which the story is set), and 'discourse' as the presentation of these events through semantics (or the telling of the story). Relating these temporalities with each other, either through authoring or reading, results in the significance of the story set against the background of the metanarrative. Depending on how temporality is artfully used in storying, it will generally result in the experience of either suspense, curiosity, or surprise (Sternberg 2003:326):

> Suspense arises from the gap between what we have been told so far and what we anticipate lies ahead. Curiosity arises from the gap between what we have been told of the past and what else we imagine might have happened. Surprise arises when a twist in the order of narrative conceals from us an event which is subsequently revealed. (Bridgeman 2007:54)

The spatiality of narrative refers to how objects/subjects are linked with locations or contexts and assist with the movements of these objects or subjects in the narrative world. 'Movement', in this instance, indicates not only physicality, but also how actors inhabit spaces in the story psychologically and socially (Bridgeman 2007:55), indicating the positioning of the actor firmly in the reality of a certain event – spaces that cannot be escaped, but need to be 'faced', so to speak. In narrative, space or location often gains prominence through its association with an event (Bridgeman 2007:56). Space without the aspect of temporality and the actors that occupy that space remains simply an empty space. Where temporality is linked with memory (past) and anticipation (future), spatiality relates to the acceptance of the reality of the event and the undeniable space which that story occupies within the metanarrative.

Both time and space, therefore, are integral to the shaping of the plot and the structuring of stories within the narrative and influence the inherent perspective of the metanarrative (Bridgeman 2007:55).

### 10.8 Narrative and the economy of Trinity

The premise of this chapter is that a resilient religion consists of a theology of resilience that encompasses a set of narratives with a religious theme. This theme provides the foundation for metanarratives to successfully fill the spaces between the incoherent stories, in order to gain meaning and purpose from it. The extent to which a person can continuously construct and reconstruct a changing, vulnerable, and frail narrative, in line with the meaning contained in the relatively stable and coherent master narrative of a resilient religion, determines his ability to be resilient in the face of trauma and turbulence, and encompasses the power inherent in a theology of resilience.

As such, trauma is depicted considering its effect on not only narrative but also identity and how a resilient religion, which similarly defines the conceptualisation of narrative and identity, can be used to process the impact of trauma and reframe the story of the trauma into the story of my trauma, while keeping the integrity of the metanarrative intact. By 'integrity' is meant specifically that the metanarrative remains a source of interpretation, purpose, motivation, and imagination, which sustains a sense of personhood and dignity, as it is experienced through the 'good' in both space and time.

Swain's (2011) understanding of the economic Trinity is used to define the thematic contours of the master narrative of religion. Specific narrative elements are suggested to be used in reframing the story of trauma into the metanarrative, by making it the story of my trauma. The economic Trinity, which represents the triune God's acts of salvation in creation, is commonly referred to, in trinitarian language, as 'Creator', 'Redeemer', and 'Sustainer' (Swain 2011:22), although Swain (2011:22) opts for the terms Earth-maker, Pain-bearer and Life-giver. These images are chosen to contour the framework for the argument of reframing the story of trauma into the metanarrative by way of the master narrative, because they depict the triune God as dynamically relating to creation.

A master narrative framed within the image of an economic trinity should engage the author in remembering, understanding, and making a choice for love and life. It is then proposed that the narrative elements, remembering and reading, should be employed during the first movement of 'earth-making', which entails the economy of creating. The narrative elements of authoring, reframing, and plotting should occur during the second movement of 'pain-bearing' with the economy of redemption. These narrative elements pave the way for the third movement of 'life-giving', supported through the economy of sustenance and proclaimed through the narrative elements of narration.

## 10.9   Earth-making and reading

### 10.9.1 The economy of creating

Swain (2011:41) refers to the movement of earth-making as a creation narrative that grounds all human narratives in relationship with God, others, and the creation as a whole. She suggests that the creation narrative is central to the religious identity narrative. As such, this image is used in this section to refer to those instances of being human in a world of suffering and adversity, grounding who we are and positioning our identity and personhood in the great narrative of the Creator (Swain 2011:36).

It is proposed that a theology of resilience uses the economy of creating to reposition the post-trauma fragile identity into the trinitarian master narrative of identity, in order to regain a sense of stability, coherence, and security. Ganzevoort (1998:10) supports the use of this, suggesting that not only identity development, adjustment, and interaction with coping should be understood in the narrative framework, but also how it relates to a so-called religious identity. He suggests that identity development contains the continuous shaping and reshaping – constructing and reconstructing – of different life stories that represent lived experiences and the meaning inherently contained within. Identity, its development, and the possibility for reconstruction should, therefore, be understood as a process and not an entity, where the process is regarded as dynamic, fluid, and dependent on specific contexts and experiences in creating meaning.

Trauma and crisis affect a person's meaning-making structure and identity (Ganzevoort 1994); 'coping' and 'identity' are thus proposed to be mutually dependent processes that correlate positively with one another. The Eriksonian (Erikson 1968) emphasis on the successful resolution of crisis before transitioning to the next stage of development is a case in point: identity development/growth is only possible through successfully coping with each crisis. Similarly, religious narratives and identity narratives inform how the self and its position and role in the world are understood (Ganzevoort 1998b:9), often referred to as a 'religious' identity. Religious orientations, beliefs, and convictions influence not only our ability to cope successfully with crises and trauma, but also the identity narratives that are often the result of such appraisal and coping. The successful development of a coherent and meaningful religious identity might result in the utilisation of better coping mechanisms. This might then become a marker for a theory on resilient religion or theology of resilience.

It should be clear by now that the theology of identity is not necessarily about construction *per se*, as much has been said regarding this process. It has been confirmed that the content of the narrative that guides identity construction and maintenance often relates to religious aspects. However, a theology of identity and relation is about the act of seeking a place (space) to (re)position identity; this space is bound to consist not as much of material matter, as of material and divine persons – community. A theology of identity and relation is the philosophy of creation and reconciliation; it is about the will to seek, find and affirm, as well as realise that space, in which this identity will be affirmed, is filled with the very being of the triune God, the God that *is*, and continues to *be*, through relationship (Swain 2011:44). A person becomes attentively aware that finding one's identity in this space of love implies that, as God continues to create, renew, and reconcile, our identities will continuously be created, renewed, and reconciled.

Earth-making (Swain 2011:44), however, implies spatiality and the physicality of the human being, purposefully created to occupy a certain space. Herein lies our identity, as human beings, as the creation of God, embody identity in God, through the breath of God that enlivened and 'spirited' this body (Swain 2011:46). The story of Creation in Genesis places created human beings in relation to both God, the created earth, and the created 'other',[4] but one in their common divine make-up (master narrative) (Swain 2011:40-51).

A second proposal for a theology of resilience that relates to the economy of creating is the notion of 'personhood'. Personhood, which implies identity and relationality, indicates that "each individual is both particular and inclusive of all that is" (Scarsella 2018:271). Scarsella confirms that persons are organised in relation, so that, without it, we do not exist. As such, when trauma attacks and destroys human relationships, it attacks and destroys the person: "There is, then, no separation between the disintegration of relationships and the disintegration of personhood" (Scarsella 2018:271). Consequently, the reframing, repositioning, and reconstructing of identity must happen in, and through spaces of relation, where the spirits of the created meet.

A theology of resilience, therefore, employs the notion that identity is relation; to be is to relate and to relate is to become. Resilience lies in the discovery that the mutual indwelling of individual identities through the fact that all were created in the *imago Dei* safeguards our identities in this specific relationality. When the traumatised experience disintegration and a loss of personhood and belonging, uncertain of who can be trusted, they can gain comfort in the mere fact that the community of believers – who do not only collectively hold onto what they know about God, and God's promise, but also hold on to what they know about human beings as God's creation and their place and purpose in this world – can confirm

---

[4] Comfort can be found in the fact that God created all separate entities to be and live in both unity and particularity. Creations are unique in their personal make-up (metanarrative).

through the sharing of historical narratives that God can ultimately be trusted.

### 10.9.2 Reading and remembering

For the traumatised person, to make use of a theology of resilience that employs the economy of creating, the story of trauma should be viewed within the story of her identity through *imago Dei* and the mutual indwelling of resulting relationality. To enable this, memory and remembering should actively be engaged.

Remembering, however, is a twofold activity, namely remembering rightly and employing sacred memories. Remembering the religious metanarratives that confirm our teleology will not have any power when the story of my trauma is also not remembered rightly. The activity will be meaningless. Remembering the traumatic event is painful, because it confirms the reality of the atrocities experienced. Volf (2006:56), however, powerfully states that remembering is imperative to reconstruct the story and plot it successfully. However, even more important is remembering rightly.

Memory is often distorted by especially negative, emotional experiences and influenced by past experiences and desires for the future. To remember rightly, according to Volf (2006:56), means to be honest about exactly what has happened. Remembering truthfully and correctly is the only path to reconciliation and experiencing any sense of healing. According to Volf (2006:76), healing is only possible when meaning can be attributed to memories, albeit painful memories. Truthfulness in remembering exposes the injustices of the trauma experienced and, in so doing, liberates the sufferer of trauma from isolation due to shame (Schreiter 1992:34-37; Volf 2006:29; Van Ommen 2019:214).

To redeem memory, engagement with the temporality and spatiality of the event becomes crucial. When a person moves with the story in time and positions the characters (including himself as an actor) firmly in the reality of the traumatic story, different aspects of character and personality emerge, creating a sense of drama, or in the case of a traumatic story, a sense of tragedy. During the experience of tragedy, a person remembers the intricacies of the event(s) more clearly (Schreider 1998:19). Memory is closely connected with emotion. Albeit painful and uncomfortable, instead of relapsing in the fleeing mode of denying these memories to escape the painful emotions, the event is fully faced.

The position of a reader can be taken to facilitate the process of remembering in a narratological manner. Hermans (20221:27) beautifully illustrates how text, independent of speech and separated by the author's intention, provides the ideal space for remembering, re-experiencing, reconstructing/reframing, and reinterpretation, as "[t]he text is the very place where the author appears" (Ricoeur 1995:109), "but the text is also distancing itself from the author" (Hermans 2022a:27). Like Bridgeman's (2007:54) proposal that the temporality between the story and discourse has an impact on the reader's interpretation, it is proposed that the sufferer of trauma, during this first phase, moves between being the reader and being the author in remembering, re-experiencing, and interpreting in a cyclic mode. In the processing of a traumatic event and, therefore, in the reconstruction of the story, a person continuously moves between varying roles: the person is, first, the actor who experienced the event; and in remembering (an aspect of temporality) the person 'reads', 'interprets' and 'authors' the story in small segments.

Reading, therefore, entails a repositioning: from being the actor who experiences to becoming the reader who observes and listens, and when ready, slowly starts to reauthor as meaning is attached to the experience. The latter part of the former statement is important, in this instance: moving from reading to interpretation to authoring is a spatial move. To 'read' means to remove oneself spatially from the locality/reality of the event. This might be very important to maintain a sense of safety and dissociate temporally from the emotional impact of memories. Equally important, however, is to use the spatial distance for reflective interpretation as a 'figurative' outsider.

The temporality of narrative and reading also allows the 'reader' to move between the memories of the traumatic event and back (or to) the sacred memories of the Christian narrative, which can continuously remind the reader (and the sufferer) of God's love, acceptance, and presence during the reliving of the suffering story. Moving forth between the memory of the painful event and the sacred memory of the master narrative of the triune God positions the reader firmly in the possibility that memories, often borrowed, can collide to create possibilities for reframing the story in the meta-narrative.

Van Ommen (2019:210-211) explains the importance of *sacred memory* in processing a traumatic event. It is proposed that sacred memory is the essence of religion and the master narrative through which relations with God, others, and self are maintained. Therefore, it becomes an important activity in affirming identity. Sacred memory addresses the narrative purpose of the structure, by drawing people into the story and the purpose of creation; it remembers the main actor and creator, God, who gives purpose. It affirms human worth through the suffering of Christ, and it gives hope by eschatologically looking to the future. It addresses the narrative purpose of acceptance, in always being a collective activity. The community are the guardians of sacred memory and live out the Christian imperative of sharing and proclaiming its functionality and inviting all into a community of belonging: "When the memories are void of meaning, we live in the hope that our identity is ultimately not defined by the wrongs we have suffered, but by our relationship with God" (Van Ommen 2019:211).

Remembering entails not only looking back, but also looking forward while considering the painful memories. Sacred memories remind us that, although we might be the actor in several stories that contribute to our metanarrative, God remains the main actor of the master narrative through which our metanarratives are formed and framed.

To move between these two types of memories (the memory of what happened to me and the memory of what happened for me), embodying the safe position of a reader allows a person to slowly come to an acceptance of what was, what is, but also what can be. Hermans (2022b:43) refers to this activity as the first task of dealing with a sense of tragedy:

> The first task is the confirmation of the pathos of not knowing, not being able to act and not feeling happy: "I don't know why, I can't change it, I feel unhappy" (Ricoeur 2007:69). If this suffering is innocent, then we must first affirm this innocence. If we are guilty of this suffering, we must first confess guilt.

Acceptance might, therefore, mean ultimately accepting our position of not knowing – and never being able to know – the reason for experiencing this tragedy in the first place (2022b:43). Acceptance of the reality of the event is one of the biggest obstacles that need to be faced during the aftermath of experiencing a traumatic event and should be the aim of this phase of 'owning the story of my trauma'. However, acceptance cannot be attained in the void of possibility. Remembering truthfully and remembering in the framework of the Sacred Memory assists a person in anticipating possibility because of what the historical master narrative promises every believer.

## 10.10   Pain-bearing and reauthoring

### 10.10.1        The economy of redemption

A theology of resilience is paradoxically grounded in the theology of suffering. The theology of suffering recognises that any discourse on suffering cannot remove the suffering person from the cause of the suffering so as to identify with righteousness that might justify suffering itself. Instead, a theology of suffering acknowledges that, although God does not require suffering to attain righteousness, God will remain with the sufferer through the suffering (Swain 2011:93). This is a call to the ministry of presence in the theology of suffering which directs us towards solidarity through expression. A ministry of presence aims to position trauma in the presence of God and God's authority through the language of suffering (Swain 2011:96).

It is suggested (Soelle 1975:70) that the language of suffering travels along three movements, namely muteness, lamentation, and change. A theology of resilience reconceptualises these movements as silence, weeping, and transfiguration, as in each lies a moment of resilience.

The state of *silence* and the act of being silent are favoured in a theology of resilience because of the nature of trauma to linger in the timeless space of silence. There is a qualitative difference between being silent and being mute. Being mute often indicates the inability to produce speech or the unwillingness to speak in an act of defeat. Silence, on the other hand, is the absence of sound or speech, but not of activity. Where muteness might indicate *inability*, silence and choosing to be silent often hide the activity's ability in silence. Retreating to silence is to enter a space of limbo, often to protect the integrity of the self. Silence is, therefore, not without function and purpose.

> Silence is the common denominator found among all victims, signifying a state of survival functioning where words fail and verbal recollections may have destroyed a fragile ego. Silence in response to massive trauma constitutes also a self-protective, self-imposed firewall to avoid total psychic fragmentation (Ritter 2014:180).

Ritter (2014:180) also states that, in silence, especially in the direct aftermath of trauma, connection and self-protection can be managed. Silence may indicate a wilful dissociation, but at times, such temporary dissociation with the expression of memory and pain is needed to calm the body and the mind. Only in silence can the noise of the world and that which tends to overwhelm be pushed aside. Swain (2011:97) reminds us that solidarity can also be experienced in silence when the unbearable becomes bearable together: "Presence, therefore, is not to be negated, even if it appears inactive.". Presence can also indicate the presence of the divine, of the Spirit, or perhaps the presence of the distant self-mindfulness of the self.

Silence, however, is not presumed to be an eternal state. Silence should move into a state of expression. After quietly waiting on answers, understanding and weeping may follow as a way of attaining that which could not be attained during silence. During weeping, or through biblical language, *lamenting*, the rawness of our pain, experiences of injustice, loss, and unfairness are expressed in the presence of others and the Divine, without any sense of shame, unfiltered and authentic. Swain (2011:97) refers to the presence in suffering and the language of suffering as the 'pain-bearing' phase, which entails expressing one's pain. Expressing pain is built on the idea of embracing one's vulnerability – the very vulnerability that puts one at risk for being pained. Too often, people respond to trauma and suffering by appearing to be invulnerable, which often worsens the situation and destabilises the integrity of personhood even further. The expression of suffering is, therefore, geared towards sustaining the integrity of the self, positioning oneself, one's body, mind and spirit in the time and space of God's promise, God's presence, and, ultimately, God's deliverance. This important proclamation prevents one from depersonalising or dissociating with one's being and reality, even though the desire to do so might be intense (Swain 2011:130; Van Ommen 2019:208). The language of suffering should, however, not remain and linger within and between the movement of silence and weeping; it should proceed to travel to the vision of change and transfiguration.

*Transfiguration* expresses much more than the word 'change'. It is a change of figure, beyond, over, 'trans' the current reality and even what was previously thought possible. It is a vision that is cemented in the Christian hope built on the transfiguration of the body of Christ from crucifixion to resurrection. Transfiguration points to an exalted position, a glorified appearance, liberated from the slavery of fear and the yoke of death.

## 10.10.2       Redeemed through lament

An economy of redemption finds its power in the theological act of lament. Lament also becomes an important aspect of a theology of resilience. Because suffering is so often a theme of the Bible, lamenting is offered as a specific spiritual practice for relating to the pain caused by the suffering, but also to relate to God – to run to God and not away from God – in expressing feelings of despair, disappointment, shame, and humiliation. Lamenting is offered as a prayer, which suggests that grievances, protests, and anger are expressed while acknowledging the One in whose presence these are expressed. Therefore, lament as a spiritual practice acknowledges the power and majesty of God as the only one who can bring forth life, who can renew and redeem. It is the final source of hope and the greatest act of vulnerability by humankind (Van Deusen Hunsinger 2015:101). According to Van Deusen Hunsinger (2015:100), "[l]ament[ing] means directing one's anguish toward God" in desperation and intense longing for deliverance, but nevertheless refusing to lose hope (Van Deusen Hunsinger 2015:99).

Hermans (2022b:43) includes the act of lament as an important task of the sufferer to deal with the experience of tragedy – the absence of happiness and the good/God:

> The lament is [,] on the one hand[,] an expression of the sorrow and emptiness that are unbearable and without end. On the other hand, it expresses the impatience of the hope of happiness that "comes", the life that fulfils (Ricoeur 2007:70).

Lamenting is, therefore, an act of sustenance. It not only asks for deliverance, but in the act itself, it also makes the unbearable bearable, and it makes relation possible by choosing not to avoid the experience of suffering and pain. It is an act that refuses to isolate and accept total and final destruction. Lamenting is powerful because the believer lays his pain, sorrow, and suffering at the feet of the all-powerful, thereby drawing from the life-giving energy found in God. Lamenting affirms the righteous and gracious nature of God and relinquishes all desires for revenge to the ultimate and only Judge (Van Deusen Hunsinger 2015:106-107). Lamenting is a crucial practice of faith that is, in itself, an element of a theology of resilience.

### 10.10.3       Accepting redemption: Reframing

In a two-part publication, 'Religious coping reconsidered, I', Ganzevoort (1998a:261) illuminates the intricacies related to coping with both crisis and trauma, and how the notion of religious coping adds a new dimension to our understanding of the power of narrative to impart resilience against the impact of both crisis and trauma.

Coping is defined as ways used by individuals in distress to deal with, make sense of, or find meaning in the difficulties they experience at that particular point in time (Ganzevoort 1998a:261; Pargament 1997). Crisis or trauma is experienced as an event (story) within a pre-existing personal narrative, within a particular historical perspective and paradigm that developed from previous experiences and the resulting interpretations (meaning-making) of these experiences (Ganzevoort 1998a:10). This presupposes that the author of the personal narrative will attempt to interpret the story of trauma or crisis to position it somewhere of significance, within the personal narrative. If a person cannot position this specific story successfully into the existing personal narrative (because no significant meaning could be gained from the story, or the story does not 'fit with the main plot of the narrative'), an existential crisis (or trauma) might be experienced. Coping theories refer to the first as 'event appraisal', and to the latter as 'resource appraisal' (Ganzevoort 1998a:11). In essence, this means that 'coping' is always aimed at preserving the personal coherent, narrative of meaning.

Several coping strategies can be employed to preserve the coherence and meaning of a personal narrative by reconsidering the position of the threatening story or event in the greater metanarrative. Reconsideration or reappraisal generally consists of either two strategies: changing the facts of the threatening story or altering the meaning of the threatening story regarding the greater meaning of the metanarrative. If any of these strategies is successful, successful coping occurs (Ganzevoort 1998a:11).

It is thus argued that the traumatised person engages in coping strategies, or a theology of resilience, by altering the meaning of the threatening story through the act of *reframing*. The notion of reframing

> means to change the conceptual and or emotional setting or viewpoint in relation to which a situation is experienced and to place in another frame which fits the 'facts' of the same concrete situation equally well or even better, and thereby changes its entire being (Capps 1990:17).

The greatest challenge of the act of reframing, and in assisting a person in reframing, is to do away with preconceived notions of 'one-size-fits-all' types of solutions. Or perhaps doing justice to this statement would be to rather acknowledge the power of society and culture to engrain within us the idea of certain perspectives and approaches being more acceptable and appropriate than others. Consequently, conformity to these perspectives and approaches are required in exchange for a sense of belonging, acceptance, and even a sense of dignity: "Reframing challenges the assumption that the solution being employed is the solution, or would be the solution if only it could be performed better. ... [R]eframing challenges the idea that the perceived solution is appropriate" (Capps 1990:18).

Reframing can take place in several ways, one of which the therapist or caregiver might suggest alternative possibilities of viewing an event or a story. However, this chapter, in arguing for a theology of resilience, proposes using the notion of reframing, by suggesting that reframing occurs specifically within the framework of specific theological themes: a theology of identity and relationality; a theology of suffering and lamenting, and a theology of hope and reconciliation. It is proposed that reframing events, stories, and narratives within the wider framework of a theology of resilience (which contains specific theological themes) provides the landscape for successfully plotting the story of trauma into the metanarrative.

Shame, often the result of experiencing trauma, is a specific issue of focus during the act of reframing. Shame, as an intensely negative affect or feeling, can only be resisted, challenged, and opposed from the perspective of self-empathy. Self-empathy is the only route/path to regaining any sense of dignity (the opposite of shame). By way of self-empathy, shame can become *accessible* rather than being intrusive, paralysing, and isolating (Sherman 2014:231). Accessing feelings of shame, observing these feelings whilst seeing oneself as an external character who experiences the event, places the shame within context and perspective, and confronts the person with questions on the justification of this shame. Placing the shame in a specific context or framework might help the person justify these feelings and reconcile them with a clear understanding of what is hoped for.

Similar to the previous suggestion, reframing the story of trauma in the framework of biblical figures and their stories of trauma might be a catalyst for creating self-empathy. The importance of self-empathy lies in its combative power against feelings of shame and the possibility of regaining a sense of dignity. Reframing the story of trauma in the wider story of trauma not only creates self-empathy, but also relates the what Nathanson (1994:304) refers to as 'shame-related scripts'. He defines 'script' as an integrated resource centre that stores all previous responses to shame-related experiences. When the feeling of shame is experienced on an *emotional* level, this resource centre is accessed to respond to this emotion. By default, many choose to respond with previously used scripts, as they are most accessible to the mind. However, these scripts can also perpetuate further experiences of shame. In this instance, real power lies not in the memory, but in the script (Nathanson 1994:304). I propose that this 'script' that sustains feelings of shame can be replaced with the scripts in the stories of the Bible. To read and re-read those narratives, to read the response of the actors of the story and the actions of God amidst these stories can replace the self-negating, shame-perpetuating scripts of the sufferer. Reframing is also closely related with remembering and is inherently dependent thereon.

A theology of resilience proposes then to reframe not only the story of trauma into the ultimate story of resurrection after crucifixion, but also the intense feeling of shame into the eschatological story of the final victory and reclaiming human dignity in the definitive goodness of God. As such, the third task of dealing with a sense of tragedy offers the possibility of separating "the reasons for believing in God from the reasons for the tragedy" (Hermans 2022b:43) as a reframing tool for distinguishing between our teleological existence and immanent earthly experience.

Narratives with such specific theological themes may provide a perspective in which experiences related to that theme might be positioned and *through which* meaning can be constructed that provides a sense of coherence and purpose (Schreider 1998:19) amidst a life story filled with complexity and incoherence. Within a religious community, these memories are commemorated, processed, understood, and finally reframed into a metanarrative of meaning, sense of dignity, and purpose.

## 10.11   Life-giving through authoring and narrating

### 10.11.1      The economy of sustaining

A resurrection mentality neither denies nor negates death but, rather, affirms that which is life-giving beyond death, a resurrection life where one, at least in the case of Jesus in the Gospels, still bears the scars of death but lives with them. This can be as profound as experiencing the presence of God and a transformational self and as simple as the life-giving things one needs to do to live in the face of a disaster in the midst of a community of care (Swain 2011:146).

A theology of suffering that encourages expression through the practice of lament and remembrance of the narratives of slavery and liberation, suffering and deliverance, crucifixion and resurrection is directed at the sustenance of hope. Christian hope lies in the character of the triune God: God the Creator who gives and continuously renews; Jesus Christ the Redeemer who shows grace and forgiveness, and the Holy Spirit who empowers and sustains. The Bible and its stories are largely a narrative of hope that testifies to God's ever-lasting presence during moments of hopelessness. The crux of this master narrative is that, through God's grace, Jesus' resurrection, and the Spirit's power to restore, the promise of a renewed life is immanent during our experiences of suffering (Van Deusen Hunsinger 2015:100).

Swain's third and final moment of her pastoral model is referred to as 'life-giving' with the activity of 'transforming'. Theologically, life-giving refers to the narrative plot of resurrection – coming back from the dead – emphasising the notion of life beyond death. For the sufferer, this narrative plot is one of hope. Hope lies in the fact that the pain, the loss, or the death is neither denied nor negated, but that there is life beyond death, albeit a life that testifies living with the irreplicable scars (Swain 2011:146). True hope acknowledges the reality of the matter, but it refuses to accept defeat and holds on to the promise that just as Jesus was resurrected, so will I. God gave the promise, Jesus lived the promise, and the Spirit continuously gives hope to hold onto the promise.

Louw (2013:13-14) argues that hope is about trust and confidence in the ontological reality that believers are transformed, restored, and renewed through the Spirit in Christ. Hope is to claim our pneumatic reality and being in Christ, to set our identity in the character of God, thereby renewing our dignity through the ultimate Source of goodness, kindness, and love.

Where hope is born, space is created for the Spirit to present the sufferer with life-giving and transformative moments. In those moments, the community of faith not only laments with the sufferer, but also listens to, and with the sufferer for visions of life and renewal. This space is not necessarily a physical space, but a space created by the community of believers – in community – where God is experienced as present, immanent, and transcendent, "with them, at times within them, and within the hands and hearts of the community" (Swain 2011:179-180).

Moreover, a theology of hope affirms the character of God in the possibility of reconciliation, even amidst pain and suffering Without hope, the idea of reconciliation cannot be fathomed. Reconciliation is not to be equated with forgiveness. Where forgiveness implies the survivor/victim to allow the story of God (and not the story of trauma) to shape his/her identity, reconciliation is initiated by God in a life-giving relationship as an act of grace to restore the sufferer's sense of dignity (Van Ommen 2019:214). God initiates reconciliation, whereas the victim initiates forgiveness.

Reconciliation, as an important religious resource (Wulf 2019:148), asks of the sufferer, the believer, to discard arguments that cannot be answered in this finite life. As such, the final task of dealing with a sense of tragedy is to "let go of the wound caused by the loss and emptiness" (Hermans 2022b:43), and reconcile the past, the present and the future with the character of God, as it is firmly grounded in eschatological hope. In a theology of hope and reconciliation, the focus is on the victim, while the aim is to restore a sense of dignity. A theology of resilience entails the ability to reconcile the story of pain and suffering with the Christian theme of hope and into God's larger narrative that creates possibilities. Opportunities for reauthoring the story of trauma lie in these possibilities.

### 10.11.2    Plotting

Through the narrative act of plotting, events are linked in a trajectory that results in the teleological resolution of the story. To plot events in a story and/or several stories in a narrative is to ultimately add meaning to the storyline from which purpose, possibilities and imaginations for the future are derived. Plotting makes a story, in fact, a *story*, and not simply raw material haphazardly connected. It transforms a story into a coherent, consistent set of trajectories that result in feelings of disclosure and resolution (Abbott 2007:43, 50).

As such, authoring, reading, deconstructing, lamenting, and reframing prepared the groundwork for plotting. In the absence of the former activities, plotting might not be possible. The story remains 'raw material', void of meaning, voided of possibilities, and experienced as a heavy yoke, with its power manifested through self-destructive language and behaviour.

Plotting entails bringing time and space together. Objects and characters have now been moved around in a changing landscape, between the past, the present, and the future (Bridgeman 2007:55). It entails that all dissociation with the landscape, time and space have now been discarded and that the protagonist (the actor/survivor) positions herself (physically, psychologically, socially, and spiritually) firmly in that space and time between events or stories. Through plotting, the author claims her position in the story, both in the present – here and now – and in the future. This entails acceptance of the temporality of spatiality and that positioning is a dynamic, active, and changing process. Comfort is found in claiming a sense of agency and realising that the author can position and reposition her-/himself as the actor or actress. This entails a conversion of paradigm and perspective to such an extent that subjective attitudes and emotions are viewed from different angles – a bird's eye view has now been obtained, which enables the structuring and restructuring of different components and characters of the events. A different perspective might imply a different landscape altogether (Bridgeman 2007:56).

In this instance, the traumatised person's perspective of the story and larger narrative is important in creating the plot (closing the gaps between the stories within the narrative). The plot will become a device (or vice) for creating constructive meaning (as a form of resilience), in order to sustain the preferred narrative filled with hope. Hope, a concept of temporality, enables the creation of a future and the motivation to sustain this narrative into the future. The positioning of the story of trauma is now ready to be plotted in the master narrative of religion where it is no longer the story of any trauma, but becomes the story of *my* trauma, just as the story of Jesus' trauma collectively became the story of our own trauma. This story will be ready and accessible to retell, to grieve, to lament on, but also to celebrate the victory attained. Ownership is now in the making.

### 10.11.3     Reauthoring

A theology of resilience that consists of hope and a spirituality of reconciliation is the driving force behind the reauthoring of the metanarrative. The story of trauma has already been viewed in the framework of the metanarrative, identity has been repositioned, and the meaning behind the trauma, with its accompanying feelings of shame, has been reframed in the ultimate story of trauma: the crucifixion that climaxed ultimately into resurrection. The gaps between the story of the trauma and the stories of the metanarrative have been filled by plotting and repositioning characters and events that sustain a coherent sense of meaning. The scene has been set for reauthoring the metanarrative into an ultimate resource for meaning making and rediscovering the good.

The influence of the community in the development and sustenance of the reauthored metanarrative cannot be disregarded. Because traumatic experiences put the individual at risk of isolation and remaining silent, the power of communities of faith to ignite and sustain a newly found sense of resilience cannot be undervalued. Such a community might just be the foundation upon which the bonds of silence and shame regarding the traumatic story are broken, as they provide a haven for the traumatised to position their story within the larger framework of the story of God with His people (Wurmser 2012:222; Wulf 2019:133).

Positive, affirming experiences with people from similar faith traditions are directly linked with a positive view of God (Wulf 2019:143). The community thus becomes the conveyors of God's image of love, grace, unconditional positive regard, and acceptance. Religious institutions provide a context filled with spiritual practices such as prayer, ritual, and worship wherein and through which individuals may transcend their crisis, trauma or otherwise stressful experiences through connecting with a Higher Being and a community who shares experiences of connecting to the transcendent Other. Such experiences offer fertile grounds for both psychological and spiritual growth (Balswick *et al.* 2016:328-329).

It is proposed that being part of a community that authentically engages in activities of empowerment, that has an attitude of enduring grace, and that is willing to foster relationships of intimacy genuinely provides a context for especially the 'wounded' to nurture a sense of the reciprocating self *(*Balswick *et al.* 2016:56-57). These qualities present the main themes of the master narrative of the community of faith, enabling an individual to transform life-limiting themes of the metanarrative into life-giving themes that may promote reauthoring.

These life-giving narrative elements are, in turn, sustained by the semantic imperatives related to the use of language in the cognition of the author through the developed image schemata. Through the meaning people attribute to the language they employ, realities are created and sustained, identities are described, experiences are labelled, and certain events are highlighted, while others are subdued (Freedman & Combs 2002:27-29). Language and its use create the framework in which meaning is constructed through, and to experiences (Demasure & Müller 2006:414). This framework can inhibit or aid a person's ability to recognise various possibilities of reauthoring the metanarrative. To renew language and reframe stories more positively requires intense cognitive effort and a decision to do so.

The notion of 'power' inherent in the use and *user* (for example, agency) of language are, therefore, important. Demasure and Müller (2006:414) confirm that relations of power are channelled through the performative and enabling characteristics of language (Loubser 2010:84). The function of power through language, according to Foucault (1973:79), is to reveal those subtle instances that communicate people's position in society and their relationships with the other (also referred to as their *facticity*), so as to make living and surviving in society possible (Loubser 2010:50). The language of trauma and experiences related to trauma will innately have power over the psychological function of the victim (survivor?). However, how the language of the victim/survivor/author/narrator determines the relationship of power that the other/the perpetrator/the secret/silence hold over the victim/survivor/author/narrator is not as apparent (Demasure & Müller 2006:413).

In the previous paragraph, various possibilities, in reference to the person who experienced trauma, are deliberately offered per illustration of the power of language. Take, for instance, how a person is referred to who has experienced trauma. If the person is a *victim*, he remains the object of pity, helpless, and forever broken, at the mercy of therapy or other health facilities that might provide a solution. If the person is a *survivor*, she becomes a person of resilience, fight, courage, and determination. If the person is the *author* of the story of trauma, he is in total control of the future possibilities. The way he tells *his* story will determine the authoring of the metanarrative and, consequently, the future possibilities that this metanarrative can provide for personal growth or regression. Similarly, if the person becomes a narrator, she is liberated from the power of silencing that the trauma held over her.

Language, therefore, creates not only realities, but also possibilities. Adversely, language can keep one forever captive in the aftermath of trauma on a subconscious level. Reframing the story of trauma into the metanarrative means that the metanarrative should be reauthored so that coherent meaning can be maintained. An authentic, supportive community can remind the author of the master narratives in which our own are framed. At the same time, conscious employment of a language of possibilities sustains a coherent frame of meaning, spatially positioned in reconciliation and temporally positioned in hope.

### 10.11.4          Narrating

To narrate the reframed story and the reauthored metanarrative is the final step in embedding the meaning attached to the story of trauma firmly into a metanarrative that can accommodate such. When narration occurs, the metanarrative has already undergone a few important spatial and temporal changes to accommodate the story of trauma successfully.

During narration, language is purposively used with the primary aim of reclaiming a sense of value, dignity, and worthiness. Narration is an act of advocacy. The authentic, supportive community is both an actor in the story's narration and an observer of the meaning of the narration. They legitimise the injustices experienced and reaffirm a person's value and dignity in God's master narrative of unconditional love, grace, and victory, providing the narrative ingredients for reconstituting meaning (Wurmser 2012:222; Wulf 2019:133). They provide the narrator with the courage to speak up against the injustices experienced, and they celebrate with the narrator the victory that has been attained through reframing, reauthoring and eventually openly and without shame retelling the story.

Dignity is the antithesis to shame. All human beings need a sense of dignity to flourish and develop in life. Dignity is regained through intimacy, where others confirm one's worth. The Master Narrative of Christianity provides such a space, community, and opportunities for intimacy where our collective dignity is confirmed by the resurrection of Christ as a result of God's relentless love for creation and God's belief in our ultimate goodness. Narrating the story of trauma in light of how the metanarrative was reauthored in front of an audience is then to actively reclaim dignity as the creation of God.

Narrating the story of trauma and how it resulted in the reauthoring of the metanarrative so as to accommodate a plot, a climax of victory in and through Christ, symbolises that ownership of the story has been taken. The story of the trauma becomes the story of my trauma as soon as it is successfully reframed into the metanarrative and when the reauthored metanarrative is retold, proclaimed, and owned.

Scarsella (2018:258) suggests using a theology that "remembers and narrates crucifixion as traumatic" to create a space for narrating stories of trauma so that the devastation thereof can be acknowledged alongside the possibility of recreation or reconstruction:

> Precisely because Christian theology is itself a process of giv-
> ing voice to what has been traumatically silenced, theology can

draw individuals and communities of faith who engage it into
that process in a way that supports such individuals and communities in bringing their own silenced trauma to voice and
pursuing processes of remaking after trauma.

Narration then is not only an act of proclaiming and claiming continuous
remaking. In the telling and retelling of the same story, different meanings
are discovered, and the metanarrative is continuously adapted to accommodate a new set of meanings. Schreider (1998:19) confirms that retelling
is aimed at gaining new perspective and not changing the story as such.

Narrating the story transforms its spatiality from the past to the present, which confirms the reality that the story is now a part of us. Narrating
and vocalising the story, however, means that claiming this story as part
of the metanarrative is now done without shame. In fact, claiming ownership of the story communicates a newly found sense of dignity borne
within the deepest hour of pain. A dignity that is based not only on the
value inherent in all creation of God, but also on the fact that victory was
attained through the story of crucifixion, which resulted in resurrection.
Dignity through resurrection.

Narrating *towards* dignity is the ultimate act of resilience to break
the silence that holds the power of shame intact.


## 10.12    A theology of resilience

A theology of resilience supports the ability of a victim of trauma to survive his/her story in several ways, by taking ownership of the story of *my*
trauma through reframing, reauthoring, plotting, and narrating. A theology
of resilience suggests that these narratological activities happen within the
framework of the economy of the Trinity, creating the narrative space in
which the story of the trauma can be viewed from the triune God's acts of
salvation in creation. Through the economy of creating, redeeming, and
sustaining (Swain 2011), the sufferer can join in God's act of creating – by
way of being the created and given the ability to create – in imagining a
narrative of possibilities amidst suffering. Through the economy of redemption, the author and narrator become aware anew that creation's stories are always redeemed through the ultimate story of crucifixion and resurrection. By accepting God's promise of sustenance, the reframed story
and reauthored metanarrative are sustained into an enduring story of life
and flourishing.

Inevitably, the notion of 'flourishing' refers to the 'good', the 'good life', or what Hermans (2022a, 27) refers to as 'morality'. The particular relationship between religion and morality creates the foundation upon which the constitution of a resilient religion is built. This relationship ensures that religion as resilience contains values related to the good life as subtext, and that the related subtext offers notions of the good life as it relates to the specific context at hand. A resilient religion's notion of the good life should establish a connection with important narrative themes of Christianity, "orient people to a future of *adventus*", and remind people of their teleology as created in the *imago Dei*. The question of a good life is reframed into the Christian notion of calling and answering to the call, which forces the called to respond in the name of God, in the name of the Good, and ultimately in the name of Agape (2022a:13-14).

The extent to which the ever-changing, changing, vulnerable, and frail narratives can be constructed and reconstructed in line with the meaning contained in the relatively stable and coherent master narrative of a resilient religion determines resilience in the face of trauma and turbulence and encompasses the power inherent in a theology of resilience. Such a theology of resilience "rests on the hypothesis that the possibility of the good (and God) is experienced in the facts of my life. The good not as an abstract idea, but as the truth 'in/of' of my life" (Hermans 2022a:18). Through storying and narration, the 'good' is connected with events and facts of our life narrative. Resilience is to actively seek a sense of good that has been lost. To seek the good/God through the journey of narration of storying is to seek "the unity between finiteness and unlimitedness, between finiteness and infinity" (Hermans 2022a:19). Spatiality and temporality that characterise storying become vehicles for re-realising the self in his/her "disproportionality". Through journeying from reframing, to reauthoring, to plotting and finally, to narrating (voicing) "the self opens towards concreteness/finite and the self opens towards unlimitedness/ infinite and the possibility of a synthesis" are reconnected. A resilient religion supports this movement from being disconnected from one's disproportionality through heart-breaking adversity to reconnecting with the 'spiritual self, by claiming back one's sense of disproportionality" (Hermans 2022a:13).

**BIBLIOGRAPHY**

Abbott, H.P. (2007). Story, plot, and narration. In: D. Herman (ed.), The Cambridge companion to narrative (Cambridge: Cambridge University Press), pp. 39-51.

Arel, S.N. (2019). Disgust, shame, and trauma: The visceral and visual impact of touch. In: R.R. Ganzevoort & S. Sremac (eds), Trauma and lived religion: Transcending the ordinary. Series: Palgrave Studies in Lived religion and Societal Challenges (Switzerland: Palgrave Macmillan), pp. 45-71.

Balswick, J.O., Ebstyne King, P. & Reimer, K.S. (2016). The reciprocating self: Human development in theological perspective. 2$^{nd}$ edition (Downers Grove, ILL: Intervarsity Press), [digital copy].

Basch, M. (1998). Understanding psychotherapy: The science behind the art. New York: Basic.

Bradshaw, J. (1988). Healing the shame that binds you. Deerfield Beach, FL: Health Communications.

Bridgeman, T. (2007). Time and space. In: D. Herman (ed.), The Cambridge companion to narrative (Cambridge: Cambridge University Press), pp. 52-65

Buber, M. & Kaufmann, W. (1970). I and Thou. New York: Charles Scribner's Sons.

Capps, D. (1990). Reframing: A new method in pastoral care. Minneapolis, MN: Augsburg Fortress.

Cooper-White, P. (2011). Many voices: Pastoral psychotherapy in relational and theological perspective. Minneapolis, MN: Fortress Press.

Day, J.M. (1991). The moral audience. On the narrative mediation of moral 'judgment' and moral 'action'. In: M. Tappan & M. Packer (eds), Narrative and storytelling. Implications for understanding moral development (CD 54) (San-Francisco, CA: Jossey-Bass), pp.27-42.

Demasure, K. & Müller, J.C. (2006). Perspectives in support of the narrative turn in pastoral care. Nederduitse Gereformeerde Teologiese Tydskrif 47(3 & 4):410-419.

Dutra, L.K., Callahan, K., Forman, E., Mendelsohn, M. & Herman, J. (2008). Core schema and suicidality in chronically traumatized population. Journal of Nervous and Mental Disease 196:71-74.

Erikson, E.H. (1968). Identity, youth and crisis. New York: Norton.

Fischer, G. & Riedesser, P. (2003). Lehrbuch der Psycotraumatologie. München and Basel: Ernst Reinhart.

Foucault, M. (1973). The order of things. New York: Vintage Books.

Frawlei-O'Dea, M.G. (2015). Gid images in clinal work with sexual abuse survivors: A relational psychodynamic paradigm. In: D.F. Walker, C.A. Courtois & J.D. Aten (eds), Spiritually oriented psychotherapy for trauma (Washington: American Psychological Association), pp. 169-188.

Freedman, J. & Combs, G. (2002). Narrative therapy with couples and a whole lot more: A collection of papers, essays and exercises. Adelaide, Australia: Dulwich Centre Publications.

Ganzevoort, R.R. (1994). Crisis experiences and the development of belief and unbelief. In: D. Hutsebaut & J. Corveleyn (eds), Belief and unbelief; psychological perspectives (Amsterdam: Rodopi), pp. 21-36.

(1998a). Religious coping reconsidered 1. Journal of Psychology and Theology 26(3):260-275.

(1998b). Religious coping reconsidered 2. Journal of Psychology and Theology 26(3):276-286.

Ganzevoort, R.R. & Sremac, S. (eds) (2019). Trauma and lived religion: Transcending the ordinary. Series: Palgrave Studies in Lived Religion and Societal Challenges Switzerland: Palgrave Macmillan.

Gergen, K.J. (1994). Realities and relationships. Cambridge, MA: Harvard University Press.

Halverson, J.R., Goodall, H.L. (Jr.) & Corman, S.R. (2011). Master narratives of Islamist extremism New York: Palgrave Macmillan.

Herman, J.L. (2011). Posttraumatic stress disorder as a shame disorder. In: R.L. Dearing & J.P. Tangney (eds), Shame in the therapy hour. (Washington, DC: American Psychological Association.), pp. 261-275.

Hermans, C.A.M. (2022a). Human experiences of heart-breaking adversity, Chapter 1 in this volume (pp.13-30).

(2022b). Processes of resilience, Chapter 2 in this volume (pp.31-46).

Jones, S. (2009). Trauma and grace. Theology in a ruptured world. Louisville, KY: Westminster John Knox Press.

Karen, R. (1992). Shame. The Atlantic Monthly 269 (February 1992, pp. 40-61), the standalone article can be downloaded from http://www.empoweringpeople.net/shame/shame.pdf, on 30 May 2022.

Loubser, J. (2010). The spiritual and psychosocial gender-specific stories of adolescent orphans affected by HIV and AIDS, in the absence of a father figure. A postfoundational practical theological approach. PhD thesis, Department of Practical Theology, University of Pretoria.

Louw, D.J. (2013). Cura vitae: The hermeneutics of spiritual healing and the beautification of life. Scriptura 112 (2013:1):1-16.

McAdams, D.P. (2001). The psychology of life stories. Review of General Psychology 5(2):100-122.
    (2006). The problem of narrative coherence. Journal of Constructivist Psychology 19(2):109-125.

McGuire, M. 2008. Lived religion: Faith and practice in everyday life. New York: Oxford University Press.

Nathanson, D.L. (1994). Shame and pride: Affect, sex, and the birth of the self. New York and London: Norton.

Nussbaum, M. (2004). Hiding from humanity: Disgust, shame and the law. Princeton, NJ: Princeton University Press.

Pargament, K.I. (1997). The psychology of religion and coping. Theory, research, practice. New York: The Guilford Press.

Rambo, S. (2010). Spirit and trauma. A theology of remaining: Louisville, KY: Westminister John Knox Press.

Richards, P.S., Hardman, R.K., Lea, T. & Berret, M.E. (2015). Religious and spiritial assessment of trauma survivors. In: D.F. Walker, C.A. Courtois & J.D. Aten (eds), Spiritually oriented psychotherapy for trauma (Washington: American Psychological Association), pp. 77-102.

Richardson, B. (2005). Beyond the poetics of plot: From Ulysses to postmodern narrative progressions. In: J. Phelan & P. Rabinowitz (eds), A companion to narrative theory (Oxford: Blackwell), pp. 167-180.

Ricoeur, P. (1995). Figuring the sacred. Religion, narrative and imagination. Minneapolis, MN: Augsburg Fortress.
    (2007). Evil. A Challenge to Theology and Philosophy. [translated by John Bowden; Introduction by Graham Ward]. London: Continuum

Ritter, M. (2014). Silence as the voice of trauma. The American Journal of Psychoanalysis74(2):176-194. https://doi.org/10.1057/AJP.2014.5

Robinson, J.A. & Hawpe, L. (1986). Narrative thinking as a heuristic process. In: T.R. Sarbin (ed.), Narrative psychology. The storied nature of human conduct (New York: Praeger), pp. 111-125.

Rogers, A. (2007). The unsayable: The hidden language of trauma. New York: Ballantine Books.

Scarsella, H.J. (2018). Trauma and theology in light of the cross. In: E. Boynton & P. Capretto (eds), Trauma and transcendence: Suffering and the limits of theology (New York: Fordham University Press), pp. 256-282.

Schreider, R.J. (1998). The ministry of reconciliation: Spirituality and strategies. New York: Orbis Books. (e-book)

(1992). Reconciliation: Mission and ministry in a changing social order. Maryknoll, N.Y.: Orbis books

Sherman. N.

(2014) Recovering lost goodness: Shame, guilt, and self-empathy. Psychoanalytic Psychology 31(2):217-235.

Shotter, J.

(1993). Conversational realities. Constructing life through language. London: Sage.

Slattery, J.M. & Park, C.L.

(2015). Spirituality and making meaning: Implications for therapy with trauma survivors. In: D.F. Walker, C.A. Courtois & J.D. Aten (eds), Spiritually oriented psychotherapy for trauma (Washington: American Psychological Association), pp. 127-146.

Soelle, D. (1975) Suffering. Philadelphia: Fortress Press.

Sternberg, M. (2003). Universals of narrative and their cognitivist fortunes (I). Poetics Today 24(2):326-328.

Swain, S. (2011). Trauma and transformation at ground zero: A pastoral theology. Minneapolis, MN: Fortress Press (Kindle edition).

Tomkins Institute. [n.d.] downloaded from http://www.tomkins.org/what-tomkins-said/introduction/nine-affects-present-at-birth-combine-to-form-emotion-mood-and-personality/ on 31 May 2022.

Tomkins, S. (2008). Affect, imagery, consciousness. New York: Springer.

Van Dalen, E. Scherer-Rath, M., Van Laarhoven, H., Wiegers, G. & Hermans, C.A.M. (2019). Tragedy as contingency acknowledgement: Towards a practical religious-scientific theory. Journal of Empirical Theology 32(2), 2019, pp.232-250

Van Deusen Hunsinger, D. (2015). Bearing the unbearable: Trauma, gospel and pastoral care. Grand Rapids, MI: Wm B. Eerdmans.

Van Ommen, A.L. (2019). Remembering for healing: Liturgical communities of reconciliation provide space for trauma. In: Ganzevoort, R.R. & Sremac, S. (eds), Trauma and lived religion: Transcending the ordinary. Series: Palgrave Studies in Lived Religion and Societal Challenges. Switzerland: Palgrave Macmillan.

Volf, M. (2006). The end of memory: Remembering rightly in a violent world. Grand Rapids, MI: Wm B. Eerdmans.

Walker, D.F., Courtois, C.A. & Aten, J.D. (2015). Basics of working on spiritual matters with traumatized individuals. In: D.F. Walker,

C.A. Courtois & J.D. Aten (eds), Spiritually oriented psychotherapy for trauma (Washington: American Psychological Association), pp. 15-28.

Wulf, C.M. (2019). Trauma in relationship – Healing by religion: Restoring dignity and meaning after traumatic experiences. In: R.R. Ganzevoort & S. Sremac (eds), Trauma and lived religion: Transcending the ordinary. Series: Palgrave Studies in Lived Religion and
Societal Challenges. Switserland: Palgrave Macmillan.

Wurmser, L. (1981). The mask of shame. Baltimore, MD: John Hopkins
University Press.
    (2012) Negative Therapeutic Reaction and the Compulsion to Dis-
appoint the Other. In: L. Wurmser & H. Jarass (eds), Nothing Good
Is Allowed to Stand. An Integrative View of the Negative Therapeutic Reaction. New York: Routledge, pp. 26-56.

# List of contributors

## Eugene Baron

Dr Eugene Baron obtained qualifications in Theology and Psychology from the University of the Western Cape and from the University of South Africa. He served as minister in the Uniting Reformed Church of Southern Africa (URCSA) and is a National Research Foundation (NRF) Y-rated researcher. He is the Editor-in-Chief of the book series *UFS Theological Explorations* (since 2022), and online Editor of the journal *Missionalia* (since 2021). He currently serves as a council member of the University of the Free State. Dr Baron is a staff member in the Department of Practical and Missional Theology at the University of the Free State (since 2019). At present, his research focuses on reconciliation, social transformation, and mission as development. His e-mail address is: barone@ufs.ac.za

## Dion Forster

Prof. Dion A. Forster is the Director of the Beyers Naudé Centre for Public Theology, and the Chair of the Department of Systematic Theology and Ecclesiology at Stellenbosch University. He holds a PhD in Systematic Theology from the University of South Africa (2006) and a second PhD in New Testament Studies from Radboud University (2017). He is a research fellow at Wesley House, Cambridge, and an associate of the Allan Gray Centre for Values-Based Leadership at the University of Cape Town's Graduate School of Business. He is also a researcher in the CNPq research team on religion and political populism in South Africa and Brazil. He serves as Editor of the *International Journal for Public Theology, Caderno Teológico, Wesley and Methodist Studies*, as well as *The Methodist Review*. His major works include 'The (im)possibility of forgiveness?' (2019); 'African public theology' (2020), and 'Reconciliation, forgiveness and violence in Africa' (2020). His email address is: dionforster@sun.ac.za

## Chris Hermans

Prof. Christiaan A.M. Hermans holds the chair in Pastoral Theology, especially Empirical Theology, at Radboud University, Nijmegen (since 2003), and the chair in Empirical Study of Religion since 2005. He is an extraordinary professor in Practical Theology and Missiology at the University of the Free State (since 2018). He is editor of the *Journal of Empirical Theology* (since 2004). His major works include 'Morele vorming' (1986); 'Wie werdet ihr die Gleichnisse verstehen?' (1990); 'Vorming in perspektief' (1993); 'Participatory learning'; 'Religious education in a globalizing society' (2003), and 'Religion and conflict' (with Antony & Sterkens) (2015). His email address is: chris.hermans@ru.nl

## Juanita Meyer

Dr Juanita Meyer is a senior lecturer in Pastoral Care and Therapy at the Faculty of Theology and Religion, University of the Free State (since 2016). She is the Head of the Department of Practical and Missional Theology. Her primary research focus is on masculinity and spirituality, as well as on the development of a pastoral theological research model for the South African context. She envisages the development of a pastoral therapy degree programme for the professional training of pastoral workers and therapists at the University of the Free State. Her email address is: MeyerJ1@ufs.ac.za

## Martin Laubscher

Dr Martin Laubscher is a senior lecturer in Homiletics and Liturgy at the University of the Free State. His research focuses on the theology and reception of Karl Barth; (South African) reformed theology; (South African) public theology; liturgy and life, as well as theologians as preachers. He is the author of *Publieke teologie as profetiese teologie? 'n Kritiese beskouing van die sosio-ekklesiologiese implikasies van die drieërlei amp in die teologie van Karl Barth* (Stellenbosch: Sun Media, 2022), and the editor-in-chief of *Acta Theologica* (since 2022). His email address is: laubscherm@ufs.ac.za

## Funlọla Ọlọjẹde

Dr Funlọla Ọlọjẹde is the postgraduate coordinator of the Faculty of Theology at Stellenbosch University and an associate with its Gender Unit. Her academic interests include Gender and Feminist Hermeneutics; Wisdom Literature; Old Testament Studies; Migration Studies, and African Biblical Interpretation. Ọlọjẹde is a fellow of the UBIAS Network. She has done research at the Princeton Theological Seminary, USA; at Alexander

## International Practical Theology

edited by Prof. Dr. Chris Hermans (Nijmegen), Prof. Dr. Maureen Junker-Kenny (Dublin), Prof. Dr. Richard Osmer (Princeton), Prof. Dr. Friedrich Schweitzer (Tübingen), Prof. Dr. Hans-Georg Ziebertz (Würzburg) in cooperation with the International Academy of Practical Theology (IAPT)

Jan Albert van den Berg; Chris A. M. Hermans (Eds.)
**Battle for the heart**
How (not) to transform church and society
The battle of the heart can be seen as the core problem of the Christian religion in modern culture. According to Augustine, the complex mixture of longings are the driving forces of human lives. These longing are not an intellectual puzzle, but rather a craving for sustenance. The contributions locate the battle for the heart and transformation of society and church in the context of an ethnic, multi-religious, socio-economical divided Africa. Where are the authentic voices of leaders who can change the heart? How to mend a 'broken' heart? How to transform congregations towards inclusion of difference? Can we embrace the dignity of difference as attitudes that enable transformation of church and society?
Bd. 23, 2020, 202 S., 39,90 €, br., ISBN 978-3-643-91306-7

Annemie Dillen; Danny Pilario (Eds.)
**Theology Facing the War on Drugs**
vol. 22, , ca. 176 pp., ca. 29,90 €, br., ISBN-CH 978-3-643-91269-5

Chris A.M. Hermans; Kobus Schoeman (Eds.)
**Theology in an Age of Contingency**
Contingency refers to an event that may be happening in future, but also may not happen. The concept plays has a long history dating from Aristotle who defined contingency as that which is possible but not necessary. The concept of contingency and related concepts as free will, the rejection of essentialisation and priority of the possible put a major challenge to theology in the 21st century. The book addresses this challenge from the perspective of practical theology. In doing so, it connects to the general debate in theology on naming God, hermeneutics, human agency and methodology.
Bd. 21, 2019, 208 S., 34,90 €, br., ISBN 978-3-643-91108-7

Jaco Dreyer; Malan Nel (Eds.)
**Practicing Ubuntu**
Practical Theological Perspectives on Injustice, Personhood and Human Dignity
*Ubuntu* is a dynamic and celebrated concept in Africa. In the great Sutu-nguni family of Southern Africa, being humane is regarded as the supreme virtue. The essence of this philosophy of life, called *ubuntu* or *botho*, is human relatedness and dignity. The Shona from Zimbabwe articulate it as: "I am because we are; I exist because the community exists." This volume offers twenty-two such reflections on practicing *ubuntu* as it relates to justice, personhood and human dignity both in Southern African as well as in wider international contexts. This work highlights the potential of *ubuntu* for enriching our understanding of justice, personhood and human dignity in a globalising world.
Bd. 20, 2017, 272 S., 34,90 €, br., ISBN 978-3-643-90848-3

Gorden E Dames
**Towards a contextual transformational practical theology for leadership education in South Africa**
"Towards a contextual transformational practical theology for leadership education in South Africa is a courageous effort by a prominent South African practical theologian to develop a framework for the theory and practice of leadership education in an African context. Taking the harsh realities of South Africa as point of departure, the author demonstrates how an indigenous South African practical theology can be developed through a critical interaction between 'Western' and African ideas."
(Prof. Jaco S. Dreyer, Professor of Practical Theology, University of South Africa)
Bd. 19, 2016, 278 S., 39,90 €, br., ISBN 978-3-643-90800-1

LIT Verlag Berlin – Münster – Wien – Zürich – London
Auslieferung Deutschland / Österreich / Schweiz: siehe Impressumsseite

von Humboldt University, Berlin, Germany, and at Vrije Universiteit, Amsterdam, The Netherlands, among other institutions. Besides her scholarly engagement, Ọlọjẹde serves as the senior pastor of the Stellenbosch parish of the Redeemed Christian Church of God. She is also the coordinator of the Circle of Concerned African Women Theologians in South Africa. Some of her publications are available at: https://www.researchgate.net/profile/Funlola_Olojede/contributions. Her email address is: funlola@sun.ac.za

## Kobus Schoeman

Prof. Kobus (W.J.) Schoeman is professor of Practical Theology at the University of the Free State (since 2009), and a National Research Foundation (NRF) C-rated researcher. He served as a full-time minister for over twenty years in three Dutch Reformed congregations. He specialises in congregational studies and leadership. His research focuses on the development of a practical theological ecclesiology and the empirical analysis of congregations. He is the editor of *Churches in the mirror, developing contemporary ecclesiologies* (SUNMedia 2020). His email address is: schoemanw@ufs.ac.za.

## Rian Venter

Prof. Rian Venter obtained a DD from the University of Pretoria. He is professor in Systematic Theology at the University of the Free State. His research work focuses on the doctrine of God and the transformation of theology at public universities. He is the editor of the volume *Theology and the post(apartheid) condition: Genealogies and future direction* (SUN MeDIA, 2016), and co-editor (with DF Tolmie) of *Making sense of Jesus: Experiences, interpretations and identities* (SUN MeDIA, 2017). His email address is: rventer@ufs.ac.za.

Pamela Couture
**We Are Not All Victims**
Local Peacebuilding in the Democratic Republic of Congo
The book chronicles the peacebuilding activities of the community led by Bishop Ntambo Nkulu Ntanda, his lay leaders and ecumenical colleagues. They respond to the conditions created by the wars in the Democratic Republic of Congo, 1996–2003, organizing relief, building social capacities, engaging in conflict transformation, and often putting risking their lives for peace. These rural Luba people in the town of Kamina and surrounding villages negotiate their understanding of Christian mandates and local tradition and practice, demonstrating that their appropriation of Christianity and local indigenous tradition can motivate practices of peace.
Bd. 18, 2016, 392 S., 39,90 €, br., ISBN 978-2-643-90796-7

Pamela Couture; Robert Mager; Pamela McCarroll; Natalie Wigg-Stevenson (Eds.)
**Complex Identities in a Shifting World**
Practical Theological Perspectives
Clear and well-defined identities are hard to sustain in a rapidly shifting world. Peoples, goods and cultures are on the move. Internet and other technologies increase the amount, the speed and the intensity of cultural exchanges. Individuals, organizations and nations develop complex identities out of many traditions, different ideals, various ways of life and many models of organization. Religious traditions both collide and interact; spiritual journeys cross religious boundaries. More than twenty authors from different backgrounds and academic disciplines offer an array of practical theological perspectives to help us understand these complex identities and negotiate this shifting world.
Bd. 17, 2015, 284 S., 29,90 €, br., ISBN 978-3-643-90509-3

R. Ruard Ganzevoort; Rein Brouwer; Bonnie Miller-McLemore (Eds.)
**City of Desires – a Place for God?**
Practical theological perspectives
Bd. 16, 2013, 216 S., 29,90 €, br., ISBN 978-3-643-90307-5

Edward Foley (Ed.)
**Religion, Diversity and Conflict**
Bd. 15, 2011, 312 S., 29,90 €, br., ISBN 978-3-643-90086-9

Heid Leganger-Krogstad
**The Religious Dimension of Intercultural Education**
Contributions to a Contextual Understanding
Bd. 14, 2011, 288 S., 29,90 €, br., ISBN 978-3-643-90085-2

Annemie Dillen; Anne Vandenhoeck (Eds.)
**Prophetic Witness in World Christianities**
Rethinking Pastoral Care and Counseling
Bd. 13, 2011, 248 S., 24,90 €, br., ISBN 978-3-643-90041-8

Hans-Georg Ziebertz; Ulrich Riegel (Eds.)
**How Teachers in Europe Teach Religion**
An International Empirical Study
vol. 12, 2009, 408 pp., 34,90 €, br., ISBN 978-3-643-10043-6

Gordon Mikoski; Richard Osmer
**With Piety and Learning**
The History of Practical Theology at Princeton Theological Seminary 1812–2012
Bd. 11, 2011, 256 S., 29,90 €, br., ISBN 978-3-643-90106-4

LIT Verlag Berlin – Münster – Wien – Zürich – London
Auslieferung Deutschland / Österreich / Schweiz: siehe Impressumsseite

**Religion – Geschichte – Gesellschaft**
Fundamentaltheologische Studien
begründet von Prof. Dr. Dr. Johann Baptist Metz (†), Prof. Dr. Jürgen Werbick,
Prof. Dr. Johann Reikerstorfer
hrsg. von Prof. Dr. Ulrich Engel OP (Institut M.-Dominique Chenu, Berlin), Prof. Dr. Judith Gruber
(KU Leuven), Dr. Michael Hoelzl (University of Manchester)

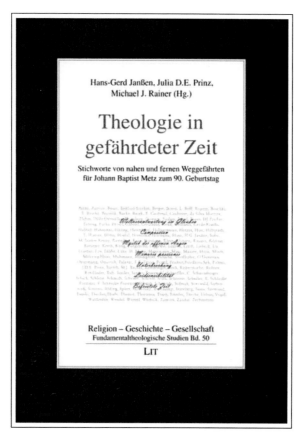

Hans-Gerd Janßen; Julia D. E. Prinz; Michael J. Rainer (Hg..)
**Theologie in gefährdeter Zeit**
Stichworte von nahen und fernen Weggefährten für Johann Baptist Metz zum
90. Geburtstag
Johann Baptist Metz (* 5. August 1928) hat seine Theologie im intensiven Austausch mit Philosophie, Geschichte, Rechts-, Politik- und Sozialtheorie, Jüdischem Denken und Welt-Literatur & Kunst
gewonnen und entfaltet – und so nicht nur in der theologischen Diskussion prägende Spuren hinter-
lassen. Seine Gottesrede lässt sich nicht aus den Katastrophen in Geschichte und Gesellschaft her-
auslösen, sondern bleibt im Kern herausgefordert angesichts der weltweit steigenden Gefährdungen:
interkulturell, sozial, politisch, ökonomisch, ökologisch … !
Dieser Band führt 150 kompakte Stellungnahmen zusammen, die Zeit-Zeichen setzen: die Beiträ-
ger_innen loten aus, in wieweit sie der Neuen Politischen Theologie und J.B. Metz als Person prägende Inspirationen und bleibende Impulse für ihre eigene Sicht auf Philosophie, Theologie, Geschichte,
Gesellschaft, Recht, Politik, Bildung und Kunst verdanken: eine ungewöhnliche Festschrift voller
Überraschungen und weiterführender Anstöße.
Bd. 50, 2. Aufl. 2019, 600 S., 39,90 €, br., ISBN 978-3-643-14106-4

**LIT** Verlag Berlin – Münster – Wien – Zürich – London
Auslieferung Deutschland / Österreich / Schweiz: siehe Impressumsseite

**Theologie Ost – West**
Europäische Perspektiven
hrsg. von Prof. Dr. Janez Juhant (Universität Ljubljana) und Prof. Dr. Albert Franz (†)


Margit Eckholt (Ed.)
**Creation – Transformation – Theology**
International Congress of the European Society for Catholic Theology (August 2021 – Osnabrück/Germany)
The social and cultural challenges posed by the increasing threat to creation (climate change, destruction of biodiversity, etc.) are the starting point for new philosophical-ethical and theological reflections on the relationship between God, human beings and the world, as presented in this volume. God's creative impulse, which transforms anew, is at work in the actions of human beings and challenges us, in view of the threat to the "house of life" earth, to go new ways that make a common and good life possible. Creation and transformation are interrelated; an ecological theology of creation and practice of sustainability to be developed in the European context is to be embedded in the horizon of a global, liberating theology.
vol. 30, 2022, ca. 568 pp., ca. 49,90 €, br., ISBN-CH 978-3-643-91488-0

Robert Petkovšek; Bojan Žalec (Eds.)
**Ethics of Resilience**
Vulnerability and Survival in Times of Pandemics and Global Uncertainty
vol. 29, 2022, ca. 240 pp., ca. 24,90 €, br., ISBN-CH 978-3-643-91211-4

Miloš Lichner (Ed.)
**Hope**
Where does our Hope lie? International Congress of the European Society for Catholic Theology (August 2019 – Bratislava, Slovakia)
In our times hope is called into question. The disintegration of economic systems, of states and societies, families, friendships, distrust in political structures, forces us to ask if hope has disappeared from the experience of today's men and women. In August 2019, up to 240 participants met at the international theological congress in Bratislava, Slovakia. The main lectures, congress sections and workshops aimed to provide a space for thinking about the central theme of hope in relation to philosophy, politics, pedagogy, social work, charity, interreligious dialogue and ecumenism.
Bd. 28, 2020, 732 S., 49,90 €, br., ISBN 978-3-643-91330-2

Robert Petkovšek; Bojan Žalecc (Eds.)
**Transhumanism as a Challenge for Ethics and Religion**
The crucial question of our time is: How to preserve humanity, humanitas, in a world of radical and not so long ago practically unimaginable technological possibilities? The book addresses this issue through its treatment of transhumanism, a diverse movement the representatives of which promise and advocate for the enhancement of human being through modern science, technology, and pharmacology. Their views differ in the degree of extremity, and they contain many ambiguities, as well as pitfalls and dangers that require an answer from both ethical and religious points of view.
Bd. 27, 2021, 236 S., 34,90 €, br., ISBN 978-3-643-91297-8

Robert Petkovšek; Bojan Žalec (Eds.)
**Ethical Implications of One God**
The Significance of Monotheism
Bd. 26, 2020, 208 S., 29,90 €, br., ISBN 978-3-643-91126-1

Tonči Matulić
**Metamorphoses of Culture**
A Theological Discernment of the Signs of the Times against the Backdrop of Scientific-Technical Civilisation
Bd. 25, 2018, 684 S., 69,90 €, br., ISBN 978-3-643-91049-3

LIT Verlag Berlin – Münster – Wien – Zürich – London
Auslieferung Deutschland / Österreich / Schweiz: siehe Impressumsseite

Chris A.M. Hermans, Kobus Schoeman (Eds.)

# Resilient Religion, Resilience
# and Heartbreaking Adversity

# International Practical Theology

edited by

Prof. Dr. Chris Hermans (Nijmegen),
Prof. Dr. Maureen Junker-Kenny (Dublin),
Prof. Dr. Richard Osmer (Princeton),
Prof. Dr. Friedrich Schweitzer (Tübingen),
Prof. Dr. Hans-Georg Ziebertz (Würzburg)

Volume 24

LIT